D1602669

Ezra Pound and the Symbolist Inheritance

Ezra Pound and the
Symbolist Inheritance

Scott Hamilton

PRINCETON UNIVERSITY PRESS

PRINCETON, NEW JERSEY

Library of Congress Cataloging-in-Publication Data

Hamilton, Scott, 1954 Dec. 31–
Ezra Pound and the symbolist inheritance /
Scott Hamilton.
    p.   cm.
Includes bibliographical references and index.
ISBN 0-691-06924-7 (cl) :
1. Pound, Ezra, 1885–1972—Knowledge—
Literature.   2. Symbolism (Literary movement)—
France.   3. French poetry—19th century—
History and criticism.   4. French poetry—
20th century—History and criticism.
I. Title.
PS3531.O82Z6413   1992
811'.52—dc20   91-20023 CIP

This book has been composed in Linotron Baskerville

Princeton University Press books are
printed on acid-free paper and meet the guidelines for
permanence and durability of the Committee on
Production Guidelines for Book Longevity of the
Council on Library Resources

Printed in the United States of America

1   3   5   7   9   10   8   6   4   2

CONTENTS

PREFACE AND ACKNOWLEDGMENTS

THE PROFOUND influence of nineteenth- and twentieth-century French verse on Ezra Pound's poetry has long been overshadowed by Pound's polemical rejection of symbolism. Pound once said that "imagisme is not symbolism," but it is apparent that he fashioned his career not only by what has become known as "'symbolism' in its profounder sense," or what Pound called "real symbolism, Cabala, genesis of symbols, rise of picture language, etc.," but also by means of "the aesthetic symbolism of Villiers de l'Isle Adam, & that Arthur Symons wrote a book about—the literwary movement." Pound's interest in the *literwary* movement can only be told by escaping the narrow confines of Anglo-American studies and by resituating Pound in his native province of comparative literature. If Pound's fascination with the occult helps to define his poetic sensibility, his early engagement with nineteenth- and twentieth-century French verse shapes Pound's practice as a modern poet.

In their reaction against Mallarmé's symbolism, the post-Symbolists showed Pound how to wage war against his own precursors. As early as 1913, Pound wrote a number of important articles on French (post)symbolist poets, and he repeatedly insisted that Gautier, Corbière, Laforgue, and Rimbaud escaped Stendhal's condemnation of poetry for "its bagwigs and bobwigs, and its padded calves and its periwigs, its 'fustian à la Louis XIV.'" Nor was Pound's bold claim gratuitous. Pound was well informed about the poetry that had been written on the fringes of Symbolism, and he had firsthand knowledge about the rich and unsettled history of French post-Symbolism. Next to F. S. Flint, Pound was the anglophone critic most responsible for introducing modern French poetry to the English-speaking public, and he soon followed the post-Symbolists in their experimentation with vers libre, their theorizing about the image, and their polemical call for a poetry that considered men and women as social beings. Thus, although Pound's symbolist inheritance is in many ways that of his English predecessors (Swinburne, Johnson, Dowson, Symons, and Yeats, among others), it is powerfully inflected by the French post-Symbolist poets' ambivalence about their own recent heritage. We can see this influence in Pound's 1912 *Ripostes*, where many of the poems are modeled on poems of such (post)symbolists as Remy de Gourmont and Henri de Régnier, and in *Lustra*, where Laurent Tailhade becomes a powerful influence.

In his crucial revision of the Symbolist canon, Pound exorcises the ghosts of Baudelaire, Verlaine, and Mallarmé by turning to Théophile Gautier, a poet who preceded, anticipated, and was celebrated by the Symbolists, and to Corbière and Laforgue, then largely unknown poets. The key figure here is Gautier, for he can be seen as a romantic, a Parnassian, or a proto-symbolist, and he allows Pound great flexibility in envisioning what poetry should be. Pound begins by invoking the Parnassianism of Gautier, Gourmont, and Régnier in *Ripostes*, but he soon discovers a satirical vein in Gautier's "Carmen" that links Gautier to Flaubert and anticipates the similarly ironic strategies of Corbière, Laforgue, Tailhade, and, later, in *Lustra*, of Pound himself. Pound's exhaustive study of modern French verse gave him poetic models and techniques that enabled him to escape his own decadent-symbolist inheritance and to discover the distinctively modern voice that he began to create in 1912.

I am thus at first concerned with classic models of influence, or, as Harold Bloom redefines the term, with source studies. My study can be seen as a straightforward literary history that revises some of our long-held commonplaces about poetic modernism (and as a developmental study of Pound's poetic). Yet Pound was an inherently imitative poet who often transcended his models because of his egotistical belief that, as Charles Olson wittily and accurately put it, he could out-talk all but Confucius and Dante. With "the beak of his ego," says Olson, Pound "breaks all down to his equals or inferiors" and maintains a belief that his own mots justes could of themselves rectify language for future generations. Contemporary theory has, of course, proven over and over again that *mots* are never *justes*, and that intertextual subversion is always present. In Pound's case, the breaks or ruptures in major poems often result from a crucial blind spot that facilitated the return of precisely those romantic elements in Gautier that Pound, as a modern poet, felt obliged to repress. In this regard, my book veers toward a study in the manner of Harold Bloom.

To sum up: there was both an inexorable and entirely logical trajectory governing Pound's borrowing from the French tradition and a paradoxical circularity (or periodicity) to Pound's poetic development. The first half of my book chronicles Pound's (re)discovery of French verse and charts the successive influence of Gautier's Parnassianism, Corbière and Tailhade's satire, and Laforgue's irony. The chapter on Laforgue marks an important shift in Pound's poetic and in my own argument, for I show that Laforgue has a less significant place in *Mauberley* than does Gautier. This time, the return of Gautier's romanticism haunts the poem and continues to haunt Pound throughout his *Draft of XXX Cantos*. Although Gautier's influence subsides in the middle cantos when Pound delegates his authority as a poet to the politicians of China and Italy, the Pisan and later cantos confirm our suspicion that any such firmly ingrained sensibility cannot be so easily repressed.

Nor is Pound's response to the French Romantic and Symbolist traditions an isolated, insignificant, or specifically modernist response. As I show in the Conclusion, Robert Duncan's similar appropriation of French Symbolist poetry reaffirms the connection between romantic, modern, and postmodern poetry. Duncan returns to Baudelaire and Mallarmé in an attempt to make sense of both modernism and his own postmodern vision. By reading Modernism as Romanticism, Duncan is able to isolate and make function in his own poetry the many aporias that beset Pound's discourse.

Pound's hesitations, mystifications, and his ultimate resignation not only provide greater definition to our vision of modernism, they enable us to compare our postmodern sensibility with that of the past. If Pound *falsely* believed that he could "make it new," we might want to withhold judgment on the radical advances that we attribute to our own postmodern discourse.

．　　●　　●

I owe debts to many scholars. My willingness to pursue such a broad topic was fostered by many critical studies and chance conversations. I am grateful to the staffs of the Lilly Library at Indiana University and the Beinecke Rare Book and Manuscript Library at Yale University for their generous assistance. I would like to thank the Division of Humanities and Social Sciences at the California Institute of Technology for the research grants that made it possible for me to visit these libraries. Finally, I would like to thank the Andrew Mellon Foundation and the California Institute of Technology for the fellowship that enabled me to complete this book.

I have profited greatly from the suggestions and criticisms of all those who have read, some anonymously, this manuscript. I would like to thank Alex Zwerdling and Joseph Duggan for their helpful comments during the early stages of its composition, and James Longenbach, Cyrena N. Pondrom, and Richard Sieburth for their responses to my near finished work. I would like to thank Anthony Zielonka and Rosy Meiron for checking my translations against the French and for their often brilliant solutions to passages that had me stymied. I would also like to thank Joy Hansen for continually upgrading my computer as quickly as upgraded programs made it obsolete. Finally, I would like to thank Robert Brown, Carolyn Fox, and Princeton University Press for their interest and encouragement.

There remain two people to whom I owe a large, if not unrepayable, debt of gratitude. Michael Bernstein, whose friendship and example as a scholar have long been a source of inspiration, supported this project from its inception with his encouraging and timely advice, and his penetrating discussions on and off the tennis courts helped to give it shape. Similarly, I cannot overstate my debt to my erstwhile colleague Ronald Bush. He unstintingly gave of his time to read innumerable drafts of the book, teaching me to write in the process, and his encyclopedic knowledge of modernism was forever at my beck and call.

Finally, more personal debts. To my wife Grace for her patience and to my son Philip, whose very early knowledge of the difference between *Flight Simulator*™ and *WordPerfect*™ cannot possibly make up for his having been deprived of "quality time." And to my parents, Bob and Dorothy, who generously helped me and who tactfully suppressed their unerring judgment regarding good and bad career moves, I would like to dedicate this book.

·   ·   ·

Portions of the Introduction and of Chapter 5 were previously published in *Paideuma* (Fall 1990), under the title "'Serenely in the Crystal Jet': A Note on Ezra Pound's Symbolist Inheritance." Portions of the Conclusion were previously published in *Sagetrieb* 4 (Fall & Winter 1985), under the title "After Strange Gods: Robert Duncan Reading Ezra Pound and H. D."

Excerpts from the following works reprinted by permission of New Directions Publishing Corporation and Faber & Faber Ltd: *The Cantos of Ezra Pound*, copyright 1934, 1937, 1940, 1948, 1956, 1959, 1962, 1963, 1965, 1968, 1970 by Ezra Pound, copyright 1973, 1986 by the Trustees of the Ezra Pound Literary Property Trust; *The Classic Noh Theatre of Japan*, copyright by New Directions; *Collected Early Poems of Ezra Pound*, copyright 1976 by Ezra Pound Literary Property Trust; *Ezra Pound*, copyright 1954, 1963 by Ezra Pound; *Ezra Pound and Dorothy Shakespear*, copyright 1976, 1984 by the Trustees of the Ezra Pound Literary Trust; *Gaudier-Brzeska*, copyright 1970 by Ezra Pound; *Guide to Kulchur*, copyright 1970 by Ezra Pound; *Instigations of Ezra Pound*, copyright 1920 by Ezra Pound; *Literary Essays*, copyright 1935 by Ezra Pound; *Pavannes & Divagations*, copyright 1958 by Ezra Pound; *Personae*, copyright 1926, 1935, 1971 by Ezra Pound; *Pound/Joyce*, copyright 1967 by Ezra Pound; *The Selected Letters of Ezra Pound*, copyright 1950 by Ezra Pound; *Selected Prose 1909–1965*, copyright 1973 by the Estate of Ezra Pound; *The Spirit of Romance*, copyright 1968 by Ezra Pound.

Permission to quote from manuscript material, copyright 1991 by the Trustees of the Ezra Pound Literary Property Trust, is granted by New Directions Publishing Corporation, agents for the Ezra Pound Literary Property Trust.

Excerpts from the following works reprinted by permission of New Directions Publishing Corporation: *Bending the Bow*, copyright 1963, 1964, 1965, 1966, 1967, 1968 by Robert Duncan; *The Flowers of Evil*, copyright 1955, 1962, 1989 by New Directions; *Ground Work* Before the War, copyright 1968, 1969, 1970, 1971, 1972, 1974, 1975, 1976, 1977, 1982, 1984 by Robert Duncan; *Ground Work* In the Dark, copyright 1987 by Robert Duncan; *The Opening of the Field*, copyright 1960 by Robert Duncan; *Roots and Branches*, copyright 1964 by Robert Duncan.

Permission to reprint from *Corbière: Selections from Les Amours Jaunes*, edited and translated by C. F. MacIntyre, copyright 1954, is granted by the Regents of the University of California.

Permission to reprint from *Poems of Sextus Propertius*, edited and translated by J. P. McCullough, copyright 1972, is granted by the Regents of the University of California.

Permission to reprint from *Poems of Jules Laforgue*, edited and translated by Peter Dale, copyright Peter Dale 1986, is granted by Anvil Press Poetry.

LIST OF ABBREVIATIONS

ABC *ABC of Reading* (New York: New Directions, 1960).

AP 1–7 "The Approach to Paris I-VII," *New Age*, n.s., 13, nos. 19–25 (Sept. 4–Oct. 16, 1913). Except for "Approach, I," this series of articles is reprinted, with commentary, in Cyrena N. Pondrom, ed. *The Road from Paris: French Influence on English Poetry, 1900–1920* (London: Cambridge University Press, 1974), 174–200.

CEP *Collected Early Poems of Ezra Pound* (New York: New Directions, 1976).

CNTJ *Classic Noh Theatre of Japan* (New York: New Directions, 1959).

CWC *The Chinese Written Character as a Medium for Poetry* (San Francisco: City Lights Books, n.d.)

GB *Gaudier-Brzeska* (New York: New Directions, 1960).

GK *Guide to Kulchur* (New York: New Directions, 1970).

Inst *Instigations of Ezra Pound* (New York: Boni & Liveright, 1920).

J/M *Jefferson And/Or Mussolini* (New York: Liveright, 1970).

LE *Literary Essays*, ed. T. S. Eliot (New York: New Directions, 1968).

P&D *Pavannes & Divagations* (New York: New Directions, 1974).

P *Personae*, rev. ed. Lea Baechler and A. Walton Litz (New York: New Directions, 1990).

SL *The Selected Letters of Ezra Pound 1907–1941*, ed. D. D. Paige (New York: New Directions, 1971).

SP *Selected Prose 1909–1965*, ed. William Cookson (New York: New Directions, 1973).

SR *The Spirit of Romance* (New York: New Directions, 1968).

T *Ezra Pound: Translations* (New York: New Directions, 1963).

The 1989 New Directions edition of the *Cantos* is used throughout this book. References are given in the text as: (1/3) to designate Canto 1, page 3. This edition includes the Italian cantos and the revised *Drafts and Fragments*. For the Pisan and later cantos, page references can be keyed to older editions by subtracting 14 pages.

Ezra Pound and the Symbolist Inheritance

EZRA POUND AND THE
SYMBOLIST INHERITANCE

Nommer un objet, c'est supprimer les trois-quarts de
la jouissance du poème qui est faite du bonheur de
deviner peu à peu; le suggérer voilà le rêve. C'est le
parfait usage de ce mystère qui constitue le symbole.
—Stéphane Mallarmé

Beauty should never be presented explained. It is Marvel
and Wonder, and in art we should find first these doors—
Marvel and Wonder—and, coming through them, a slow un-
derstanding (slow even though it be a succession of lightning
understandings and perceptions) as of a figure in mist, that
still and ever gives to each one his own right of believing,
each after his own creed and fashion.
Always the desire to know and to understand more deeply
must precede any reception of beauty. Without holy curiosity
and awe none find her, and woe to that artist whose work
wears its "heart on its sleeve."
—Weston St. Llewmys (*CEP*, 58)

To hold a like belief in a sort of permanent meta-
phor is, as I understand it, "symbolism" in its pro-
founder sense. It is not necessarily a belief in a perma-
nent world, but it is a belief in that direction.
Imagisme is not symbolism. The symbolists dealt in
"association," that is, in a sort of allusion, almost of
allegory. They degraded the symbol to the status of a
word. They made it a form of metonymy.
—Ezra Pound (*GB*, 84)

POUND'S 1914 polemic championing imagism and its later offshoot,
vorticism, over "'symbolism' in its profounder sense" has more or less
shaped subsequent critical debates about his poetry and about mod-
ernism in general. According to Pound, such Symbolists as Baudelaire,
Verlaine, and Mallarmé, poets who decisively shaped the English Dec-
adent and Aesthetic movements out of which Pound himself evolved,

were improper models for modern poets and could only lead to a de-
rivative poetry. In a September 1913 letter to Harriet Monroe, for
example, he severely criticizes the two French poets who had perhaps
most influenced late nineteenth- and early twentieth-century English
poetry: "There are few enough people on this stupid little island who
know anything beyond Verlaine and Baudelaire—neither of whom is
the least use, pedagogically, I mean. They beget imitation and one can
learn nothing from them" (*SL*, 23). His lack of regard for Mallarmé is
equally apparent in this 1913 letter to Dorothy Shakespear: "I have
been reading your Mallarmé. He seems to me (the prose) worse than
dear Henry James. It's all upside down. The Vers I haven't tried yet."[1]
All of which is neatly and succinctly summed up in Pound's confident
assertion in January 1914 that "there's nothing to be studied about
symbolism."[2]

Pound's *via negativa* has been so deeply ingrained in our discussions
of modernism that the attempt to disentangle his various dicta from
modernist literary history as it is currently conceived might seem a
dubious, if not futile, critical enterprise. Pound's battle cry—
"Imagisme is not symbolism"—was taken up by May Sinclair in the
Egoist,[3] the official mouthpiece of a nascent modernism, and became a
commonplace in subsequent modernist histories. Thus, when Frank
Kermode suggested that the *Cantos* were the only possible mode of a
long symbolist poem, he was criticized severely by Donald Davie and
by Herbert Schneidau.[4] In Hugh Kenner's monumental *Pound Era*,
the idea that Pound might have begun with a symbolist predisposition
seemed to have been definitively buried. Potential symbolist influ-
ences were enshrined in modernist prehistory, "a geological epoch," as
it were, that might certainly contain some interesting archaeological
finds, but would not alter our understanding of the origins of a mod-
ernist poetic. "Commencing from the post-Symbolist nineties," ac-
cording to Kenner, "Pound worked his way clear of systematized sug-
gestiveness until his chief point of contact with 19th-century French
verse was Théophile Gautier of the direct statement ('Carmen is thin')
and his most Symbolist procedure an isolating of single words, not
necessarily English."[5] From the perspective of Kenner's model,
imagism, vorticism, and objectivism all derive from Pound's rejection
of the "mushy technique" and "impressionism" (*GB*, 85) of the French
Symbolists, and all three movements define themselves by their quest
for the clarity and hardness of a purely objective and transparently
referential language.

These critics are responding in good faith to Pound's own pro-
nouncements ex cathedra and are undoubtedly correct in their at-
tempt to dissociate imagism from symbolism as Mallarmé defined it in

the epigraph to this chapter; that is, to divorce the "thing" from the "ineffable *idée*," the clarity and precision of the image from the "arabesque" of the symbol.[6] Indeed, Pound's imagist theories and adherence to a scholastic understanding of language—following Aquinas and Dante, his *nomina sunt consequentia rerum* (*GB*, 92)—were crucial to his reorientation of modernist poetry. Imagism, in theory, was an attempt to dissociate poetry from a more romantic quest for an *au-delà* and to ground knowledge upon our concretely realized experience of *this* world. As William Carlos Williams suggested very early on, Pound's *Cantos* force us to consider them "in relation to the principal move in imaginative writing today—that away from the word as symbol toward the word as reality,"[7] and he later gave Pound's imagist dictum its definitive form in this memorable line from *Paterson*: "Say it! No ideas but in things."[8]

Nevertheless, despite this longstanding critical tradition arguing for an "objectivist" Pound, despite the proliferating number of critical interpretations demonstrating with ever-increasing thoroughness the centrality of Pound's historical and economic vision to the *Cantos*, and despite its reliance on a wide-ranging, comparative study of literature, I do want to suggest that this official version of modernism is curiously Anglocentric. Applying literary criticism's version of the "deep-pockets law," this official history transforms Pound's rejection of symbolism into a blanket condemnation of modern French poetry and of those English poets, many of whom were Pound's literary idols, who succumbed to the pernicious influence of the French. Although no critic will deny that Pound began his career in the Decadent tradition of *l'art pour l'art* and *poésie pure*, Pound's derivative "juvenalia," that is, anything he wrote up until his twenty-seventh year when he published *Ripostes* (1912), is still condemned as a youthful infatuation with an obsolescent literary past. As a result, we are almost compelled to talk about a poetic modernism emancipated from the bonds of literary history and arising ex nihilo as a predominantly American (or Celto-American) phenomenon.

Yet before *Ripostes*, Pound, especially with his series of troubadour masks, found himself at an impasse that paralleled the one facing young French poets of the same period. Pound's antiquarian spirit is subject to the same caveat addressed to his contemporaries by Tristan Derème: "On n'écrit plus, non plus, de sonnets sur Cléopâtre ou sur les troubadours et rares sont les mains qui ouvrent encore la porte de ces magasins de décors que l'on nomme l'antiquité ou le Moyen-Age" [One no longer writes sonnets on Cleopatra or the troubadours, and rare are the hands that still open the door of those decorating shops that we call antiquity or the Middle Ages].[9] And because Pound did

radically transform his poetry in *Ripostes*, with its emphasis on the con-
temporary world, as well as its more vigorous language that begins to
eliminate the Pre-Raphaelite diction and the Decadent posturing of
his previous verse, it would certainly be very appealing indeed to lo-
cate Pound's modernity at a precise and biographically verifiable mo-
ment in his career—to say, for example, that Ford's rolling on the floor
triumphed over Yeats's evenings, or that imagism emerged from a
fortuitous meeting between Pound, Aldington, and H. D. in a London
tea shop. Unfortunately, it is doubtful that even Ford's acrobatic feat
would constrain someone like Pound to discard the cultural bric-a-
brac he had so assiduously collected, and if we faithfully accept
Pound's historiography, we risk replacing a history of the *development*
of poetic modernism with a *big bang* theory that charts the tremors and
aftershocks of Ford Madox Ford's tumble on the floor. Thus, I think
we need to look elsewhere if we are to account for the modern voice
that begins to appear in Pound's poetry.[10]

Not coincidentally, Pound donned the modernist mantle at pre-
cisely the moment that he became interested in contemporary French
poetry in 1912 (and probably earlier through the intervention of F. S.
Flint). Next to Flint, Pound was most responsible for disseminating
knowledge to English and American readers about developments in
France. Pound wrote numerous articles on French verse between
1913 and 1934, the most significant of which include "The Approach
to Paris" (1913), "Irony, Laforgue, and Some Satire" (1917), "The
Hard and Soft in French Poetry" (1918), "A Study in French Poets"
(1918), "Paris Letters" (1920), the French issues of *The Little Review*
(1921–1924), and his unpublished "French Poets: A Postscript"
(1934).[11] This last retrospective note, though brief and otherwise unil-
luminating, is significant because it continues to underscore, as late as
1934, this important French influence in a manner uncolored by
Pound's early modernist polemics:

> The reader in 1934 will be puzzled by the amount of attention given to
> Jammes. That belongs to an almost forgotten transition. Perhaps no one
> who wasn't in London about 1912 will understand one's interest in 'that
> sort of thing'. That sort of thing being an attempt to get rid of wooded
> and rhetorical phraseology. . . . From 1911 to 1917 or '18, my sifting out
> of French verse implied search for what we didn't know. Writing from
> Paris after 1920, I was merely reporting on current publication that was
> good enough to merit interest or respect outside of Paris.

Kenner's more or less strategic dismissal of the French influence on
Pound has obscured the international nature of modernism. We must
at all times remember that just as Pound was attempting to extricate

himself from the decadent poses and the Celticism of the Aesthetes, so too the French post-Symbolists were attempting to escape the legacy left them by Mallarmé. As Kenneth Cornell has argued, the post-Symbolists reacted against Mallarmé's aesthetic because it was overly hermetic and failed to provide a "comprehensive view of life,"[12] and because it presented entirely private emotions that could only be interpreted with great difficulty, if at all. This opposition to Mallarmé's symbolism led the post-Symbolists away "from the confession of individual emotion to a conscious consideration of man as a social being."[13] Searching for a way out of this symbolist deadlock, argues Enid Starkie,

> Writers now turned to the iconoclastic poets of the eighteen seventies for inspiration, to those who had written then, but had not been fully appreciated or understood during the Decadent or Symbolist movements; to Tristan Corbière, Charles Cros, Lautréamont and Jean Richepin; and to those later poets who resemble them, to Laurent Tailhade, and Jules Laforgue; and Jules Laforgue's literary heir, Guillaume Apollinaire.[14]

Significantly, these poets are precisely those whom Pound himself championed, further suggesting the link between the post-Symbolist revolt described above and Pound's imagist revolt in 1912. Although Pound openly rejected both Baudelaire's and Mallarmé's conception of poetry, his interest in such poets as Tristan Corbière, Jules Laforgue, Laurent Tailhade, and Jules Romains certainly links him to the critical problems raised by a symbolist aesthetic.

Cyrena Pondrom, in her important *Road from Paris: French Influence on English Poetry, 1900–1920*, has chronicled both the influence of modern French poetry on Anglo-American modernism and Pound's much-debated role in the dissemination of knowledge about French poetry to his English and American publics.[15] English interest in French verse was curbed by the scandals surrounding the Decadence, but it reawakened during the second decade of the twentieth century, and, as early as 1908, F. S. Flint was writing about Baudelaire, Mallarmé, and Verlaine, and was "advocating in the course of a series of articles on recent books a poetry in vers libre, akin in spirit to the Japanese."[16] At this same time, T. E. Hulme had founded the Poets' Club and was writing "imagist" poems modeled, as he suggests in his "Lecture on Modern Poetry" (1909), on the French vers libre of Kahn.[17] Flint soon came into contact with Hulme, and after seceding from the Poets' Club Hulme suggested in March of 1909 that they form a Second Poets' Club along with Edward Storer, F. W. Tancred, Joseph Campbell, Florence Farr, and, in April of that year, Ezra Pound. As Flint describes it, "what brought the real nucleus of this

group together was a dissatisfaction with English poetry as it was then
. . . being written. We proposed at various times to replace it by pure
vers libre; by the Japanese *tanka* and *haikai.* . . . There was also a lot of
talk and practice among us, Storer leading it chiefly, of what we called
the Image. We were very much influenced by modern French symbol-
ist poetry."[18] And as a direct result of this "talk and practice," Flint
published *In the Net of the Stars* (1909), modeled on the verse of Ver-
haeren and Régnier.[19]

Interest in French developments continued to simmer during the
early years of the second decade until it exploded in 1912 with Flint's
monumental "Contemporary French Poetry,"[20] an extensive survey of
French post-Symbolism which, as Pound admitted, "everybody had to
get" (*SL*, 35). Flint's study introduced English readers to the largely
unfamiliar world of French poetry, commencing with the vers libre of
Gustave Kahn, Henri de Régnier, and Henri Ghéon, and including
what for English readers would be much more esoteric figures like
André Spire, Georges Périn, Georges Duhamel, Tancrède de Visan,
Henri Hertz, as well as movements like Jean Royère's *Néo-Mallarmisme*,
the *Néo-Paganisme* of Théo Varlet and Paul Castiaux, Jules Romains's
Unanimisme, Nicolas Beauduin's and Jean Thogorma's *Paroxysme*, Flo-
rian-Parmentier's *Impulsionnisme*, Marinetti's *Futurisme* and Lucien
Rolmer's *École de Grâce*, and, finally, the poets associated with *L'Abbaye
de Créteil:* René Arcos, Charles Vildrac, Henri-Martin Barzun, Alexan-
dre Mercereau.

Pound followed Flint's lead in 1913 by publishing his own "Ap-
proach to Paris," creating the illusion of a common front linking the
imagist movement and French post-Symbolism, as well as setting the
stage for the bitter recriminations regarding the honor of precedence
that would arise with the breakup of the imagist movement.[21] And
because Pound's discussion of such poets as Romains, Vildrac, Spire,
Régnier, and Barzun merely reiterates Flint's in some ways, the vari-
ous partisan claims that Flint was instrumental in introducing Pound
to French poetry have gained in credibility, as Pound himself back-
handedly admits in a letter to his mother: "Flint, in return for being
resurrected, has put me on to some very good contemporary French
stuff: Remy de Gourmont, de Régnier, etc."[22] In his "History of
Imagism," Flint belittles Pound's knowledge of modern French poetry
at the time he joined the Poets' Club, saying that "he could not be
made to believe that there was any French poetry after Ronsard," and
suggests that Pound only became interested in French verse in 1912.[23]
Similarly, John Gould Fletcher maintains that his remarks to Pound in
the summer of 1913 "seemed to impress him with the thought there
might be something in the symbolists after all, whom he had never

actually read. . . . When I next saw him he was already enthusiastic over de Gourmont, Corbière, and the early Francis Jammes."[24]

Nevertheless, such claims are misleading because Pound would certainly have been exposed to French poetry through the Poets' Club, especially if that was the group's principal interest as Flint maintains, and Richard Aldington admits that the Pound of 1912–1914 "gave [him] Verlaine [and] the Symbolistes."[25] Moreover, even if Flint did break the ground, Pound's discussion of Romains and Vildrac goes far beyond both Flint's analysis of poetic practice and his understanding of literary history. In fact, Pound was subsequently praised by Romains for the depth of his insights: "Une grande sympathie pour ma manière de sentir les choses de l'univers et de l'art vous à donné, certes, à mon égard une indulgence excessive. Mais j'ai en tant de fois à souffrir de l'incompréhension de mes compatriotes, que vos paroles ne peuvent manquer d'être les bienvenues" [Your great sympathy for my way of experiencing the things of the universe and of art has certainly led to an excessive indulgence toward me. But I have so often suffered the incomprehension of my compatriots that your remarks can only be welcome ones].[26] More importantly, Flint's and Pound's studies differ significantly. Whereas the former discusses only the post-Symbolists, the latter pays great attention to poets outside the purview of Flint's study (to Corbière, Tailhade, Jammes, and to Gautier en passant) and gives a surprisingly strong emphasis to poets connected with the Symbolist *cénacle*, to Gourmont and Régnier. And given the strength of his individual analyses, I think we have to attribute Pound's somewhat peculiar emphasis on what he himself calls "back numbers" to a specific program shaped by his own poetic interests rather than to any deficiency in his knowledge of contemporary developments in France. Although he tends to vacillate between, on the one hand, the quasi-symbolist melodic structures of Gourmont or Régnier and, on the other, a "modernist" prose constatation and the "strict, chaste, severe" syntax and "clarification of the speech" of Corbière, Tailhade, and Romains (*AP* 3, 607), the tension created by the joining of these mutually opposed lines of descent is not a contradiction deriving from mere ignorance, but an important catalyst for Pound's developing poetic. In other words, we can begin to see in his selection a series of strategic choices containing the rudiments of a canon that would remain intact throughout his career and, I will argue, would help to shape his own poetic. Pound's "Approach to Paris" outlines a poetic program that foretells his eventual break with the imagists and his subsequent redefinition of imagist practice.

Pound's first important revision of Hulme's and Flint's account of French poetry was his attempt to give new life to Parnassianism. Both

Hulme and Flint viewed the Parnassians as the manifestation of an evolutionary process wherein, as Flint describes it, "School followed school: Romanticism, Parnassianism, Naturalism, each in turn denied its forerunners and was denied; and the latest comer of all, Symbolism, which denied all." "What," asks Flint, "was symbolism?":

> First of all, a contempt for the wordy flamboyance of the romanticists; secondly, a reaction against the impassive descriptiveness of the parnassians; thirdly, a disgust of the 'slice of life' of the naturalists. Ultimately, it was an attempt to evoke the subconscious element of life, to set vibrating the infinity within us, by the juxtaposition of images. Its philosophy, in fact, as M. Tancrède de Visan has shown in that profound book, *L'Attitude du Lyrisme Contemporain*, was the philosophy of intuitiveness: it has been formulated by Bergson.[27]

And Symbolism, Flint argues, again echoing Hulme, "is itself in process of evolution into other, different forms,"[28] which, for both Hulme and Flint, ultimately meant the more "perfect" poetic form of vers libre. As Hulme puts it, ignoring the Symbolists altogether, "With the definite arrival of this new verse in 1880 came the appearance of a band of poets perhaps unequalled at any one time in the history of French poetry."[29]

But where Hulme describes the Parnassian school as a "reaction from romanticism [that] has come rapidly to decay,"[30] and Flint maligns the "impassive descriptiveness" of the Parnassians, who, "exhausted," "sank into an idiocy of echolalia,"[31] Pound broadly extends the notion of a specifically Parnassian poetry by applying the label to Régnier, whom he considers "the last of the Parnassians, or at the least the last one who counts" (*AP* 5, 663). Pound also counters the Parnassians' critics by upholding Régnier as a model for modern poets: "It is fairly obvious that there exists in Paris a numerous and clamorous younger generation who consider M. De Régnier a back number. It is equally obvious that there are among the English writers many who have not attained to any standards more recent than those employed by this author" (*AP* 5, 663). And where Hulme and Flint classify Monde, Prudhomme, de Lisle, de Vigny, Banville, and Heredia as Parnassians, Pound extends the notion of Parnassianism even further to include not only Régnier, but also, and even more importantly, Théophile Gautier: "If the Parnassians were following Gautier they fell short of his merit. Heredia is perhaps the best of them. He tries to make his individual statements more 'poetic'; his whole, for all this, becomes frigid. Samain follows him and begins to go 'soft', there is just a suggestion of muzziness" (*LE*, 285).[32] In many respects Pound's definition of Parnassianism corresponds to subsequent reappraisals of the movement by recent critics like Pierre Martino:

Si l'on faisait commencer l'histoire du Parnasse en 1866—année où parut la première série du *Parnasse contemporain*—, on rendrait cette histoire bien peu intelligible, et elle serait vite inexacte. On s'obligerait d'abord à ne point parler, ou très peu, de Théophile Gautier, de Théodore de Banville, de Baudelaire, de Leconte de Lisle, dont, à cette date, les oeuvres, du moins les belles, étaient presque entièrement parues. Ce sont eux pourtant qui, aujourd'hui, représentent le plus complètement l'idéal parnassien; ils le définirent eux-mêmes fort nettement, et ils le réalisèrent en des oeuvres de grand prestige; auprès d'eux, un Sully Prudhomme, un Glatigny, un Dierx, un Coppée, même un Heredia ne font pas grande figure. Et puis, ce qui est aussi grave peut-être, on serait disposé, à cause du tour que prit à ce moment-là, et pour un peu de temps, la bataille littéraire, à définir le mouvement parnassien comme une révolte contre le romantisme.

[If one began the history of the Parnassians in 1866, the year in which appeared the first *Parnasse contemporain*, one would render this history a little unintelligible, and it would soon become inaccurate. One would be obliged not to talk about, or to talk very little about, Théophile Gautier, Théodore de Banville, Baudelaire, Leconte de Lisle—poets whose works, at least their best works, had almost entirely appeared by this time. These poets, however, are those who today represent most completely the Parnassian ideal; they defined this ideal in a very concise manner and realized it in very prestigious works. After them a Sully Prudhomme, a Glatigny, a Dierx, a Coppée, even a Heredia, is not a major figure. Moreover, and perhaps even more important, one would be obliged, because of the turn taken in the literary revolt at that moment, and only for a brief time, to define the Parnassian movement as a revolt against the romantics.][33]

Pound's broadening of Parnassianism to include Gautier was a decisive move in his appropriation of the French tradition. First, it enabled him to salvage some of his previous literary heroes like Swinburne and Lionel Johnson and still continue his search for a modern voice. Gautier's importance to Pound is signaled at the outset of his "Approach to Paris" when he says that "Lionel Johnson alone would seem to have reached the polish and fineness of 'Emaux et Camees' in those few poems of his where he seems to be moved by emotion rather than by critical spirit" (*AP* 2, 557), an argument that is repeated with even more force in Pound's 1915 "Preface to the *Poems of Lionel Johnson*":

One thinks that he had read and admired Gautier, or that at least, he had derived similar ambition from some traditional source. One thinks that his poems are in short hard sentences. The reality is that they are full of definite statement. . . . The impression of Lionel Johnson's verse is that of small slabs of ivory, firmly combined and contrived. There is a constant feeling of neatness, a sense of inherited order. Above all he respected his art. (*LE*, 363)

Pound's attempt to link the poetry of his predecessors to that of Gautier was by no means an original one. In an essay with which Pound was surely familiar, Henry James had already compared Gautier to Robert Browning: "There are a host of reasons why we should not compare Gautier with such a poet as Browning; and yet there are several why we should."[34] What James singles out in this essay is Gautier's "pagan *bonhomie*" and "Homeric simplicity": "His world was all material. . . . His faculty of visual discrimination was extraordinary. His observation was so penetrating and his descriptive instinct so unerring, that one might have fancied grave Nature, in a fit of coquetry, or tired of receiving but half-justice, had determined to construct a genius with senses of a finer strain than the mass of the human family."[35] James's endorsement of Gautier thus legitimizes Pound's prior Hellenism and at the same time points toward a modern poetic tradition sanctioned by the master himself. By following Gautier, Pound could still retain his own pagan *bonhomie* without succumbing to the impressionistic "muzziness" of the nineties because Gautier's Parnassianism was firmly grounded upon a descriptive clarity that had similarly escaped the rhetoric of romanticism.[36] "For poets who were repelled by feeble visual and auditive imagery or by jejune poetic terms," says John Porter Houston, "the descriptive style with its well-defined, if limited vocabulary, and normality of epithets, meant firmness, clarity, and concreteness."[37]

Gautier was indeed a seminal figure for Pound because he had already outlined in his poetry the terms of the debate between Ford Madox Ford and Yeats and had been able to mediate between these opposed demands for a quotidian realism and a Parnassian longing for ideal beauty. In poems like "Symphonie en blanc majeur,"[38] Gautier discovers an absolute beauty within the quotidian world of the *salon* and yet manages to escape the frigid sterility of that ideal world through his lively play of correspondences. Describing a beautiful woman playing the piano, Gautier transposes this cascade of fragile notes and tremolos into a color symphony "en blanc majeur" and fashions a poésie pure to rival the purity of music. In terms very similar to those used by Mallarmé in his "Le Vierge, le vivace et le bel aujourd'hui," Gautier compares this beautiful woman to a "femme-cygne" of Nordic legends. She is "Blanche comme le clair de lune/Sur les glaciers dans les cieux froids," and this frigid purity brings the seemingly despairing poet to ask himself: "Oh! qui pourra mettre un ton rose / Dans cette implacable blancheur!" [As white as the moonlight on glaciers in cold skies. . . . Oh! who can add a rose tint to this implacable whiteness!]. But this question is merely a rhetorical one, for Gautier himself has already given life to the "implacable blancheur" of this winter landscape:

> Son sein, neige moulée en globe,
> Contre les camélias blancs
> Et le blanc satin de sa robe
> Soutient des combats insolents.
>
> Dans ces grandes batailles blanches,
> Satins et fleurs ont le dessous,
> Et, sans demander leurs revanches,
> Jaunissent comme des jaloux.
>
> [Her breast, a globe of molded snow,
> Against her white camellias
> And the white satin of her gown
> Begins its insolent skirmishes.
>
> In this great winter campaign,
> Satin and flowers are routed,
> And, without demanding revenge,
> Turn yellow like jealous lovers.]

These proliferating images of whiteness—her white breast, the snow, camellias, and white satin—are vivid and concrete realizations of an absolute purity, and as they begin their "combats insolents" they take on a life of their own and escape Mallarmé's "songe froid de mépris / Que vêt parmi l'exil inutile le Cygne" [chill dream of contempt donned by the swan in its futile exile].[39] As David Kelley has remarked, "Cette coulée ininterrompue de fantaisie en mouvement sert simultanément d'affirmation et de négation de l'idéal" [This uninterrupted flow of mobile fantasy serves simultaneously to affirm and to negate the ideal].[40] As we shall see, Pound's *Ripostes* is heavily influenced by this aspect of Gautier's poetic, especially such poems as "The Alchemist," where Pound undertakes this same quest for a concretely realized idealization of the quotidian.

Even more significantly, in this same "Approach to Paris" series where Pound compares Gautier and Lionel Johnson, he singles out a line from Gautier's "Carmen" ("Carmen est maigre—un trait de bistre") as a forerunner of Laurent Tailhade's satirical *Poèmes Aristophanesques* and, by association, the poetry of Tristan Corbière (*AP* 5, 662). By emphasizing Gautier's prose-like "constatation of fact," Pound is able to derive from Gautier's Parnassian search for "ideal beauty" a "satirical realism" approaching the idioms of Flaubert, Joyce, and Lewis. If we turn to Pound's poetry from the *Lustra* period, we see that his own "satirical realism" depends heavily upon this other, "realist" Gautier. In "Albâtre," Pound's monochrome "Symphonie en blanc mineur," he scants Gautier's mythopoeic vision and satirizes a pretentious bourgeoise "in the white bath-robe which she calls a peignoir," who is accompanied by "the delicate white feet of her little white dog" (P, 88). Instead of Gautier's "albâtre où la mélancolie/ Aime à retrouver ses pâleurs" [alabaster where melancholy loves to rediscover its pallor],[41] Pound resorts in the end to a flat monotone: "Nor would Gautier himself have despised their con-/trasts in whiteness" (P, 88). Thus, his peculiar transformation (or deformation) of Gautier enables him to create a poetic genealogy descending from Gautier that not only includes the symbolism of Régnier and Gourmont, but also leads directly to the satirical realism of Corbière, Laforgue, and Tailhade, a line of descent that recapitulates Pound's vision of the modern novelistic tradition stemming from Flaubert. Pound discovers in Gautier's poetry an originary node similar to the one most critics see in Baudelaire, one which permits the joining of the artist, the visionary, and the realist in a single figure. Whereas Marcel Raymond has proposed a genealogy linking Baudelaire and subsequent poet-priests (Mallarmé, Valéry) and poet-visionaries (Rimbaud)[42]; and where Francis Burch has extended that Baudelairean genealogy to include such "poet-realists" as Corbière, Laforgue, Apollinaire, Pound, and Eliot[43]; Pound ignores Baudelaire altogether, but nevertheless preserves a nascent symbolism by discovering in Gautier the wellspring of all viable modern French poetry.[44] In other words, there are in fact three Gautiers in Pound's pantheon: the Parnassian-Symbolist championed by Mallarmé, the romantic protosymbolist praised by Baudelaire, and the realist poet whom Pound likens to Flaubert.

    Evidence of Gautier's Parnassian influence on Pound can be found as early as *Riposies* (1912). Numerous critics have pointed out Régnier's influence on "The Return" and Gourmont's on "The Alchemist" (1912).[45] But in addition to these poems, Pound's "Apparuit," "carven in subtle stuff," is a *transposition d'art* very much akin to Gautier's "À une robe rose." Another Gautieresque echo, though perhaps circumstantial, can be found in Pound's "Pan is Dead," which contains the same Plutarchian reference adopted by Gautier in his "Bûchers et Tombeaux." Finally, Gautier's "Nostalgies d'obélisques" would seem to have suggested Pound's treatment of the ascetic life in "The Tomb at Akr Çaar" (P, 56–57), a very unusual poem for Pound because of its Egyptian framework.[46] Both poems adopt a "monumentalized" voice that transcends time, and both contain explicit temporal references that suggest a parallel between the two poems: "On a mis mon secret, qui pèse / Le poids de cinq mille ans d'oublis" [They hid my secret, which has borne the weight of five millennia's oblivion]; "I am thy soul, Nikoptis. I have watched / These five millennia." Moreover, both poems make central the act of interpreting the mysterious hiero-glyphs or the "emblèmes dorés et peints" [painted and gilded em-blems]: "Là-bas, il voit à ses sculptures / S'arrêter un peuple vivant, / Hiératiques écritures, / Que l'idée épelle en rêvant" [He sees the living people below stop dead before his sculptures, dreaming of this hier-atic writing that spells out the idea image by image]; "I have read out the gold upon the wall, / And wearied out my thought upon the signs."

More important, we can see in a comparison of the two poems the beginnings of a fundamental rift that will shape Pound's critical ap-propriation of Gautier. In Gautier's "Nostalgies d'obélisques," the ob-elisk in Paris holds a disdain for the shabby modern world of Paris, "l'abri des corruptions" [the abode of corruptions], and looks back to the ancient grandeur of Egypt: "Je te pleure, ô ma vieille Égypte, / Avec des larmes de granit!" [I cry for you, o my ancient Egypt, / With tears of granite!]. The "obélisque de Luxor," on the other hand, envies his brother in Paris because he has escaped the eternal solitude of the vast, sterile desert and is surrounded by life:

> Que je voudrais comme mon frère,
> Dans ce grand Paris transporté,
> Auprès de lui, pour me distraire,
> Sur une place être planté!
>
> . . . .
>
> Les fontaines juxtaposées
> Sur la poudre de son granit
> Jettent leurs brumes irisées;
> Il est vermeil, il rajeunit!
>
> Des veines roses de Syène
> Comme moi cependant il sort,
> Mais je reste à ma place ancienne,
> Il est vivant et je suis mort!
>
> [Would that I were like my brother,
> Transported to that great city,
> Near him, guarding a city square,
> With all Paris there to divert me!
>
> . . . .
>
> Bathed in his granite dust,
> The two juxtaposed fountains
> Reciprocate with rainbow mist.
> He reddens and grows young again!

His rosy Syenitic face
Is still like mine; but because he's fled
And I stay in my ancient place,
He is living and I am dead!]

As David Kelley has suggested, "le paradoxe de 'Nostalgies d'obélis-
ques' est aussi et surtout celui de la situation du poète au dix-neuvième
siècle" [the paradox voiced in 'Nostalgies d'obélisques' is above all that
of the poet in the nineteenth century].[47] For Gautier, to flee from
modern life is to succumb to artistic death; yet to embrace life means
to run the risk of giving in to the triviality of a social existence. In
Pound's poem, on the other hand, the soul, although it could flee "the
jagged dark" for "the glass-green fields," decides to remain in the
tomb because "it is quiet" there. Whereas Gautier leaves the central
paradox in play, Pound ignores any possible dialectical resolution and
opts for a relatively simple ascesis. Instead of Gautier's subtle balanc-
ing of the ideal and real worlds, of the subjective and objective, Pound
sunders these realms.

Although I do not wish to put too much weight on a slight poem like
"The Tomb at Akr Çaar," I want to argue that it is symptomatic of a
pattern that begins to emerge in Pound's own poetry. Pound's poetic
development mirrors his skewed critical appropriation of Gautier.
Whereas *Ripostes* was written under the influence of the Parnassian
Gautier, *Lustra* evolves out of Pound's (mis)reading of "Carmen" and
redeploys Gautier's realism for satirical purposes shaped largely by
the satires of Corbière and Tailhade. Pound then gives this Corbi-
èrean aesthetic a further inflection in *Mauberley* by adopting the ur-
bane irony of Jules Laforgue. And indeed, at every point, and with
every poet, we will find a surprisingly similar series of conjunctions
and disjunctions that will help us to see not only precisely what Pound
gained from his study of French poetry, but also what he was com-
pelled to ignore.

If we turn, for example, to some of the other unexpected elements
of the French tradition upon which he builds, we can argue that
Pound's reading of Corbière not only initiates his call for a poetry of
realism, but that Corbière's poetry also suggests to him the possibility
and legitimacy of a collage method approaching that of the dadaists.
Examined in this light, Pound's "objective" language, his ideogramic
method so often associated with his discovery of the Fenollosa manu-
scripts, is as much the result of his interest in French poetry. At the
same time, however, we can see that Corbière's associative techniques
pose a threat to Pound in that they raise the idea of an unconscious
mind, later exploited by the Surrealists and by Joyce in *Finnegans*

Wake, but rejected by Pound. Similarly, Pound's treatment of Laforgue is predicated on his ironizing or eliminating altogether Laforgue's explicit references to Nirvana and the Unconscious. Pound's discussions of the externalized, "objective" representation evident in the poets he champions will thus help us to recontextualize his subsequent treatments (and his emergent fear) of a self-implicating, romantic subjectivity, of an in-depth language, and of "l'éternel féminin."

Still, it would seem that Pound invariably returned to, and was therefore probably initially attracted by, what repelled him as a modernist. Despite Pound's championing of the realism of Gautier, Corbière, and Tailhade, we will find inscribed in *Mauberley* precisely that problematic, and admittedly problematized, fascination with "l'éternel féminin" and that romantic subjectivity he attempted to purge from Gautier's poetic.[48] Although Pound legitimizes his poetics of externalization by referring to half of Gautier's aesthetic program, he leaves open the possibility that the subjective, visionary aspect of Gautier's poetry, what Baudelaire described as his "immense connaissance innée de la *correspondance* et du symbolisme universels,"[49] would reappear as a "return of the repressed." Indeed, this suspicion that there might be a strong element of repression at work in Pound's appropriation of the French tradition helps, I think, to explain the lingering sense, even in the face of an overwhelming critical consensus arguing for an "objectivist" Pound, that his poetry has symbolist underpinnings.[50] Although Pound's growing obsession with economic history would tend to suggest that he has forever shed his Decadent mantle, his frequent references to a doctrine of signatures in the late cantos indicate, perhaps, an illicit and unacknowledged return to that symbolist worldview from which he attempted so vigorously to separate himself. But because any such argument risks being seduced by the siren song of symbolism, risks running aground upon the theoretical foundations of the Symbol, I prefer to chart a safer course and limit my discussion to Pound's confrontation with, and ostensible rejection of, the French Symbolists.

.   .   .

As T. S. Eliot remarked of Pound, "He showed a discriminating taste among the minor poets of the 'Symbolist Movement'. But he ignores Mallarmé; he is uninterested in Baudelaire."[51] Whereas Eliot would argue that Baudelaire's technical mastery made him "the greatest exemplar in *modern* poetry in any language,"[52] Pound the archmodernist finds this "shaggy influx" or "Baudelairian 'vigour' . . . too facile a mechanism" (*P&D*, 75). Similarly, where Eliot would praise Baudelaire's "theological innocence,"[53] Pound seconds Henry James's evaluation of his moral stance: "A good way to embrace Baudelaire at a glance is to say that he was, in his treatment of evil, exactly what Hawthorne was not—Hawthorne, who felt the thing at its source, deep in the human consciousness. Baudelaire's infinitely slighter volume of genius apart, he was a sort of Hawthorne reversed."[54]

While Eliot's discussion is undoubtedly colored by his own critical position, the disparity between Pound's and Eliot's views of French Symbolism is so great that it become almost incomprehensible.[55] Moreover, given Gautier's and Baudelaire's estimation of one another's work, Pound's antagonism toward Baudelaire and his unbounded admiration for Gautier become somewhat perplexing.[56] Although it is entirely possible that Pound has rejected in advance Eliot's arguments on behalf of Baudelaire's theological dualism, it would seem that Pound's hostility has an even deeper source.

On the surface, at least, Pound seems less concerned with what James describes as Baudelaire's "groping sense of the moral complexities of life"[57] than with his poetic technique. Here as elsewhere, Pound follows James's account of French romantic poetry quite closely. James strongly contrasts Gautier and Baudelaire, much to the detriment of the latter: "Gautier was perfectly sincere, because he dealt only with the picturesque and pretended to care only for appearances. But Baudelaire (who, to our mind, was an altogether inferior genius to Gautier) applied the same process of interpretation to things as regards which it was altogether inadequate; so that one is constantly tempted to suppose he cares more for his process—for making grotesquely-pictorial verse—than for the things themselves."[58] Baudelaire's vision of evil, says James, "begins outside and not inside, and consists primarily of a great deal of lurid landscape and unclean furniture. This is an almost ludicrously puerile view of the matter. Evil is represented as an affair of blood and carrion and physical sickness— there must be stinking corpses and starving prostitutes and empty laudanum bottles in order that the poet shall be effectively inspired."[59]

Like James, Pound begins his discussion with the "much finer question . . . of the contrast between Gautier and Baudelaire" (*P&D*, 74), that is, the inimitability of the former and the relative translatability of the latter. Pound echoes James's condemnation of Baudelaire when he derides the "decayed-lily verbiage" of the Decadence: "Vomit, carefully labelled 'Beauty', is still in the literary market, and much sought after in the provinces" (*P&D*, 74). Then, regarding Baudelaire's "shaggy influx," Pound says:

Any decayed cabbage, cast upon any pale satin sofa will give one a sense
of contrast. I am not saying that Baudelaire is nothing but cabbages cast
upon satin sofas, but merely that in many poems one "unpleasant" ele-
ment is no more inevitable than another, and that for a great many of his
words and lines other words and lines might be substituted; and that he
can be translated very roughly without losing any of his quality. (P&D,
75)

When Pound criticizes another poet's style, however, such ostensibly
technical discussions often serve to conceal deeper issues that hit
rather close to home. For example, although he criticizes Henri de
Régnier for needing "two thousand odd pages to say that he delights
in gardens full of statues and running water and that Greek mythol-
ogy is enchanting" (AP 5, 663), we will find upon closer observation
that it is to those poems "full of statues" that Pound turns as models
for his own verse. Thus, before uncritically accepting Pound's (or,
more charitably, Walter Villerant's) examples of Baudelaire's "de-
cayed cabbages," we might want to search for an underlying motiva-
tion for his reaction (or, more correctly, his overreaction) to Baude-
laire's "Une Nuit que j'étais près d'une affreuse Juive":[60]

> One night stretched out along a hebrew bitch—
> Like two corpses at the undertakers—
> This carcass, sold alike to jews and quakers,
> Reminded me of beauty noble and rich.
> Although she stank like bacon in the flitch,
> I thought of her as though the ancient makers
> Had shown her mistress of a thousand acres,
> Casqued and perfumed, so that my nerves 'gan twitch. . . .
>
>   (P&D, 74)

But for one observation, Pound's description of his translation is
fairly just: "I finished the sonnet without much mental effort in fifteen
minutes of a May morning, threw away the MSS., and this is all that
comes back to me. It seems fairly Baudelairian but is nowhere inevita-
ble, nor does it seem to me greatly worth recovering" (P&D, 75). Al-
though this early poem is very arguably not one of Baudelaire's best,
the "decayed cabbages" Pound has thrown up here are entirely home-
grown. The poem contains no "bacon in the flitch" or "twitching
nerves," and Baudelaire's complex vision of a "triste beauté" has been
reduced to a clichéd "beauty noble and rich." Although intended as
"criticism by translation," Pound's version fails to bare the principal
features of Baudelaire's poetic technique. Seemingly fascinated by the

image of the "affreuse Juive," Pound so exaggerates every subsequent image that his translation soon devolves into a pointless, and largely monochromatic, parody that completely misses the dialectical tensions that make the poem interesting.

Indeed, although Pound would probably not have known or cared that the "Juive" was Baudelaire's mistress, Sara, or that she is featured in a much more attractive light in other poems, or that the "reine des cruelles" is possibly Jeanne Duval,[61] it is nevertheless overwhelmingly clear that Baudelaire wants to suggest a strong contrast between two very different types of women and types of love, between the cadaverous prostitute *à corps vendu* and the "triste beauté" of the "reine des cruelles"; and between "désir" and "amour":

> Une nuit que j'étais près d'une affreuse Juive,
> Comme au long d'un cadavre un cadavre étendu,
> Je me pris à songer près de ce corps vendu
> A la triste beauté dont mon désir se prive.
>
> Je me représentai sa majesté native,
> Son regard de vigueur et de grâces armé,
> Ses cheveux qui lui font un casque parfumé,
> Et dont le souvenir pour l'amour me ravive.
>
> Car j'eusse avec ferveur baisé ton noble corps,
> Et depuis tes pieds frais jusqu'à tes noires tresses
> Déroulé le trésor des profondes caresses,
>
> Si, quelque soir, d'un pleur obtenu sans effort
> Tu pouvais seulement, ô reine des cruelles!
> Obscurcir la splendeur de tes froides prunelles.
>
> [A hideous Jewess lay with me for hire
> One night: two corpses side by side we seemed
> And stretched by that polluted thing I dreamed
> Of the sad beauty of my vain desire.
> I thought upon her brow clad round with fire
> And matchless strength, her native majesty,
> Her perfumed helm of hair whose memory
> Makes me toward Love's heights to reaspire.
> For fervently I would have rained, my Sweet,
> Fond kisses over all thy form divine
> Even from thy black tresses to thy feet,
> If some soft evening, with a single tear,
> O cruel queen, thou couldst have dimmed the clear
> Cold splendour of those icy eyes of thine.][62]

Although not as complex as some of Baudelaire's other love poems, "Une Nuit" anticipates the representation of desire evident in "La Chevelure," wherein, as Leo Bersani has suggested, "The mobility of the desiring imagination makes the identity of the desiring self problematic. The movement away from the woman's physical presence is also a movement away from any fixed center of being in the poet. . . . the poet himself is set afloat among his fantasies, and the more intensely he desires the less possible it becomes to say anything conclusive about his desires."[63] "Une Nuit" begins with a cultural transgression, heightened by the suggestion of necrophilia, creating a sexual frisson that will generate and ultimately deny the poet's various, and increasingly displaced, representations of desire. Moved by this sordid sexual encounter, the poet dreams of "la triste beauté" and represents to himself an image or memory (*souvenir*) of "sa majesté native," which serves to reawaken or revive his love. Almost immediately, therefore, Baudelaire suggests an unbridgeable gap between presence and a re-presented past, between sexual desire (*désir*) and what begins to seem like a chivalric Love for a warrior-princess, and that gap grows even wider when we discover that the poet's love never had been reciprocated (*Car j'eusse . . . si*), and never will be since the "reine des cruelles" is incapable of dimming the splendor of her cold eyes. Thus, his love for her is an idealized one that becomes all the more desirable because she is unattainable.

But Baudelaire soon recognizes that there is a darker side to his idealization of the Beloved. His vision is merely a narcissistic projection of his fantasy onto the Beloved, and his request amounts to a demand for love that completely disregards her subjective world wherein tears are not obtained "sans effort" or without cause. And to add insult to injury, one might well imagine that it is actual sexual desire that withholds the poet's dream of "la triste beauté" ("Je me pris à songer . . . A la triste beauté dont mon désir se prive"), and that it is only with the cessation of desire that the poet can recover his "memory" of her, which undergoes a further displacement with its transformation into sexual fantasy. But, if sexual desire makes it impossible to uphold such imaginary constructs, the ardent passion depicted in his fantasy will inevitably repeat the macabre desire with which the poem began. What we see, in other words, is a desiring subject who is never actually present in his desire, as well as the futile circularity of desire weaving its fantasies around an imaginary or idealized object, which must itself be anchored, via a series of displacements, to a real, though debased, world.

Mario Praz's exhaustive analysis of the "romantic agony" leaves no doubt as to Baudelaire's central role in the reshaping of our modern

conceptions about Beauty. As Praz convincingly demonstrates, the ro-
mantics, and Baudelaire in particular, sought a "tainted beauty" that
commingled ugliness, corruption, horror, and death, and, anticipating
Freud, they considered "pain as an integral part of desire."[64] Such a
conception of Beauty signals the breakdown of fixed hierarchies—
"Enfer ou Ciel, qu'importe?"[65]—and a resultant fluidity of vision. As
Baudelaire writes in his *Journaux Intimes:* "J'ai trouvé la définition du
Beau, de mon Beau. C'est quelque chose d'ardent et de triste. . . . Une
tête séduisante et belle . . . c'est une tête qui fait rêver à la fois,—mais
d'une manière confuse,—de volupté et de tristesse" [I've found the
definition of the Beautiful, of my Beautiful. It's something ardent and
sad. . . . A seductive and beautiful head . . . a head that makes one
dream simultaneously—but in a confused manner—of sensual plea-
sure and sadness].[66]

We can therefore begin to see why Pound would rebel against the
"metaphysical muddle" precipitated by Baudelaire's dreaming "d'une
manière confuse," for it affords him no "bust thru from quotidian into
'divine or permanent world'" (*SL*, 210). For Pound, there can be no
blurring of boundaries, and he attempts to straightjacket Baudelaire
by insisting on the distinction between beauty and ugliness: "The cult
of beauty is the hygiene, it is sun, air and the sea and the rain and the
lake bathing. The cult of ugliness, Villon, Baudelaire, Corbière,
Beardsley are diagnosis. Flaubert is diagnosis" (*LE*, 45). Thus, when
he reconsiders poetry's diagnostic potential in 1918, he excommuni-
cates the "cult of ugliness" from the poetic realm: "Most good prose
arises, perhaps, from an instinct of negation; is the detailed, convinc-
ing analysis of something detestable. . . . Poetry is the assertion of a
positive, i.e. of desire, and endures for a longer period" (*LE*, 324).

Moreover, while Pound's development of his theory of the persona
and his later Scholastic understanding of *atasal*—"the identification of
the consciousness WITH the object. . . . union with the divine" (*GK*,
328)—argues for a similar concern with a more or less problematic
location of the *self*, Pound nonetheless seems to fear such a fluid con-
ception of the self and of the imagination. From the beginning, Pound
shows how acutely aware he is of the precarious nature of his various
personae: "In the 'search for oneself,' in the search for 'sincere self-
expression,' one gropes, one finds some seeming verity. One says 'I
am' this, that, or the other, and with the words scarcely uttered one
ceases to be that thing" (*GB*, 85). Although Pound intends this in a
positive light, we can immediately see the epistemological quagmire
suggested in the movement from one sentence to the next; a "seeming
verity" that "ceases to be that thing" the moment it is spoken is scarcely
a strong foundation for a self in search of itself. Pound is clearly un-

comfortable in this threateningly fluid world and cannot tolerate the angst accompanying the search for *un coeur mis à nu;* thus, instead of a "fairly Baudelairean" translation of "Une Nuit," we are left with a fairly Poundian reaction formation. Pound cheapens Baudelaire's complicated representation of sexual desire by reducing it to the base physicality of twitching nerves and then proceeds to muddy the picture with unnecessarily emphatic prejudices. It would appear that Pound's "decayed cabbages" are a form of rhetorical ornamentation (hypocrisis) serving to obscure rather than to reveal some hidden truth.

But does Pound really escape a Baudelairian vision by asserting that Gautier was the wellspring of all viable modern French poetry? Don't Gautier's "white camellias on white satin dresses" manifest the same tensions as Baudelaire's "decayed cabbages cast upon pale satin sofas," albeit in a more chaste or sanitized form? Gautier's "Caerulei Oculi," for example, contains an "eminently Medusean"[67] sense of Beauty and foregrounds the romantics' threatening conjunction of death and desire:

> Mon âme, avec la violence
> D'un irrésistible désir,
> Au milieu du gouffre s'élance
> Vers l'ombre impossible à saisir.
>
> [My soul, led by the violence
> Of an irresistible desire, vainly
> Leaps into the whirlpool's current
> Toward the shadow that cannot be seized.][68]

And because this poem also subtends Pound's *Mauberley*, we might well have to revise radically our understanding of Mauberley's (and Pound's) dilemma. Moreover, Pound continues to reinscribe this romantic dislocation of the self in his later representations of women (most notably in his portrait of Queen Bess in Canto 91), a consideration of which might help us explain Pound's need to anchor his poetry in a real world divorced from a desiring subject and to speak in a series of increasingly authoritarian voices.

In view of this near identity of a Gautieresque and Baudelairian vision, I want to suggest that the presence of Gautier in Pound's pantheon might provide another, somewhat paradoxical inflection to both his French canon and his own poetic. Whether or not Gautier lies behind Pound's subtle qualification of the "doctrine of the image" ("Direct treatment of the 'thing,' whether subjective or objective"), his rediscovery of Gautier enables him to justify on theoretical grounds his subsequent return to those symbolist arabesques disallowed by the strict application of the imagists' program. In order to make this point clear, however, we must return briefly to the literary tradition from whence Pound arose. After all, Pound didn't take his *alchimie* straight from the Symbolists, but absorbed it from the Aesthetes.

· · ·

Pound would have imbibed those arch-Symbolists Verlaine and Mallarmé through Dowson, to whom he pays homage in "The Decadence," and through Symons and Yeats. Pound fondly quotes an occasional poem by Verlaine in an early letter (1911 or 1912) to Dorothy Shakespear, saying "Ça c'est la chose qu'on appelle le style," and allusions to Mallarmé crop up in his poetry even late in Pound's career.[69] And in Pound-Villerant's criticism of Baudelaire's "shaggy influx," we could easily substitute Swinburne's name without rendering it meaningless. Indeed, Swinburne's fondness for antithesis and synaesthesia derives largely from Baudelaire, a debt that he duly acknowledges in "Ave Atque Vale."[70] In short, by including Gautier in his pantheon and by rehabilitating Swinburne, Pound introduces the possibility that the poetic *parole pleine* arising from this Swedenborgian theory of correspondences will, despite his rejection of Baudelaire, continue to resonate within his own poetic. Examined chronologically, Pound's 1914 polemic against symbolism amounts to a diversionary tactic whereby he faults the Symbolists for precisely those poetic crimes he had discovered earlier, though somewhat belatedly and most reluctantly, in the Pre-Raphaelites and Aesthetes; by shifting the attack to the French Symbolists, he in essence places his literary heroes hors de combat, the better to reinstate them to their *officium poetae* at a later date.

Because we tend to remember only his self-deprecatory remarks about his own Swinburnisms, his Rossettitis, and his Browningese, we also conveniently tend to ignore Pound's extravagent praise of Swinburne in "Swinburne Versus His Biographers" (1918), which would seem almost a throwback to the Decadence after his arguments on behalf of a cubist or collage aesthetic in *Gaudier-Bzreska*.[71] And although we could conceivably argue that Pound's scrupulous concern for truth lies behind this scathing attack on Edmund Gosse (and the literary establishment in general) for his sanitized *Life of Algernon Charles Swinburne*,[72] Pound's essay goes much further in its celebration of Swinburne. In fact, Pound's attempted rehabilitation of Swinburne, the poet who almost single-handedly introduced Pound's much-detested Baudelaire to England, enables him to attack T. E. Hulme's "Doctrine of the Image" and thereby to salvage his cherished melopoeic mode and to reinstate a poetics that goes beyond the mere "juxtaposition of distinct images in different lines" called for by Flint and Hulme.[73]

Pound begins by criticizing Swinburne, and his many, just criticisms remain unchallenged and still serve as literary commonplaces. "Swinburne's actual writing is very often rather distressing" (*LE*, 292), says Pound; "the whole of his defects can be summed up in one—that is, inaccurate writing" (*LE*, 293).[74] But Pound does not dismiss Swinburne: "It is the literary fashion to write exclusively of Swinburne's defects. . . . Defects are in Swinburne by the bushelful: the discriminating reader will not be able to overlook them, and need not condone them; neither will he be swept off his feet by detractors" (*LE*, 294). On the contrary, Pound suggests that his virtues, "largely dug from the Greek," outweigh his many faults, which are "mostly traceable to Victor Hugo" (but, surprisingly, not to Baudelaire). First, he has a noteworthy historical importance for Pound: "At any rate we can, whatever our verbal fastidiousness, be thankful for any man who kept alive some spirit of paganism and of revolt in a papier-mâché era, in a time swarming with Longfellows, Mabies, Gosses, Harrisons" (*LE*, 293). Second, and remember that this article was published after Pound had embarked on the *Cantos* and *Propertius*, he claims that Swinburne's poems (in particular, "A Ballad of Life," "The Ballad of Death," and "The Triumph of Time") "are full of sheer imagism, of passages faultless" (*LE*, 293). Third, says Pound, "No one else has made such music in English, I mean has made his kind of music; and it is a music which will compare with Chaucer's" (*LE*, 293). And finally, in a phrase reminiscent of his discussion of Henry James,[75] Pound celebrates Swinburne's "passion not merely for political, but also for personal, liberty" (*LE*, 294).

Especially striking is his second claim that Swinburne's poetry is "full of sheer imagism," and we might learn something about Pound's brand of imagism if we turn to a representative stanza from one of the poems, "A Ballad of Life," of which he approves:

> I found in dreams a place of wind and flowers
>> Full of sweet trees and color of glad grass,
>> In midst whereof there was
> A lady clothed like summer with sweet hours.
> Her beauty, fervent as a fiery moon,
>> Made my blood burn and swoon
>> Like a flame rained upon.
> Sorrow had filled her shaken eyelids' blue,
> And her mouth's sad red heavy rose all through
>> Seemed sad with glad things gone.[76]

This passage would certainly seem to go against the grain of Pound's dictum that a poet "use no superfluous word, no adjective that does not reveal something" (LE, 4). Swinburne's use of *sweet* and *glad* are instances of the pathetic fallacy wherein the poet projects his own emotions onto the landscape (or, in this case, dreamscape), and his "colour of glad grass" mixes an abstraction with an overwrought concrete image as does Pound's most famous "Don't": "Don't use such an expression as 'dim lands *of peace*'" (LE, 5). [77] Moreover, Swinburne's use of synaesthesia in the description of the "lady clothed like summer with sweet hours" is extended considerably in his description of the effect that this lady's beauty has upon him. Her "fervent beauty" is almost an oxymoron (as is the "fiery moon") that blurs perceptual boundaries in order to suggest the "sense of sudden liberation" (LE, 4) occuring at that "precise instant when a thing outward and objective transforms itself, or darts into a thing inward and subjective" (GB, 89). Swinburne's perception of the lady's outward beauty is internalized, becoming a fervent or ardent passion within the poet, making his "blood burn" and, with yet again another shift of register, making him lose consciousness "like a flame rained upon." Despite the force of this last Dantescan epic simile that vividly redefines and arrests the complex and protean vision, and despite other fine similes in this poem ("The next was Shame, with hollow heavy face / Coloured like green wood when flame kindles it"), we cannot ignore this poem's reliance on a romantic rhetoric and its use of a symbolist synaesthesia made popular by Baudelaire. In short, this poem does not correspond to Hulme's doctrine calling for the "piling-up and juxtaposition of distinct images in different lines";[78] on the contrary, it tends more to resemble the "heavy, crude pattern of rhetorical verse" anathematized by Hulme.[79] Thus, if Pound can argue that Swinburne's poetry is "full of sheer imagism," he has revised considerably Hulme's and his own imagist proscriptions.

Pound's regard for Swinburne goes against Hulme's imagism in another interesting and highly significant manner. In "A Lecture on Modern Poetry," Hulme maintains that the poetry of "extreme modernism" was meant to be "read and not chanted":

> We have thus two distinct arts. The one intended to be chanted, and the other intended to be read in the study. . . . I am not speaking of the whole of poetry, but of this distinct new art which is gradually separating itself from the older one and becoming independent. . . .
>
> The effect of rhythm, like that of music, is to produce a kind of hypnotic state, during which suggestions of grief or ecstasy are easily and powerfully effective. . . . This is for the art of chanting, but the procedure of the new visual art is just the contrary. It depends for its effect not

on a kind of half sleep produced, but on arresting the attention so much
so that the succession of visual images should exhaust one.[80]

And yet, Pound praises Swinburne for precisely "his kind of music,"
and we can see what he means if we return to the above stanza from "A
Ballad of Life." It is held together by an intricate web of alliteration
and assonance of the sort that Pound prized in the poetry of Henri de
Régnier, and, to be sure, being a "dream," the poem induces Hulme's
much-detested, hypnotic "half sleep" as a result of its many sibilants,
liquids, and unvoiced consonants. Sound patterns are repeated
throughout the stanza with subtle variations and build upon one an-
other in the movement from one line to the next: "I found in dreams
a place of wind and flowers / Full of sweet trees and colour of glad
grass." Moreover, the initial consonants of terminal words are often
carried over to the next line: "sweet ʰours. / ᴴer beauty, **fer**vent as a
fiery ᵐoon, / ᴹade ᵐy **b**lood **b**urn and swoon." As we can see, "A Ballad
of Life" is quite obviously a poem wherein sound values are of para-
mount importance and often override considerations of "le mot
juste." As Pound says in qualifying his praise of Swinburne, "The
word-selecting, word-castigating faculty was nearly absent. Unusual
and gorgeous words attracted him. His dispraisers say that his vocabu-
lary is one of the smallest at any poet's command, and that he uses the
same adjectives to depict either a woman or a sunset" (*LE*, 293–94);
but, he continues, "There are times when this last is not, or need not
be, *ipso facto* a fault. There is an emotional fusion of the perceptions,
and a certain kind of verbal confusion has an emotive value in writing"
(*LE*, 294).

We will continue to see throughout Pound's career the manifest in-
fluence of these two Swinburnian "virtues," his "sheer imagism"
(Pound's phanopoeia) and his "rhythm-building faculty" (Pound's
melopoeia), which, curiously enough, are always associated by Pound,
either directly through his criticism or indirectly through allusions,
with the poetry of Gautier. In his 1912 "Prolegomena," for example,
Pound links Swinburne and Gautier by borrowing the notion of l'art
pour l'art from Gautier's preface to *Mademoiselle de Maupin:* "As for
there being a 'movement' or my being of it, the conception of poe-
try as a 'pure art' in the sense in which I use the term, revived with
Swinburne" (*LE*, 11). And the Lady in Pound's "Apparuit" (1912),
"clothed in goldish weft," "casting a-loose the cloak of the body," her
"throat aflash with / strands of light inwoven about it" (*P*, 64–65), ech-
oes not only Gautier's "À une robe rose" (D' où te vient cette robe
étrange / Qui semble faite de ta chair),[81] but also Swinburne's exem-
plary (for Pound) "Ballad of Death": "Make thee soft raiment out of
woven sighs / Upon the flesh to cleave." Again, in his 1918 "Swinburne

Versus His Biographers," Pound praises Swinburne's "Hymn to Pros-
erpine," a poem in which Swinburne laments Christianity's triumph
over the pagan gods, as does Gautier in "Bûchers et Tombeaux," and
as Pound will in *Mauberley*. Finally, and more surprising still, Pound
wanted his wife Dorothy to send him his copy of Swinburne's *Poems
and Ballads* during that period when he was revising *A Draft of XVI
Cantos* and beginning work on cantos 17–27,[82] thus raising the possi-
bility that Swinburne and Gautier's ghosts may be lurking somewhere
in that landmark modernist text. Indeed, when Pound describes his
Cantos as his "chryselephantine poem,"[83] he most fittingly pays hom-
age not only to Swinburne, but to what Swinburne has described as the
"chryselephantine verse" of Théophile Gautier[84]—and, by extension,
to Charles Baudelaire and the entire symbolist tradition that Pound
had rejected with such vehemence. Even after he has made his new
start in the Malatesta Cantos, Pound reverts to the romantic compo-
nent underlying Gautier's poetry, not to Gautier's imagist poetics
voiced in "L'Art" so often cited by orthodox Poundians—"sculpte,
lime, cisèle"—but to the quasi-hallucinatory metamorphoses set forth
in his "Affinités secrètes" and "Club des haschischins."

There is one further insight to be gained from Pound's discussion
of Swinburne's poetic. When discussing Swinburne's melopoeia, and
more particularly his "emotional fusion of the perceptions, and . . .
[his] verbal confusion [having] an emotive value," Pound qualifies his
praise in a manner that is quite revealing about his own fears as a poet:
"But this is of all sorts of writing the most dangerous to an author, and
the *unconscious* [my italics] collapse into this sort of writing has
wrecked more poets in our time than perhaps all other faults put to-
gether" (*LE*, 294). Ironically, Pound's acknowledgement of the dan-
gers of a Swinburnian (or symbolist) poetic can in retrospect be seen as
a warning to himself intended to forestall his own "unconscious col-
lapse into this sort of writing," for, as the *Cantos* progresses, Pound's
melopoeia becomes increasingly suspect the more it begins to approx-
imate the "divine energy" he sought as a means to attain his paradise
and the more this unconstrained play of language begins to over-
whelm his desire for a univocal relationship between words and
things.

Reacting violently in the middle cantos against his prior "spirit of
romance," Pound advances his ideogrammic juxtaposition of *docu-
menta*—i.e., objective and externally verifiable "facts"—as a means to
contain or eliminate the subjective basis of his lyric mode. Not content
to remain in a decentered universe of verbal signs, he returns to a
realist language that had seemingly been exploded by nineteenth-cen-
tury epistemology. Whether fortunately or not, Pound's discovery of
the Fenollosa manuscripts, although prepared for by his interest in

Corbière's "collage" method, provides him with a linguistic foundation which suggests the possibility of an adequation between word and world, and his subsequent adaptation of a static Chinese historiography, itself filtered through the French Enlightenment, enables him to represent a conservative revolution wherein myth and history become interchangeable.

With the fall of Mussolini, however, Pound's program could no longer offer even the hope of being empirically verified, and his sense of presence and plenitude enters an Eliotic world of negation and absence, as it were, by the back door. Paradoxically, Pound's interest in French Symbolism returns with a vengeance in the *Pisan Cantos*, so much so that these cantos constitute almost a second edition of his "Study in French Poets." He now turns for consolation to those Symbolists whom he had ostensibly rejected, to Verlaine, Baudelaire, and Mallarmé. Moreover, his poignant references to Laforgue in the Pisan and later Cantos suggest a fuller appreciation of the more mature, and not merely ironic, Laforgue. Finally, Pound's renewed interest in the Neoplatonism and mysticism of his early career suggests a need to assure himself that his poem will have a more or less transcendental ground. Pound's later Neoplatonism brings with it a noticeable attenuation of his mythological vision and, instead of suggesting an earthly *hypostasis*, seems to engage an au-delà wholly at odds with his earlier Hellenism.[85]

When considered a little more closely, Pound's understanding of "'symbolism' in its profounder sense" as "association," "as a sort of allusion, almost of allegory," as the degradation of "the symbol to the status of a word," as "a form of metonymy," is less a persuasive critical dissociation than an indication of a real conflict at the center of Pound's poetry. Pound did, as Kenner suggests, work his way clear of a predominantly symbolist aesthetic, and he did this largely by creating a counter-canon of nineteenth-century French "poet-realists" (Gautier, Corbière, Laforgue, Tailhade, Romains). But by elevating Gautier to the status of a "germinal master," Pound cannot forever avoid the symbolist vision at the heart of Gautier's aesthetic. If, as Michel Foucault suggests, Mallarmé and the symbolists were attempting, via Baudelaire's correspondences, to find their "way back from the representative or signifying function of language to this raw being that had been forgotten since the sixteenth century,"[86] Pound, ever the literalist of the imagination, traverses this same "futile yet fundamental space" in the *Cantos* with his modernist ideograms and his medieval doctrine of signatures.

Chapter One

POUND'S GRADUS AD PARNASSUM

> "From the colour the nature
> & by the nature the sign!"
> —(90/619)

> Manier savamment une langue, c'est pratiquer une espèce de sorcellerie évocatoire. C'est alors que la couleur parle, comme une voix profonde et vibrante; que les monuments se dressent et font saillie sur l'espace profond; que les animaux et les plantes, représentants du laid et du mal, articulent leur grimace non équivoque; que le parfum provoque la pensée et le souvenir correspondants; que la passion murmure ou rugit son langage éternellement semblable.
> —Charles Baudelaire, "Théophile Gautier," *Oeuvres*

GAUTIER soon became Pound's *miglior fabbro*, serving both as a personal inspiration and as a germinal master anticipating his own version of modernism. Gautier's influence begins to be felt as early as 1912 and continues unabated throughout the twenties. In the 1913 letter to Harriet Monroe where Pound criticizes Baudelaire and Verlaine, he continues by saying that "Gautier and de Gourmont carry forward the art itself" (*SL*, 23). Later, in a 1920 letter to James Joyce, Pound writes, "I cling to the rock of Gautier, deluding myself perhaps with the idea that he did journalism for years without becoming an absolute shit" (*P/J*, 174). And as late as 1928, Pound could still say, "Gautier j'ai étudié et je le révère" (*SL*, 218). According to Pound, Gautier's poetry of the thirties "did in France very much what remained for the men of 'the nineties' to accomplish in England. An examination of what Gautier wrote in 'the thirties' will show a similar beauty, a similar sort of technique" (*LE*, 285). Put simply, "Théophile Gautier is, I suppose, the next man who can write" (*SL*, 89). Pound's insistence that Gautier was sixty years ahead of his time is crucial to his vision of modernism, for if *Émaux et Camées* constitutes yet another advance, Gautier becomes a "modernist" by default, and Pound can truly go back to the future.

However, as Ford Madox Ford's dramatic criticism of *Canzoni* made abundantly clear to Pound, modern poetry could no longer sustain itself by taking the highroad of l'art pour l'art because it was now competing with the prose realism practiced so well by Ford. As Pound would later argue, "During the last century or century and a half, prose has, perhaps for the first time, perhaps for the second or third time, arisen to challenge the poetic pre-eminence. That is to say, *Coeur Simple*, by Flaubert, is probably more important than Théophile Gautier's *Carmen*, etc." (*LE*, 26). But the equivocation in this statement— that is, "Coeur Simple" is *probably* more important than "Carmen"— insists less on the works' differences than it does on the close proximity of Gautier's poetic to what Pound would later define as "prose constatation." Pound believed that he had found in Gautier a poet who had bridged the gap between poetry and prose: "Perfectly plain statements like his 'Carmen est maigre' should teach one a number of things" (*SL*, 89).

Pound's unshakeable belief in Gautier's "perfectly plain statements" indicates a close relationship between Gautier's poetic and Pound's own Imagist doctrine of 1912, and both Pound's and Eliot's homages to "Carmen" help to substantiate his later claim that "la *technique* des poètes français était *certainement* en état de servir d'*éducation* aux poètes de ma langue—de temps de Gautier, jusqu'à 1912" [the technique of the French poets was certainly available as a means to educate poets writing in my language from the time of Gautier until 1912] (*SL*, 217). Without attempting to adjudicate between the respective literary merits of Flaubert's "Coeur simple" and Gautier's "Carmen," I think it would be safe to say that what Pound values in "Carmen" is the direct subject-verb syntax comprised of weighted substantives and the minimal use of poetically descriptive adjectives. The poem opens with a flat constatation worthy of Catullus and is governed by the simple copula:

> Carmen est maigre,—un trait de bistre
> Cerne son oeil de gitana.
> Ses cheveux sont d'un noir sinistre,
> Sa peau, le diable la tanna.
>
> Les femmes disent qu'elle est laide,
> Mais tous les hommes en sont fous
>
> [Carmen is thin,—charcoal eyeliner
> Rings her gypsy eye.
> A sinister black her hair
> And the devil tanned her skin.
>
> The women say she's ugly,
> But all the men are crazy about her][1]

Gautier's chiseled style highlights the phrase, the "perfectly plain statement," and gains in density with his emphasis on substantives and his use of a realistic and often highly technical vocabulary.[2] Even Baudelaire adopts almost Flaubertian terms to describe Gautier as "ce magnifique dictionnaire dont les feuillets, remués par un souffle divin, s'ouvrent tout juste pour laisser jaillir le mot propre, le mot unique" [this magnificent dictionary whose pages are turned by a divine breath and open to the exact word, the only word].[3] And when images and metaphors are employed, they are more frequently descriptive than they are a means of access to an imaginary realm. As David Kelley has suggested, Gautier's poetry contains "gammes d'images évocatrices dont l'effet est d'éblouir le lecteur et de l'empêcher d'en approfondir les possibilités de signification" [a whole set of evocative images that work to dazzle and blind the reader and to prevent him or her from getting to the bottom of their meaning].[4] Gautier's "angoisse provoquée par la profondeur métaphysique," says Kelley, results in "une forme de superficialité, celle d'une vie païenne, faite de sensations et de surfaces" [Gautier's anxiety provoked by a metaphysical depth (results in) a form of superficiality, that of a pagan sensibility made up of sensations and of surfaces].[5] This description of Gautier's poetry is suggestive of Pound's as it begins to evolve into his later style: despite Pound's emphasis on the verbal nature of language, his poems also begin to acquire a real density with his imagistic juxtaposition of image on image, particularly with his use of kennings that intensify the substantive weight of his diction.

Once again, however, we begin to see that peculiar bipolarity at the center of Gautier's poetic and his role in the evolution of modern French poetry. Marcel Voisin has argued that Gautier constitutes an essential link between French poetry of the eighteenth and twentieth centuries.[6] Beginning with a stock romanticism and a markedly neoclassical diction, Gautier soon originated an individual style that would have a profound influence on subsequent Symbolist poets. But it is Baudelaire who perhaps best describes Gautier's complex admixture of a prose realism and a nascent symbolism when he immediately qualifies his discussion of "ce magnifique dictionnaire":

Si l'on réfléchit qu'à cette merveilleuse faculté Gautier unit une immense intelligence innée de la *correspondance* et du symbolisme universels, ce répertoire de toute métaphore, on comprendra qu'il puisse sans cesse, sans fatigue comme sans faute, définir l'attitude mystérieuse que les objets de la création tiennent devant le regard de l'homme. Il y a dans le mot, dans le *verbe*, quelque chose de *sacré* qui nous défend d'en faire un jeu de hasard.

[If one considers that Gautier adds to this marvelous faculty an immense and innate knowledge of correspondences and of universal symbolism, this catalog of every metaphor, one will come to understand that he can, without cease, without tiring and without fault, define that mysterious attitude that the objects of creation hold before the eyes of man. There is in the word, in the *logos*, something sacred that prohibits us from making of it a game of chance.][7]

Enlisting Gautier's uncanny knack for finding "le mot juste" in the Symbolists' quest for "le Verbe sacré" and their attempt to "définir l'attitude mystérieuse que les objets de la création tiennent devant le regard de l'homme," Baudelaire captures here that "sorcellerie évocatoire" that makes Gautier such an important transitional figure in the history of modern French poetry.

In his *Ripostes*, Pound too attempts to express this "attitude mystérieuse," or, to use Pound's terms, this "Marvel and Wonder" (*CEP*, 58). Moreover, Pound's important transitional volume manifests this same wavering between a visionary realm and a realistic modern surface, between a quasi-symbolist "poésie pure" and a modern spoken idiom. Pound's "Alchemist: Chant for the Transmutation of Metals" (1912), for example, derives from both Gourmont's symbolist invocation in "Litanie de la rose" of the woman-rose "absente de tout bouquet"[8] and, I would argue, Gautier's "Symphonie en blanc majeur." In "The Alchemist," Pound transforms both nature and language into a mysterious "alembic" (*CEP*, 226) wherein things undergo a metamorphosis and become what P. E. Tennant, referring to Gautier, describes as "a jewel-case to be plundered by the artist-connoisseur":[9]

> Sail of Claustra, Aelis, Azalais,
> As you move among the bright trees;
> As your voices, under the larches of Paradise
> Make a clear sound,
> Sail of Claustra, Aelis, Azalais,
> Raimona, Tibors, Berangèrë,
> 'Neath the dark gleam of the sky;
> Under night, the peacock-throated,
> Bring the saffron-coloured shell,
> Bring the red gold of the maple,
> Bring the light of the birch tree in autumn
> Mirals, Cembelins, Audiarda,
> > Remember this fire.
>
> Elain, Tireis, Alcmena
> 'Mid the silver rustling of wheat,

> Agradiva, Anhes, Ardenca,
> From the plum-coloured lake, in stillness,
> From the molten dyes of the water
> Bring the burnished nature of fire;
> Briseis, Lianor, Loica,
> From the wide earth and the olive,
> From the poplars weeping their amber,
> By the bright flame of the fishing torch
> > Remember this fire.
> > > > (*CEP*, 225)

Pound's "Alchemist" is a "Symphonie en or majeur," and the purifying fire described therein is a mere transposition into another key of Gautier's northern landscape and vision of absolute beauty. And just as Gautier sets forth a play of correspondences between Parian marble, mica, ivory, alabaster, "l'argent mat, la laiteuse opale,"[10] Pound uses his mineral imagery (gold, copper, amber, bronze, the "pallor of silver," the "milk-white bodies of agate") to much the same effect. Both Gautier and Pound are "luminous" poets whose characteristic mineral imagery and images of reflecting light and water invariably suggest the existence of, and a pathway to, a crystalline world of the Hellenic gods.[11]

But even in this most patently symbolic and artificial of Pound's poems, his natural descriptions nevertheless contain a Gautieresque specificity that anticipates much of his later poetry. Pound greatly extends his range of floral and mineral imagery in this particular poem, and the variegated landscape and mellifluous *alchimie du verbe* are always securely anchored by the extended catalog of trees ("larches of Paradise," "the red gold of the maple," "the light of the birch tree in autumn," "the poplars weeping their amber") and the vivid description of the natural setting: "the plum-coloured lake," "the molten dyes of the water," "Rain flakes of gold on the water, / Azure and flaking silver of water." Thus, despite the residue of a Gautieresque symbolism, Pound shows that he has learned his lesson well, and that he can successfully integrate Gautier's "realism" into his own verse.

For the first time, Pound manages in *Ripostes* to avoid the patently decorative, where colors and flowers, for example, are mere stage props for a secondhand literary vision. In lieu of Pound's early roses, willows, and "bright white drops upon a leaden sea . . . Evan'scent mirrors every opal one" (*CEP*, 7), a precise and less interchangeable diction begins to appear in poems like "Effects of Music Upon a Company of People":

> A soul curls back,
> > Their souls like petals,

> Thin, long, spiral,
> Like those of a chrysanthemum curl
> Smoke-like up and back from the
> Vavicel, the calyx,
> Pale green, pale gold, transparent,
> Green of plasma, rose-white,
> Spirate like smoke,
> Curled,
> Vibrating,
> Slowly, waving slowly.
> O Flower animate!
> O calyx!
> O crowd of foolish people!
>
> (*CEP*, 199)

Reminiscent of H. D.'s, the floral imagery here is much more specific than the generic roses of his early poetry, and the botanical terms anticipate Pound's later use of them in the *Cantos*.[12] Moreover, Pound's use of color is so qualified that the description paradoxically becomes both extremely concrete and extremely ephemeral. Moving from the pale green of the calyx to the pale gold of the chrysanthemum (literally, golden flower), Pound establishes a vivid contrast or dissociation held together by a qualifying "paleness" that transforms the flower into an ethereally transparent thing: "Vavicel, the calyx, / Pale green, pale gold, transparent." Pound then modifies this color opposition, developing the suggested translucence in the previous line by conjoining a hard crystalline substance, a translucent variety of chalcedony, with a gaseous one: "Green of plasma, rose-white." The pale gold has now become "rose-white, / Spirate like smoke," enabling Pound to return to his initial analogy between the soul and the "chrysanthemum curl / Smoke-like up and back from the / Vavicel." Because Pound is now able to interrelate successfully his various descriptive elements and analogies, the golden color does not escape the bounds of the poem to become just another one of the blazons that plagued his early poetry.

This newfound control is even more readily apparent in "Apparuit." Although it is often singled out by critics as a last manifestation of Pound's Rossettian diction,[13] "Apparuit" can also be seen as another instance of Gautier's influence, adopting as it does the rose-white, crimson-alabaster contrast so evident in Gautier's "'sculpture' of rhyme" (*P*, 186):

> Golden rose the house, in the portal I saw
> thee, a marvel, carven in subtle stuff, a

portent. Life died down in the lamp and flickered,
        caught at the wonder.

Crimson, frosty with dew, the roses bend where
thou afar, moving in the glamorous sun,
drinkst in life of earth, of the air, the tissue
        golden about thee.

Green the ways, the breath of the fields is thine there,
open lies the land, yet the steely going
darkly hast thou dared and the dreaded aether
        parted before thee.

Swift at courage thou in the shell of gold, cast-
ing a-loose the cloak of the body, camest
straight, then shone thine oriel and the stunned light
        faded about thee.

Half the graven shoulder, the throat aflash with
strands of light inwoven about it, loveli-
est of all things, frail alabaster, ah me!
        swift in departing.

Clothed in goldish weft, delicately perfect,
gone as wind! The cloth of the magical hands!
Thou a slight thing, thou in access of cunning
        dar'dst to assume this?

                                        (*P*, 64–65)

Like Gautier's "À une robe rose,"[14] "Apparuit" objectifies the poet's fleeting vision in a painterly fashion through the play of color, light, and a virtual arabesque of line and movement. The opening stanza situates the vision and establishes the governing color scheme as well as the fulgurant light which permits the apparition: "Life died down in the lamp and flickered,/Caught at the wonder." Containing a curious echo of the concluding quatrain of Baudelaire's "Les Bijoux,"[15] "Apparuit" moves from the darkness of the portal to the radiant, sun-lit world of the woman. The poem enacts a progressive idealization and etherealization of the woman whereby she "cast[s] a-loose the cloak of the body," loses all solidity, becoming a fragile, airy, "slight thing."

But despite this poetic rarefaction, descriptive adjectives take on weight by virtue of their isolated position as the central image in each stanza, becoming almost substantives: "Golden rose the house"; "Crimson, frosty with dew"; "Green the ways."[16] Instead of a "crimson dew . . . fallen on the leaf" ("Canzon: The Yearly Slain," *CEP*, 133),

Pound abstracts from the flower a specific and especially vivid attribute, its crimson color, which is in turn made very realistic, almost tactile, when Pound incorporates the sense of coldness and of wetness into his description: "Crimson, frosty with dew." Compare, for example, the second stanza of "Apparuit" with two instances of Pound's use of the rose image in his 1911 *Canzoni:*

> Ah! red-leafed time hath driven out the rose
> And crimson dew is fallen on the leaf
> Ere ever yet the cold white wheat be sown
> That hideth all earth's green and sere and red
> ("Canzon: The Yearly Slain," *CEP*, 133)

> Who is she coming, that the roses bend
> Their shameless heads to do her passing honour?
> Who is she coming with a light upon her
> Not born of suns that with the day's end end?
> ("Sonnet: Chi É Questa?" *CEP*, 143)

In the first example, we might wonder about the appropriateness of Pound's descriptive language; the color red is so pervasive that it afflicts not only the rose, but "red-leafed time," the "crimson dew" and the "earth's . . . red" as well. The description conveys absolutely no sense of an objective reality; rather, we are privy to a subjective vision not far removed from that of the speaker in Tennyson's *Maud*. In the second example, the roses must be personified in order to evoke the sense of mystery surrounding this lady with an aura "not born of suns that with the day's end end," and that personification contravenes every poetic principle that Pound stands for. In "Apparuit," on the other hand, the weight of the dew enables Pound to suggest that the roses do in fact bend "to do her passing honor" without his having to resort to personification. His new descriptive techniques permit him to transform the external world into something that is at one and the same time both extremely concrete and extremely ethereal. In the last line of the second stanza, for example, the concrete image of the golden raiment is reabsorbed in the type of abstract color symphony popularized by Gautier in his "Symphonie en blanc majeur."

This Gautieresque wavering between the concrete and the abstract in "Apparuit" should reconfirm our suspicion that Pound's critical arguments need to be approached with some caution. Because of Pound's emphasis on Gautier's satirical prose constatation, on his "Carmen est maigre," we tend to forget that the strength of Gautier's poetry arises from his ability to rescue an ideal beauty from a quotidian reality and still maintain the dialectical tension between the realms of the ideal and the real. In other words, against the realistic diction

that reinvigorated nineteenth-century French verse, we must oppose
his doctrine of l'art pour l'art, which leads ultimately to a symbolist
poésie pure; against his portrait of "Carmen," we must place his nu-
merous portraits of an "Aphrodite éthérée":

> A l'horizon monte une nue,
> Sculptant sa forme dans l'azur:
> On dirait une vierge nue
> Émergeant d'un lac au flot pur.
>
> Debout dans sa conque nacrée,
> Elle vogue sur le bleu clair,
> Comme une Aphrodite éthérée,
> Faite de l'écume de l'air.
>
> On voit onder en molles poses
> Son torse au contour incertain,
> Et l'aurore répand des roses
> Sur son épaule de satin.
>
> Ses blancheurs de marbre et de neige
> Se fondent amoureusement
> Comme, au clair-obscur de Corrège,
> Le corps d'Antiope dormant.
>
> [A cloud on the horizon
> Is sculpting its form in the azure:
> Or should we say a naked virgin
> Emerging from a lake that's pure?
>
> Standing in her nacre shell,
> She sails upon the blue clear
> Like an Aphrodite become ethereal,
> Made from the spray of the air.
>
> Uncertain still her body's contour,
> We see her soft and undulant poses,
> And on her satin shoulder
> Dawn scatters a thousand roses.
>
> Her doubled whiteness of marble and snow
> Embrace and blend together lovingly,
> A chiarascuro painting by Correggio
> Of the body of the sleeping Antiope.][17]

Pound's abstract yet concretely realized descriptions of the beloved
in "Apparuit" and other poems contain strong echoes of Gautier's

representations of Aphrodite in his many transpositions d'art, with their painterly emphasis on spatial relations, reflecting surfaces, and, in this instance, the sfumato rendering of this "Aphrodite éthérée." Gautier's description of Correggio's "nue, / sculptant sa forme dans l'azur," must inevitably remind us of a number of Pound's early poems such as "Gentildonna" (1913), which contains a similar manifestation of this feminine beauty:

> She passed and left no quiver in the veins, who now
> Moving among the trees, and clinging
> > in the air she severed,
> Fanning the grass she walked on then, endures:
> Grey olive leaves beneath a rain-cold sky.

> (P, 93)

Just as Gautier continually returns to this "femme mystérieuse . . . Au bord des flots retentissants" [mysterious woman . . . At the edge of the resounding sea],[18] so too does Pound describe his Beloved as an ethereal goddess who, like Gautier's Aphrodite, separates herself from an elemental nature. Another slight variation on this technique occurs in Pound's "A Virginal" (1912):

> No, no! Go from me. I have left her lately.
> I will not spoil my sheath with lesser brightness,
> For my surrounding air hath a new lightness;
> Slight are her arms, yet they have bound me straitly
> And left me cloaked as with a gauze of aether;
> As with sweet leaves; as with a subtle clearness.
> Oh, I have picked up magic in her nearness
> To sheathe me half in half the things that sheathe her.

> (P, 67)

Although Pound's characteristic hubris enables him to have already possessed the woman, and although Pound ultimately grounds her in the natural world—"As white their bark, so white this lady's hours"—the bulk of the poem attempts to suggest the divine presences so central to the haunting, visionary passages in the *Cantos*.[19]

Also like Gautier, Pound is concerned with both the stasis and the fluidity inherent in the idea of metamorphosis. Curiously, however, critics discussing Gautier's influence on Pound tend to ignore this dual aspect of metamorphosis, preferring to emphasize the stasis implicit in Gautier's definition of the poem as a cameo or medallion, and programmatically summarized in his "L'Art": "Sculpte, lime, cisèle." Although Gautier's poetry is often characterized as consisting entirely of plastic, two-dimensional decorative tableaux, Tennant rightly argues that a "static or cinematographic effect is often conveyed by Gautier through his painter's habit of eyeing landscape in terms of organized planes of observation: 'ici . . . là', 'à gauche . . . à droite', 'plus loin', 'au premier plan', 'd'un côté . . . de l'autre', 'au milieu.'"[20] If we allow that Gautier's poetry contains the movement implicit in the idea of a "cinematographic effect," Pound's interest in the "moving image," developed extensively in his metamorphic passages, recapitulates this aspect of Gautier's "painterly" representation, and Pound's descriptive techniques once again approach those of Gautier. Whether or not Pound derives his ideogramic juxtaposition of "planes in relation" from the cubists or vorticists, his postimagist poetry is largely characterized by a scenographic representation which suggests both depth and movement through its use of deictic markers (*near, far*):

> Olive grey in the near,
> >   far, smoke grey of the rock-slide,
> Salmon-pink wings of the fish-hawk
> >   cast grey shadows in water,
> The tower like a one-eyed great goose
> >   cranes up out of the olive-grove
>
>   (2/10)

In addition to this introduction of perspective, the image of the tower suggests another parallel between the two poets. As Tennant observes, "Gautier's scenic imagery tends to crystallise around certain geometrical, linear motifs, of which the commonest are the angular (serrated skylines spiked with towers and angled roofs) and the sinuous. . . . Like the flame, Gautier's arabesques, deriving from the *figura serpentinata* of Renaissance mannerism, defy matter and rise upwards to eternity."[21] As we have already seen, Pound is similarly fascinated with such *figurae*—flames, smoke-wreathes, etc.—as well as with architectural monuments: "Bright tips reach up from twin towers" (*Homage to Sextus Propertius, P,* 209); this type of imagery is already evident in early poems like "Provincia Deserta," which Pound singles out as a forerunner of the descriptive techniques in his later poetry:[22]

> I have seen the torch-flames, high-leaping,
> Painting the front of that church;
> Heard, under the dark, whirling laughter.
> I have looked back over the stream
> >   and seen the high building,
> Seen the long minarets, the white shafts.
>
> .   .   .   .

I have seen the fields, pale, clear as an emerald,
Sharp peaks, high spurs, distant castles.

(*P*, 125–26)

Although Pound's adaptations of Gautier's descriptive techniques will be developed much more extensively in the *Cantos*, where we will find many poignant depictions of churches, temples, and cities, even these early manifestations suggest, as we shall see in another context, a strong similarity between Gautier's "rêverie méditerranéen"[23] and the visionary world of Pound's *Cantos*.

Thus, the question of Gautier's influence is not resolved by simply examining Pound's explicit borrowings from Gautier. Indeed, even without such proof, we can see strong evidence of Gautier's influence in Pound's movement from a quasi-symbolist mode to an imagistic hardness, from a patently decorative description to a much more concrete realism tempered with an abstract formalization. But if we demand proof of an extensive Parnassian influence on Pound, we need only extend our discussion to include Henri de Régnier, a poet Pound acknowledged to be "the last of the Parnassians, or at the least the last one who counts" (*AP* 5, 663). In view of Pound's overwhelming praise of Gautier, he seems to extend greatly the scope of Gautier's Parnassian influence when he says elsewhere "that there is no one who writes English as well as De Régnier writes French, or whose work has the quality of seeming so *modo pumice expolitum*" (*AP* 5, 663),[24] and I think it is here that we can assess the early influence on Pound of contemporary French poetry.

·   ·   ·

In his more or less double-edged estimation of Régnier, Pound rightly argues that "his melody presents nothing that is any longer new or startling. The perfection of his melody will interest none save the lovers of melody. . . . If his work has the beautiful fineness it is of no importance—save to the lovers of beauty" (*AP* 5, 663). Although Régnier's vers libre is based on the unit of expression or the grammatical unit which determines the line length, the play of repetition and assonance gives his poems a melodic fluidity that extends beyond the limitations of his quite concise verse form. "Odelette I," which Pound acknowledges "to have long been recognized as M. de Régnier's declaration of his intent" (*AP* 5, 663), adopts once more the classical echoes which permeate his poetry and that of the symbolists in general. The poet/faun, animating the forest with his reed pipe, replays the mythical metamorphosis so central to the symbolist imagination after Mallarmé's "L'Après-midi d'un faune":

> Un petit roseau m'a suffi
> Pour faire frémir l'herbe haute
> Et tout le pré
> Et les doux saules
> Et le ruisseau qui chante aussi;
> Un petit roseau m'a suffi
> A faire chanter la forêt.

> [A little reed sufficed
> To make the tall grass tremble
> And all the meadow
> And the soft willows
> And the babbling brook;
> A little reed sufficed
> To make the forest sing.][25]

The repetition of the first line, as well as the anaphoric middle lines, provides a sense of closure which anchors the play of assonance and internal rhyme; in addition, each line is itself balanced by what amounts to a hidden caesura that divides the line into two half lines joined by internal rhymes. The first two lines are structured by means of assonance and alliteration so that *petit/suffi* and *faire frémir/l'herbe haute* echo one another and provide a balanced cadence. In lines three and four, the anaphoric repetition of "et" is set off against the chiasmic construction of the two lines: "Et tout[1] le pré[2] / Et les[2] doux[1] saules." The third anaphoric line differentiates itself from the first two by the inclusion of the culminating verb phrase, but the assonance contained in "ruiss*eau*" and "*saules*" provides an echo that links the two lines and, in turn, permits the parallelism between lines five and six (a repetition of the first line): "Et le *ruisseau* qui chante *aussi* / Un petit *roseau* m'a *suffi*." Régnier's "method of rhyme, and of the blending of rhyme-sounds" (*AP* 5, 663) establishes a series of incremental differences that preserve his Parnassian unity of vision. Given that this reed was picked at "la fontaine où vint l'Amour / Mirer, un jour, / Sa face grave" [the fountain where came Love / One day to mirror / His grave face], the poem admirably embodies its mythological theme within the "being" of language.

Curiously, however, although Pound tends to emphasize Régnier's stylistic advances, and although he rightly warns us that no one "should need two thousand odd pages to say that he delights in gardens full of statues and running water and that Greek mythology is enchanting" (*AP* 5, 663), it is precisely this aspect of his verse to which Pound turns in his own *Ripostes*. In his various discussions of Régnier, Pound mentions a number of his poems, mostly from *Jeux rustiques et divins*, which express the central intuition that the divine world of the Hellenic gods still exists "derrière l'écho, / Debout parmi la vie universelle" [behind the echo, / Standing among universal life].[26] René Taupin has already suggested that some of Pound's poems in this volume, namely "N.Y.," "A Girl," and "The Return," are modeled on Régnier's poems, and Pound's high praise for the introductory poem to *Médailles d'argile* has led Taupin to remark on the similarity between this poem and Pound's own "Return."[27] Juxtaposing two stanzas, Taupin shows just how closely Pound follows Régnier:

> *Une à une*, vous les comptiez en souriant,
> *Et* vous disiez: Il est habile;
> *Et* vous passiez en souriant.[28]

> See, they return, *one, and by one,*
> With fear, as half-awakened;
> As if the snow should hesitate
> *And* murmur in the wind,
>   *and* half turn back, [italics mine]

                                                      (*P*, 70)

Although Pound does not adopt the more rigid principles of the rhythmic constant used in his own "Girl" or in Régnier's odelettes, his translation of "une à une" and his anaphoric substitution of *and* for *et* would indicate that he has Régnier's poem very much in mind. Pound also adopts the strategy of direct address often used by Régnier in this and other poems; whereas Régnier tells his reader to "écoute," Pound says to his reader: "See, they return." Finally, both poems emphasize the borderline existence of the divine realm and the necessity of creative vision in order to evoke the presence of these gods.

While I have already discussed the Gautieresque echoes in "Apparuit," we should also note that "Apparuit" is in many respects very much like Régnier's "Odelette III," with its evocation of a similar experience occasioned by the arrival of dawn:

> Tu frapperas.
> La porte est haute sous les roses et le lierre
>
> . . . .
>
> La maison noire et solitaire
> Qui maintenant chante et luit
> Sous les roses, à l'aube claire.

Je t'attends assis en chantant,
Je t'attends, car c'est le printemps;
Les vitres pâlissent, et le pavé pâle
S'éclaire et blanchit de dalle en dalle,
Et l'ombre s'accroupit aux angles;
Entre,
Toi qui à ma porte es venue,
Souriante et nue.
.   .   .   .   .   .
Veux-tu que je te donne
Le gobelet de hêtre et l'assiette d'étain,
Le fruit, le pain,

Un peu d'eau pure,
Et rester là?

[You will knock.
The tall door is beneath the roses and ivy
.   .   .   .
The dark and solitary house
Now sings and glistens
Beneath the roses, in the clear dawn.

I await you, sitting and singing,
I await you, because it's Spring;
The windows grow pale, and the walk
Becomes lighter and whiter stone by stone,
And the darkness crouches in the corners;
Enter,
You who have come to my door,
Naked and smiling.
.   .   .   .
Do you want me to give you
The beechwood cup and tin plate,
Fruit, bread,
A little pure water,
Do you want to stay?][29]

   In Régnier's poem, the poet beckons the woman, "souriante et nue,"
to approach the dark and solitary house, which now begins to reflect
the clear dawn as the windows and the pavement become lighter with
the retreat of the shadows, and he asks her to await with him the ap-
proaching autumn. Unfortunately, time is fleeting, and, realizing that
she cannot stay, the poet acquiesces and allows her to go among men.
Although Pound's poem is more successful than Régnier's because it

eschews the patently allegorical, it is difficult to ignore the fact that the narrative framework of "Apparuit" bears a striking similarity to "Odelette III," that the poem sets forth a similar constellation of images, and that it evokes the same fleeting experience of temporal vision. "Apparuit" depicts the emergence of the house from darkness— "Golden rose the house"—and contains a similar sensitivity to the play of light and shadow with the approach of dawn: "then shone thine oriel and the stunned light/faded about thee" (*P*, 64–65). Moreover, "clothed in goldish weft," "The cloth of the magical hands," Pound's woman actually "drink[s] in life of earth" before departing, "gone as wind." And like "Odelette III," "Apparuit" no longer echoes the boisterous Provençal aubade; instead, it is more subdued and wistful, more concerned with the borders of perception than with the Provençal clarity of sound and image, and, despite Pound's dissociation between Provence and Hellas, more Hellenic or plastic than medieval.[30]

Thus, over and above the new emphasis in *Ripostes* on concrete imagery and Gautier's "'sculpture' of rhyme," several themes and tones from a different register begin to appear in Pound's poetry. Whereas many of Pound's early poems contain worn-out literary tropes that can never realize a visionary presence because they continue to refer to the world of art and literature,[31] Pound's evolving realism now begins to charge minutiae with emotional overtones:

> It is, and is not, I am sane enough,
> Since you have come this place has hovered round me,
> This fabrication built of autumn roses,
> Then there's a goldish colour, different.
>
> And one gropes in these things as delicate
> Algae reach up and out, beneath
> Pale slow green surgings of the underwave,
> 'Mid these things older than the names they have,
> These things that are familiars of the god.
>
> ("Sub Mare," *CEP*, 194)

Although "Sub Mare" contains Pound's standard tropes (roses, goldish color, delicate things), they are muted and naturalized, and they gain in resonance the more meticulous the description. Moreover, the poem contains a new instance of aquatic or submarine imagery, one which will assume a considerable importance in Pound's later poetry, especially the *Cantos*, but which, at this point in his career, is so novel that it forces us to look to outside sources for an explanation. Interestingly, "Sub Mare" was first published in February 1912—

that is, at about the same time that Pound first admits to having read Régnier's work.[32] Not coincidentally, one of Régnier's central images is that of algae, or seaweed, the ebb and flow of which evokes the poet's memories of the past, of his childhood, of both the joy and the melancholy that occur with the passing of time:

> Douces pensées!
> Comme la mer chantait, ce soir-là, sur la grève
> Le refrain éternel des Heures brèves!
> Douces pensées,
> Pareilles à des algues enlacées,
> Algue d'argent souple et bleui,
> Algue d'or que le flot verdit,
> Double serpent du caducée,
> Thyrse d'oubli,
> Joie éparse, douleurs passées
> En mes pensées.
>
> Celle-là qui sourit est venue,
> Sur sa barque de fleurs, qui penche,
> Des jours lointains de mon enfance;
> Je l'ai connue
> Assise jadis à la porte
> De la vieille maison ouverte sur la mer,
> Elle m'apporte
> Son rire clair . . .
> Le flot roule, parmi les algues,
> Des conques d'émail et de nacre;
> On y entend toute sa vie,
> On y écoute son passé vivant,
> Écume, marée et vent,
> Sa joie et sa mélancholie
>
> [Sweet thoughts!
> As the sea sang that evening on the sand
> The eternal refrain of brief hours!
> Sweet thoughts,
> Similar to algae entwined
> And pliant, silver and blue,
> Golden algae that the waves made green,
> Double serpent of the caduceus,
> Thyrsus of forgetfulness,
> Scattered joy, and past sorrows
> In my thoughts.

That smiling one has come
On her flowery barque, which tilts
Under the long gone days of my childhood;
I knew her formerly
Sitting at the door
Of the old house looking out on the sea,
She brought me
Her bright smile . . .
The tide rolls in, among the algae,
And the enamelled and nacre shells;
One hears her entire life,
Foam, tide and wind,
Her joy and her melancholy][33]

Both "Odellete III" and "Sub Mare" conjoin a woman with the sea to evoke the visionary presence of the gods, and of Aphrodite in particular, as well as the actualized presence of the past, and, more importantly, both poems are, to borrow Pound's phrase, somehow "different" in that they depend upon our acknowledging the real nature of the seascape being described: "la vieille maison ouverte sur la mer" and the "Pale slow green surgings of the underwave."

Thus, despite his various caveats about Régnier's tendency to drift off into description, it does nevertheless appear that Pound was extremely interested in some of the thematic aspects of such Parnassian verse. All of these poets so highly praised by Pound—Gautier, Gourmont, and Régnier—set forth a subjective lyricism that has led to or evolved out of Symbolism. Their quest to develop and extend the idea of "la *correspondance* et du symbolisme universels" permits Pound, who defines the image as being either "subjective or objective" (*LE*, 3), to continue to indulge in his prior mystical tendencies set forth in *The Spirit of Romance* or in his later "Religio" (*P&D*, 96–98). Taken together, such Parnassian echoes indicate that, even though his critical pieces on contemporary French poetry only began to appear in late 1913, Pound was in fact indebted to Gautier, to Gourmont, and to Régnier for the new beginning evident in *Ripostes*. Both Gautier's and Régnier's poetry contain the pronouncement so familiar to Pound, that "les dieux vivent dans l'homme" [The gods live in man].[34]

The Hellenic world of the gods, the figure of Helen, who is an archetypal figure for such poets as Samain,[35] Régnier, and, following their lead, Pound himself, all of these elements help to account for Pound's interest in contemporary French poetry as a model for the imagist poets of 1912. The overwhelming number of such similarities and echoes argues for a shared sensibility between the Parnassians and Pound, a sensibility which would include the Hellenic legends, the Parnassian special effects cherished by these poets, and Pound's, Gautier's, and Régnier's love of Venice and of the Mediterranean in general. Given that Pound began his poetic career with homages to Venice in his *San Trovaso Notebook*, and continued to evoke the majesty of Venice long thereafter, we are forced to acknowledge the lasting indebtedness to a Parnassian sensibility. That Pound did in fact see something more than the "prose hardness" that led him to compare Gautier and Flaubert, that Pound saw in Gautier something more than the "perfectly plain statement," is undeniable.

What seems to have misled critics is Pound's insistence on the stylistic aspects of these poets in his critical writings, an insistence which tends to overshadow the thematic elements that infiltrate his own poetry. All of the poets discussed above yield to Pound's double-edged appreciation of form and content and, in this sense, are central to Pound's emerging poetic because they mark the dividing line between Pound's own quasi-symbolist leanings and his subsequent imagist practices. For example, whereas Pound's imitation of Gourmont's *Litanies* in "The Alchemist" suggests that his poem serves as a bridge between symbolism and imagism, containing as it does a nebulous network of associations conjoined to a precise lexical configuration,[36] an objective critical view of Gourmont would differ markedly depending on whether it privileged his *Litanies* or his *Problème du Style*. Pound, however, characteristically gives them equal weight and thus becomes caught up in a somewhat tortuous aesthetic gyration. In the case of all of these poets, there arises a real disparity between Pound's critical appraisals of their poetry and his adaptations of the various motifs which help us to surmise why Pound actually became interested in their work.

·   ·   ·

While Pound tends to imitate poems that are somewhat outside the scope of his critical overview of French poetry, his critical emphasis tends to lie with those stylistic traits that he believes will lead him beyond Parnassus. For example, whereas Pound imitates Régnier's distinctly Parnassian poems, in his critical writings he emphasizes only the stylistic aspects like the "limpidity of syntax" he discovers in Régnier's "Le Vase." This poem, which was considered by contemporary critics to be Régnier's "chef-d'oeuvre,"[37] is an instance of prose constatation which, despite the Decadent thrust provided by his use of dream and legend, avoids completely the Symbolist obscurity of some of Régnier's other poems. "Le Vase" contains none of Mallarmé's proleptic syntax, and each line provides a self-contained unit of meaning couched in a straightforward grammatical pattern. Augmenting the narrative continuity provided by the poem's temporal framework, this syntactical progression marks time just as the sculptor-poet's "Marteau lourd sonnait dans l'air léger, / . . . Rythmant le matin clair et la bonne journée":

> Un jour, encore,
> Entre les feuilles d'ocre et d'or
> Du bois, je vis, avec ses jambes de poil jaune,
> Danser un faune;
> Je l'aperçus aussi, une autre fois,
> Sortir du bois
> Le long de la route et s'asseoir sur une borne
> Pour prendre un papillon à l'une de ses cornes.
>
> Une autre fois,
> Un Centaure passa la rivière à la nage;
> L'eau ruisselait sur sa peau d'homme et son pelage;
> Il s'avança de quelques pas dans les roseaux,
> Flaira le vent, hennit, repassa l'eau;
> Le lendemain, j'ai vu l'ongle de ses sabots
> Marqué dans l'herbe

[Still another day, between the ochre and gold leaves of the woods, I saw a faun with shaggy yellow legs dancing; I caught sight of him also, another time, coming out of the wood, along the road, and sitting down upon a stump to take a butterfly from one of his horns.

Another time, a centaur crossed the river swimming, the water streamed from his man's skin and his horse's coat; he advanced a few steps into the reeds, snuffed the wind, whinneyed, and crossed back over the water; the next day I saw the prints of his hoofs stamped in the grass.][38]

The extreme care with which Régnier marks the narrative progression—"un jour," "une autre fois"—is echoed by the simple subject-verb-object syntax and the extreme insistence on perception as the instigator of vision: "j'entendais," "je vis," "je l'aperçus." As a whole, this emphasis on perception as the foundation of both narrative and a visionary stance becomes the basis for much of Pound's own verse, particularly "Provincia Deserta." Finally, in the lines Pound quotes as an example of Régnier's "limpidity of syntax," notice the prosodic variety possible even within a prose syntax; the hesitating cadence of the first line—"Il s'avança de quelques pas dans les roseaux"—is submitted to an extreme form of compression in the next line with its two caesurae governed by the syntactical parallelism established in the first: "[Il] Flaira le vent, hennit, repassa l'eau." Despite the symbolist backdrop, "Le Vase" is very much a "prose" poem which justifies, perhaps, Amy Lowell's prose translation of the poem in her *Six French Poets*. In this and the other poems Pound refers to, Régnier manages to avoid the preciosity Pound warns against:

> It would seem as if the French versifiers had become so engrossed in matters of craftsmanship as to forget that the first requisite of a work of art is that it be interesting. . . . It is certain that the method of constatation drifts off imperceptibly into description and that pages of poetic description can have no interest save for those particularly interested in the things described, or for those interested in language as language. (*AP* 5, 663)

Once again, therefore, we encounter this dichotomy between Pound's emphasis on a "modern tone" comprised of Régnier's "limpidity of syntax," and his actual borrowings which tend to suggest that the metamorphic road to the visionary realm constitutes the chief thrust of Régnier's poetry.

As Pound continues to refine his poetic, however, he also becomes more attuned to, and is able to incorporate into his own poetry, the specifically modern aspects of Régnier's verse. For example, Pound, possibly following van Bever, discovers another instance of what he takes to be a "modern tone" whereby Régnier "has joined himself to the painters of contemporary things" (*Inst*, 40) in "L'Accueil," a poem which eliminates completely the decadent tone so characteristic of Régnier's verse and bares the poet and his innermost sentiments to the scrutiny of his guests:

> Tous deux étaient beaux de corps et de visages,
> L'air franc et sage
> Avec un clair sourire dans les yeux,
> Et, devant eux,
> Debout en leur jeunesse svelte et prompte,
> Je me sentais courbé et j'avais presque honte
> D'être si vieux.
>
> . . . . . .
>
> Et tous deux me regardaient, surpris de voir
> Celui qu'ils croyaient autre en leur pensée
> Se lever pour les recevoir
> Vêtu de bure et le front nu
> Et non pas, comme en leur pensées,
> Drapé de pourpre et lauré d'or.

[Both had beautiful figures and faces,
And an air fresh and wise
With a bright smile in their eyes,
And, in front of them,
Standing in their svelt and timely youth,
I felt that I stooped and was almost ashamed
To be so old.

.   .   .   .   .

And both looked at me, surprised to see
A person other than they had expected
Rise to meet them
Dressed in sackcloth and with a bare head
And not, as they had imagined,
Draped in purple and laureled in gold.][39]

Here, according to Pound, "we find him leading perhaps onward toward Vildrac, and toward a style which might be the basis for a certain manner F. M. Hueffer has used in English *vers libre*, rather than remembering the Parnassians" (*Inst*, 44). Pound's appreciation of this poem helps to account for one of Pound's very infrequent attempts to express directly his own sentiments in "Villanelle: The Psychological Hour" (1915), where "with middle-aging care" the poet prepares for a visit from two friends; yet, the poet is characteristically spared this task by the ironic note informing him that his friends are leaving England. This poem provides a telling instance of the difficulty Pound has in discovering an authentic "personal" voice: Pound is clearly uncomfortable with this confessional mode, since it implicates him, and he tilts the balance toward an ironic presentation of the self that anticipates *Mauberley*. We can thus begin to understand Pound's attraction to Gautier's supposedly satirical presentation directed outward against others.

The double-bind described in the preceding pages, as well as the ensuing shift in Pound's aesthetic, is clearly set forth in his 1913 homage to Albert Samain in "The Garden" (*P*, 85). This poem has an undeniably curious status given that Pound chooses to include as an epigraph the first line of Samain's introductory poem to *Au Jardin de L'Infante*, which, as Pierre Martino notes, "a rendu assez populaire une poésie mièvre, alanguie, indécise, triste" [has made popular a poetry that is affected, languishing, indecisive, sad].[40] Although Pound comments favorably on this poem in the *Little Review* (Feb. 1918), he comes increasingly to see an inherent softness in Samain's poetry. Whereas Remy de Gourmont, seeing in Samain a sincerity and a delicateness of craft, contends that "toutes les âmes sont amoureuses de cette 'infante

en robe de parade'" [all souls are enamored of this *Infanta* in full rega-
lia], Pound argues in the February issue of *Poetry* that Samain "begins
to go 'soft', there is just a suggestion of muzziness" (*LE*, 285).[41] The
question that arises immediately, therefore, is what valence we should
give to Pound's use of the epigraph "en robe de parade" in this
poem—is it ironic?—and whether we can discern some sort of conti-
nuity between Pound's poetry in 1913 and his critical appreciation of
Samain as it evolves in 1918.

Pound's use of epigraphs is not generally disrespectful. When
Pound quotes Browning, Swinburne, or Yeats, for example, we can
safely assume that the epigraph situates that particular poem and pro-
vides an intellectual framework within which Pound will work; if, on
the other hand, Pound intends an epigraph in a satirical vein, it is
generally obscure or anonymous. By quoting Samain, Pound creates a
context that resonates throughout his own poem; indeed, Pound does
not merely limit himself to a passing reference to Samain, but pro-
ceeds to transpose the setting of Samain's poem into his own. Both
works present a woman of aristocratic bearing walking in a garden,
exiled and shut off from any connection to a social reality. Pound's
lady, surrounded by the "unkillable infants of the very poor" and by
the poet himself, displays her aristocratic "end of breeding" through
her exquisite and excessive boredom. Similarly, Samain's *âme/infante*
listens to "d'ensorcelants poèmes" read by "Son page favori," and, "re-
doutant la foule aux tumultes de fer, / Elle écoute la vie—au loin—
comme la mer . . ." [listens to "enchanting poems" read by her "favor-
ite page," and "shunning the tumultuous crowd with its weapons
drawn,/She listens to life, far away, like the sea . . ."].

Pound's decision to quote only the second half of Samain's opening
line in his epigraph is in this respect quite telling. Whereas Samain sets
forth a metaphorical comparison which conveys a more or less interi-
orized, subjective state ("Mon âme est une infante"), Pound prefers to
evoke only the external, social codes pertaining to dress: "en robe de
parade." Thus, we can see that Pound's quest for an "objective,"
imagistic presentation or social portrait amounts to a desire to repress
the subjective core of Samain's poem:

> Elle est là résignée, et douce, et sans surprise,
> Sachant trop pour lutter comme tout est fatal,
> Et se sentant, malgré quelque dédain natal,
> Sensible à la pitié comme l'onde à la brise.
>
> Elle est là résignée, et douce en ses sanglots,
> Plus sombre seulement quand elle évoque en songe

Quelque Armada sombrée à l'éternel mensonge,
Et tant de beaux espoirs endormis sous les flots.

[She is there, resigned, sweet and knowing all,
Knowing too much to fight as all is fatal,
And finding herself, despite some native disdain,
Sensible to pity, like the wave is to the breeze.

She is there, resigned, sweet in her sobs,
More somber only when she dreams
Some Armada sunk in the eternal lie,
And so many beautiful hopes lost beneath the waves.][42]

This strangely inverted anticipation of Pound's portrait of Queen Elizabeth in Canto 91 develops a psychological dimension absent in, yet wholly relevant to, Pound's own poem. Samain's *infante* is the perfect embodiment of the decadent personality evident in Pound's early poetry and, thus, raises the question of Pound's position in "The Garden."

One standard way of interpreting Pound's poem would be to argue that it is entirely concerned with the relationship between aesthetics and social reality.[43] From this perspective, one would emphasize the contrast between the wealthy and the poor; the woman's aristocratic position has now become an entirely marginal one as "she walks by the railing of a path in Kensington Gardens" surrounded by "a rabble/Of the filthy, sturdy, unkillable infants of the very poor." Whereas the numerically substantial presence of the poor will enable them to inherit the earth, Pound's "woman of substance" is "dying piecemeal/of a sort of emotional anaemia" because she fears any chance social interaction that occurs outside the confines of her class identity. She is exquisitely decadent, the "end of breeding" in both senses, and cannot tolerate the infusion of new blood, new experiences, or new social realities. According to this interpretation, therefore, we must assume that the speaker is highly critical of the upper classes and enacts his revenge upon them by means of his violent simile in the first line of the poem.

While the above interpretation is both coherent and plausible, it does not quite account for the speaker's position in the poem. The speaker's characterization of the woman's boredom as "exquisite and excessive" contains a discursive judgment that reenacts the decidedly ambivalent simile in the first line of the poem: "Like a skein of loose silk blown against a wall." The transition from liquids and sibilants in the first half of the line to the voiced consonants in the second abruptly divides the line in two, with the suggestion of a trochaic rhythm in this acephalous line becoming decidedly iambic as the beautifully diaphonous silk threads are blown violently against the wall. Our expectations are overturned because, although we realize that Pound simply wants to suggest the extremely fragile and unsubstantial nature of the woman, the beauty of this image awakens our aesthetic sensibility as well as our sympathy. We can, of course, account for the violence of this simile by saying that the speaker is expressing the resentment occasioned by the woman's having equated him with the rabble surrounding her, since the much feared indiscretion can only occur because the speaker exists outside of the woman's social realm, but this explanation only highlights the speaker's own marginal position in society. We cannot assume that the speaker fully accepts the social and aesthetic implications of the triumph of the poor; after all, it is the speaker who sets forth the pejorative description of the "rabble." Moreover, we cannot assume that this "rabble" would constitute a fit audience for Pound's poetry, and we know that Pound would not especially care for a typological reenactment of biblical themes. Thus, the poet is in a very tenuous position; like the woman, who is incapable of adapting to the emerging political and social position of the working classes, Pound is incapable of anything more than a naturalistic description of mere externals: "filthy, sturdy, unkillable infants." On the other hand, Pound is capable of entering into the woman's mind and of understanding the conventions of her world. Thus, in addition to the poet's criticism of the woman's isolation from social realities, we can detect a hint of nostalgia for an age that is slowly dying.

If we accept this interpretation, we can see just how tenuous Pound's position is at this juncture in his career. Not only does this poem indicate a distinct tension underlying the relationship between the social and aesthetic realms, but it also voices an uncertainty about whether to privilege a satirical presentation over a decadent one. Thus, our understanding of the role of a Parnassian aesthetic in Pound's own developing poetic is complicated by Pound's seeming intent to transform the dialectical tension in Gautier's poetry into a simple bifurcation between a symbolist or Parnassian mode and a modernist aesthetic. Once we recognize that much of the appeal of Gautier's poetry arises from his ability to maintain a dialectical tension between a symbolist mode and what Pound rightly calls a "modern tone," we can say that Pound commits a real critical blunder when he suggests that Gautier's poetic vision is wholly embodied in his "Carmen." Nonetheless, Pound's suggestion that this is indeed the case enables us to discern in Pound's own poetic development a gradual trajectory whereby Pound himself moves from a mode of symbolism implicit in the above-mentioned poets to a "modernism" based wholly on satire.

Whereas the attraction of Gautier's "Carmen" results largely, I think, from a poetic technique which enables Gautier to balance a quotidian bourgeois existence against a romantic idealization of "l'éternel féminin," both Pound and Eliot in their versions of the poem opt for only half of the equation. Gautier by no means sets forth the purely satirical representation adopted by Pound in "To a Friend Writing on Cabaret Dancers" and Eliot in his "Whispers of Immortality." Instead, Gautier acknowledges the double-edged nature of Carmen, who, in a sense, becomes beautiful through hyperbole:

> Elle a dans sa laideur piquante
> Un grain de sel de cette mer
> D'où jaillit nue et provocante,
> L'âcre Vénus du gouffre amer.
>
> [Her piquant ugliness contains nonetheless
> A grain of the salt of that sea
> From which the naked Venus of the bitter abyss
> Bursts forth provocatively.][44]

Against the "trait de bistre," Gautier juxtaposes the powerfully erotic line: "Et de ses yeux la lueur chaude / Rend la flamme aux satiétés" [And the hot glimmering of her eyes / Sets fire to satiety]. It is precisely Gautier's ability to wed opposites that makes the poem the success that it is; Gautier's strategy in *Émaux et Camées* is not simply an extension of his doctrine of l'art pour l'art, but an attempt to reconcile a shabby bourgeois existence with the ideal demands of an art which seeks out beauty. As David Kelley has remarked in another context, Gautier "cherche à se servir du 'joli', du sentimental et du badin pour créer un poème à résonances éternelles et universelles sans toutefois être infidèle à la trivialité qui permet à ces manifestations du mauvais goût de résumer l'ambiance affective, la vie même, du siècle" [attempts to make use of the "cute," the sentimental, and the humorous to create a poem with universal or eternal resonances, but which is not unfaithful to the triviality that enables these manifestations of bad taste to sum up the emotional life of the century].[45] Gautier's subtle balancing of tawdriness and erotically charged images lends the poem a piquancy that leads Pound to call it "deathless":

> Et, parmi sa pâleur, éclate
> Une bouche aux rires vainqueurs;
> Piment rouge, fleur écarlate,
> Qui prend sa pourpre au sang des coeurs.

Ainsi faite, la moricaude
Bat les plus altières beautés,
Et de ses yeux la lueur chaude
Rend la flamme aux satiétés.

[And in the midst of her palour,
A conquering smile explodes;
Pimento red, scarlet flower,
Taking its color from the heart's blood.

Thus made, this swarthy lass
Conquers the most haughty beauty,
And the hot glimmering of her eyes
Sets fire to satiety.]

In Pound's "To a Friend Writing on Cabaret Dancers," however, he tends to downplay any aesthetic idealization in order to achieve an unsentimentalized "realism," which, despite Pound's argument that "the underlying statement is very humane and most moral" (*SL*, 82), verges toward a satirical "naturalism":

The prudent whore is not without her future,
Her bourgeois dulness is deferred.
              Her present dulness . . .
Oh well, her present dulness . . .
Now in Venice, 'Storante al Giardino, I went early,
Saw the performers come: him, her, the baby,
A quiet and respectable-tawdry trio;
An hour later: a show of calves and spangles,
"*Un e duo fanno tre*,"
              Night after night,
No change, no change of program, "*Che!*
"*La donna è mobile*."

                                                            (*P*, 160)

Although laden with explicit references to Gautier's "Carmen," and to his "Coquetterie posthume" and "Les Joujoux de la morte," Pound's "To a Friend" opts for only half of Gautier's compromise between poetry and a prose world. As Pound argues in defense of the poem, "The thing the bourgeois will always hate is the fact that I make the people *real*. I treat the dancers as human beings, not as 'symbols of sin'. That is the crime and the 'obscenity'"(*SL*, 82). While Pound does, perhaps, treat these people realistically, there is nonetheless a slight difference between realism and the modicum of sympathy necessary to realize a meaningful portrait; his portrait of the dancers does not quite manage the delicate balancing act achieved by Gautier. In fact, as I will argue in the next chapter, Pound's homage is much closer in spirit to Corbière's contumely.

If we accept the idea that Gautier is continuously striving to reconcile a polarized world of art and bourgeois existence, Pound's own post-imagist poetry voices only a wearisome contempt for the middle-class values of a post-Edwardian England. Whereas Gautier's "Symphonie en blanc majeur" contains a compelling play of correspondence and analogy that transforms the world of the salon into a veritable mythopoeic vision, Pound's "clin d'oeil à ce poème," his "Albâtre," contains a number of scathing comparisons which completely undermine the more serious intent of Gautier. Whereas Gautier desires to rescue an ideal beauty from a quotidian world, Pound remains content simply to attack bourgeois pretense:

> This lady in the white bath-robe which she calls a peignoir,
> Is, for the time being, the mistress of my friend,
> And the delicate white feet of her little white dog
> Are not more delicate than she is,
> Nor would Gautier himself have despised their contrasts in whiteness
> As she sits in the great chair
> Between the two indolent candles.
>
> (P, 88)

Having been attracted initially to that aspect of Gautier's aesthetic which would lead ultimately to the symbolist orientation of Mallarmé, a Parnassianism which enabled Pound to retain some of the Pre-Raphaelite coloring of his early verse without having to give up any claim to being modern, Pound soon adopts the satirical side of Gautier's poetry without being able to retain the sense of mystery and affirmation at the heart of Gautier's bourgeois tableaux. But given what we have already seen of Pound's often conflicted development, it should come as no surprise that the tension between satire and Parnassus does not end when Pound falls under the spell of Corbière, Tailhade, and Laforgue, but continues, indeed increases, in *Mauberley* and the early cantos.

Chapter Two

POUND'S GRADUS A PARNASSO:
MISANTHROPY, POUND, AND SOME
FRENCH SATIRE

> Poëte—Après! . . . Il faut *la chose*:
> Le Parnasse en escalier
> —Tristan Corbière

> The Twelve Tables penalized satire.
> —(97/692)

ALTHOUGH Pound reverently returns to the Parnassians in his later critical writings,[1] his poetry after *Ripostes* demonstrates the fruits of his interest in the satirical Théophile Gautier, in Tristan Corbière, Laurent Tailhade and, still later, Jules Laforgue.[2] This manifest influence of the French satirical poets on Pound's *Lustra* necessitates that we at least ask ourselves whether Pound's critical conjunction of heterogeneous, if not irreconcilable, poetic modes has shaped the extreme tonal swings and the diverse subject matter in *Lustra*. In other words, the consideration of the new "masters" in Pound's ideogram of good writing might help to explain the change in emphasis in *Lustra*, as well as the critic's difficulty in generating a stable interpretative framework or set of expectations with which to approach it.[3]

Pound's confusing juxtaposition in his critical writings of mutually exclusive poetic modes—i.e., Realism and Romance, Parnasse and Satire—can also be seen in the transition from *Ripostes* to *Lustra*. The aggressive stance in *Lustra* is signaled at the outset by the programmatic opening poem, "Tenzone," which casts the poet as a centurion setting about to terrify the "virgin stupidity" of the reader. No longer "homesick after [his] own kind" ("In Durance," *CEP*, 86), the poet has apparently abandoned his quest for an audience:

> Will people accept them?
> (i.e. these songs).
> As a timorous wench from a centaur
> (or a centurion)
> Already they flee, howling in terror.

Will they be touched with the verisimilitudes?
    Their virgin stupidity is untemptable.
I beg you, my friendly critics,
Do not set about to procure me an audience.

I mate with my free kind upon the crags;
    the hidden recesses
Have heard the echo of my heels,
    in the cool light,
    in the darkness.

                    (P, 83)

Pound's plea to his friendly critics not to procure him an audience has already been inscribed in the opening of the poem with his peremptory answers to his own questions. Contrary to what we might expect, the poet's quest for universally recognizable verisimilitudes has become a wholly private affair; his supposedly alienating desire to represent society as it really is leads to his curious withdrawal to the hidden recesses upon the crags, where he mates with his "own free kind," not the "timorous wench[es]," but where, ironically, the only sound heard is the echo of his retreat.

Similarly, where the Hellenic vision in *Ripostes* was more wistfully passive, the visionary stance in *Lustra* is strangely aggressive. Pound's vision of the Beloved or of beauty now contains the recognition of the inevitability of death or destruction ("Actaeon," "April"), and desire includes a threatening potential for dissolution ("The Spring"). And where *Ripostes* was dominated by a modern, conversational tone, and by Hellenic visions or modernist and imagistic metamorphoses, *Lustra* expands the satirical and epigrammatic vein embryonic in that earlier volume ("Phasellus Ille," "An Object," "Quies").[4] In effect, the Hellenic and imagist poems in *Lustra* serve largely to provide relief from the vehemently satirical tone so prevalent throughout the volume. The conversational tone of "Portrait d'une Femme" is transformed into an "objectively impersonal" (i.e., satirical) description of externals ("Les Millwin"), a self-congratulatory distinction between "us" and "them" ("The Garret"), or the scathing attacks on the bourgeoisie and the "hypocrite lecteur" ("Albâtre," "The Bellaires," "The Cake of Soap," "Tenzone," "The Condolence," "Salutation 2nd," etc.).

In this respect, the title of Pound's *Lustra* is particularly apt because it captures this shift in his poetic. As Pound writes in a letter to Elkin Mathews, "Dell in Chicago was the first man to see that I was writing . . . in latin tradition as distinct from greek" (P/J, 285). Latin here implies epigrammatic rather than Hellenic, and, more particularly, the satirical tradition, which, as Remy de Gourmont has argued, was also the tradition of Laurent Tailhade: "Latin de race et de goûts, M. Tailhade a droit à ce beau nom de rhéteur dont se choque l'incapacité des cuistres; c'est un rhéteur à la Pétrone, également maître dans la prose et dans les vers" [Latin by race and by taste, M. Tailhade has every right to the title of a rhetor, for he has shocked and offended those incompetent pedants and prigs; he's a rhetor à la Petronius, a master of both prose and verse].[5] There is indeed a further irony in Pound's choice of a title in that *lustrum*, in addition to being a "purificatory sacrifice," can also mean: (1) a slough, bog, haunt, den of beasts; (2) a wood, forest, wilderness; (3) a house of ill-repute; and, figuratively, (4) debauchery.[6] With its satirical epigrams on modern British mores, *Lustra*, despite Pound's altruistic arguments to the contrary, is very much an attempt to *épater le bourgeois* through its matter-of-fact representation of modern life: "Nine adulteries, 12 liaisons, 64 fornications/ and something approaching a rape" ("The Temperaments," *P*, 100). This portrait of Florialis, a "man . . . so quiet and reserved in demeanour/That he passes for both bloodless and sexless," ironically underscores the hypocritical behavior and, when contrasted with the bombastic Bastidides, the insipidity of the upholders of public virtue.

The mannered impersonality of this "presentative method" which Pound has inherited from Laurent Tailhade is, he says, "equity"; it is "as communicative as Nature [or] as uncommunicative as Nature," and, thus, "is irrefutable because it does not present a personal predilection" (*AP* 5, 662). By presenting a catalog of so-called "facts," the poet wants us to believe that he is presenting a "nature" free of any oppressive ideological content; hence, the Whitmanian voice of liberation in *Lustra*. And yet no one could argue that the poems of either Pound or Tailhade contain no "personal predilection." The title of Pound's volume alone indicates that he has arrogated to himself the function of maintaining public morality, for, according to the definition taken by Pound from C. T. Lewis's *Elementary Latin Dictionary*, a *lustrum* is "an offering for the sins of the whole people, made by the censors at the expiration of their five years of office" (*P*, 80).

At the same time, however, we never have the sense that Pound wholeheartedly supports or sympathizes with "the whole people." As Pound wrote in an attempt to circumvent Elkin Mathews's censorship of *Lustra:* "I do not write as that pandar to public imbecilities Mr Chesterton, nor yet for the Meynell's nurse-maid. I write for a few hundred people who are familiar with the classics and who are bored to death with modern inanities because the latter have no directness" (*P/J*, 278). Although the poems in this volume are intended as a form of expiation for, or exorcism of, the sins of the bourgeois philistines against whom Pound rails, his salutations to the reader depend upon bald assertion and the too easy assumption of superiority. In the following poem, for example, we might ask what it is that stands behind and legitimizes this inversion of "the great chain-of-being":

SALUTATION

O generation of the thoroughly smug
    and thoroughly uncomfortable,
I have seen fishermen picknicking in the sun,
I have seen them with untidy families,
I have seen their smiles full of teeth
    and heard ungainly laughter.
And I am happier than you are,
And they were happier than I am;
And the fish swim in the lake
    and do not even own clothing.

(*P*, 86)

As Hugh Witemeyer has argued regarding the emergence in *Lustra* of a radically new Whitmanian persona, such "songs" as "Salutation," "Salutation the Second," or "Commission" argue for a spiritual aristocracy of poets rather than a general democratic embrace.[7]

Turning to Tailhade, if we examine his "Dîner champêtre," we might well agree with Pound that "perhaps the most characteristic phase of Tailhade is in his pictures of the bourgeoisie," but we would, I think, puzzle over Pound's characterization of the poem as being "one depicted with all Tailhadian serenity" (*Inst*, 52):

DÎNER CHAMPÊTRE

Entre les sièges où des garçons volontaires
Entassent leurs chalands parmi les boulingrins,
La famille Feyssard, avec des airs sereins,
Discute longuement les tables solitaires.

La demoiselle a mis son chapeau rouge vif
Dont s'honore le bon faiseur de sa commune,
Et madame Feyssard, un peu hommasse et brune,
Porte une robe loutre avec des reflets d'if.

Enfin ils sont assis! Or le père commande
Des écrevisses, du potage au lait d'amande,
Toutes choses dont il rêvait depuis longtemps.

Et, dans le ciel couleur de turquoises fanées,
Il voit les songes bleus qu'en ses esprits flottants
A fait naître l'ampleur des truites saumonées.

[A Rustic Dinner

Between the seats where free-lance waiters
Stack their customers on the bowling green,
The Buttocks family, with an air so serene,
Had a hard time choosing among the empty tables.

The daughter wore her bright red cardinal's hat
To honor the good hatter of her town,
And wearing a yew-colored otter gown,
Madam Buttocks was mannish, dark, and fat.

Seated at last! Father commands
Crayfish and soup with milk of almond,
All the things he'd desired so long.

And in the faded turquoise heaven,
His reeling mind sees blue dreams brought on
By the copious meal of trout and salmon.][8]

There is, of course, a certain serenity in this poem, since we are
privy to a quasi-symbolist vision of the infinite, the faded turquoise sky
which contains M. Feyssard's "blue dreams"; unfortunately, this vision
of the "infinite" was precipitated by "l'ampleur des truites saumonées"
of which he had dreamt so long. Moreover, if we consider Tailhade's
description of Mme Feyssard, we can see the purely materialist or ani-
malistic basis for this vision. Wearing an otter coat with the red glint of
a yew, she is described as being a little dark and masculine. Once we
come to terms with the bizarre description of the "robe loutre avec de
reflets d'if" referring us back to the bad taste of her daughter's bright
red hat and forward to her husband's otter-like dreams of fish, we
begin to realize that Tailhade has gone a little out of his way in his
search for "le mot juste," for an objective and impersonal description.
Despite "the opulence of the vocables," this is a damning portrait of
the bourgeoisie. In the end, despite Pound's elaborate critical smoke
screen, we realize that what he means by "serenity" is simply "a per-
sonal satire impersonalized by its glaze and its finish" (*Inst*, 51) and that
this "serenity" results from the poet's unspoken superiority.
    Similarly, if we consider one of Pound's "objective" portraits of the
bourgeoisie, "Les Millwin," we can see exactly what he means by such
"impersonalized" facts "worthy of record":

The little Millwins attend the Russian Ballet.
The mauve and greenish souls of the little Millwins
Were seen lying along the upper seats
Like so many unused boas.

The turbulent and undisciplined host of art students—
The rigorous deputation from "Slade"—
Was before them.

With arms exalted, with fore-arms
Crossed in great futuristic X's, the art students
Exulted, they beheld the splendours of *Cleopatra*.

And the little Millwins beheld these things;
With their large and anaemic eyes they looked out upon this
    configuration.

Let us therefore mention the fact,
For it seems to us worthy of record.

(P, 94)

Like Tailhade's characterization of the Feyssards, Pound's description of the little Millwins hinges upon the calculatedly impressionistic color scheme (mauve and green) and the unflattering invocation of *la mode* ("Like so many unused boas"). The anaemic Millwins are contrasted with the "rigorous deputation from 'Slade',," who "Exulted, [as] they beheld the splendours of *Cleopatra*." Given Pound's presentation, we cannot quite be sure whether the "configuration" that the Millwins' "large and anaemic eyes looked out / Upon" is the Russian Ballet or the art students' "fore-arms / Crossed in great futuristic X's," but we do know that the little Millwins would be unable to make heads or tails of whatever they beheld. At the same time, we are certainly not intended to uphold the exultant art students as model concertgoers, and we are left to wonder what "fact" is, in fact, "worthy of record."

The poetic "I" in this poem, or rather the royal "we," leaves very little room for the spectacle surrounding the Russian Ballet itself; indeed, the poem suggests that Pound's presence at the Russian Ballet has nothing to do with the art of dance, but with the lambasting of both the pseudo-connoisseurs who transform art into popular fashion and those who blithely follow along.[9] While Thomas H. Jackson has rightly qualified Hugh Kenner's discussion of "the immolation of auctorial personality"[10] in this poem by arguing that "[i]t is wrong to assert that the poem is untainted by the attitudes of the poet,"[11] Jackson himself perhaps overstates his case when he concludes that the "technique of juxtaposition displayed [in *Lustra*] precludes any rhetorical appeal to readers to accept the poet's interpretation as their own."[12] Where Tailhade seems awfully good-natured by comparison, Pound's contempt is palpable, and we are left with little option but to similarly condemn the spectacle before us or to join the ranks of the unenlightened.

In *Lustra*, Pound makes explicit what has been implicit even in his early poems: that the interlocutee matters very little. Whereas the early Eliot labors to escape the shadow of Laforgue's ironic monologues in which much of the pain is self-inflicted, Pound is incapable of recognizing the Other and proceeds to transform the You into an It, irony into satire; there is little room here for an ironic, self-implicating and self-correcting *Ich-Spaltung* or splitting of the ego, as it were, no possibility for Pound to say, like Prufrock, "Let us go then, you and I." Moreover, the relatively simple dualism suggested by Pound's dissociation between the "cult of beauty" and the "cult of ugliness" (*LE*, 45) provides no inherent stability, and the sanitizing power of satire crosses the supposedly impregnable boundary into the realm of the beautiful. In Pound's "Dans un Omnibus de Londres," for example, Pound repeats the central motif in his "Picture," a poem describing Jacopo del Sallaio's *Venus Reclining* ("The eyes of this dead lady speak to me"), but here the beautiful eyes of the goddess are irreverently associated with, framed and contained by, the banal presence of a nondescript woman:

> Les yeux d'une morte
> > M'ont salué,
> > Enchassés dans un visage stupide
> Dont tous les autres traits étaient banals

> [The eyes of a dead lady
> > Greeted me,
> > Enshrined in a stupid face
> In which all the other traits were banal.]

(P, 156)

What we realize is that the poem succeeds (or fails) in providing what little solace it does provide, not by virtue of the epiphanic nature of this divine apparition, but in direct proportion to our willingness to trust the poet's discernment, to accept the possibility that the poet can in fact separate the wheat from the chaff, the beautiful eyes from the banal traits. The concept of le mot juste becomes in this case a misnomer if we seek an objective representation based on something more than our trust in Pound's vision; the value judgment contained in this description is voiced a little too strongly to enable us to see anything more than a strained vision, a striving to attain and fix the epiphanic moment, which, as Proust tells us, and as Pound demonstrates again and again in the Pisan and late cantos, is ultimately less fulfilling than the accidental or involuntary memory of the experience.

As with Pound's "Ortus," the process of bringing beauty to life is entirely one-dimensional, depending on the poet to name the unnamed and reflecting only the naming subjectivity:

How have I laboured?
How have I not laboured
To bring her soul to birth,
To give these elements a name and a centre!
She is beautiful as the sunlight, and as fluid.
She has no name, and no place.
How have I laboured to bring her soul into separation;
To give her a name and her being!

Surely you are bound and entwined,
You are mingled with the elements unborn;
I have loved a stream and a shadow.

I beseech you enter your life.
I beseech you learn to say "I,"
When I question you;
For you are no part, but a whole,
No portion, but a being.

(P, 85–86)

Although seemingly quite benevolent, Pound's endeavor to bring the women to life, beauty to light, the poem into existence, contains sinister overtones as all the actions emanate from Pound, especially since Pound adopts the topos of a real woman (H. D.?) and not simply "beauty";[13] the woman-poem becomes a stillborn Galatea, and there is no sense here, as there will be later in Pound's poetry, that the object has its own immanent form: "the stone knows the form" (74/444). Although he pleads for the soul's "separation," Pound's unwillingness to admit that this "whole" has a "being" apart from the naming subjectivity is quite tellingly hinted at in the lines—"I beseech you to say 'I' / When I question you"—where the gesture at subjectivity is overwhelmed by the grammatical subject, where the "I" of "being" is in essence only a quotation, a second-order existence proferred by a poet who ultimately rejects the notion that poetry should concern itself with such "airy nothings."[14]

Already evident in "Portrait d'une Femme" (1912), this wholly subjective strategy permits absolutely no intersubjectivity. There is mordant speech, perhaps, but no dialogue, since others are always subjected to the poet's controlling metaphors:

Your mind and you are our Sargasso Sea
. . . .
No! there is nothing! In the whole and all,
Nothing that's quite your own.
              Yet this is you.

(P, 57–58)

If we compare Pound and Eliot's two "Portraits," we can see that
Pound maintains the relentlessly cynical tone that Eliot strives for yet
gives up in the almost Jamesian realization that he himself has been
implicated, painfully so, in another person's life. If poems like "Por-
trait d'une Femme" are, as Schneidau argues, "clear forecasts of the
mature style,"[15] that modern tone or mature style also brings with it
the loss of depth of feeling.

Thus, the realization on the part of a number of critics that Pound's
sensibility has become somewhat impoverished in *Lustra* results, not
from any intrinsic loss of Pound's poetic powers, since he is still capa-
ble of producing some very effective and powerful poems, but from
the blurring of the two antithetical foci in *Lustra:* (1) Pound's new
quest for an impersonal "presentative method" capable of adequately
addressing the contemporary world, and (2) Pound's prior interest in
a subjectivity capable of naming the unnamed. *Lustra* certainly con-
tains the mordant subjectivity for which he praises Corbière, but it is
a subjectivity that transforms dialogue into monologue, the I-You re-
lationship into one predicated on I-They (or -It), a relationship, more-
over, containing the perhaps unearned corollary that the "I" and the
"We" are by definition homologous. The poems in *Lustra* become dis-
cordant precisely because Pound's objective, "presentative method" is
composed of a mordant subjectivity directed, cynically and harshly,
against others.

Numerous critics have attempted to situate this jarring transforma-
tion of Pound's aesthetic in a broader historical perspective that in-
cludes the advent of vorticism as well as Pound's close association with
Wyndham Lewis and James Joyce. Such critics emphasize the "mascu-
line" precision accompanying a broad range of endeavors deriving
ultimately from the "prose method" of Flaubert's "mot juste," and yet
it is difficult indeed, if not a little parochial, to overlook the French
poets who have by this time obtained a position of prominence in
Pound's "ideogram." As René Taupin rightly argues, "Corbière, Tail-
hade lui donnent, l'un un modèle d'intensité, l'autre, de modernisme
dans l'art de peindre les moeurs" [Whereas Corbière gives Pound a
model of intensity, Tailhade gives him a model for the art of depicting
modern mores].[16] He singles out this quatrain in Tailhade's
"Gensdelettres"—

> Coeur de lapin, ventre de porc, nez de gorille,
> Incarnation des plus saumâtres Vichnous,
> Dubut de Laforest qu'une gale essorille,
> Étant un pur gaga, rayonne parmi nous.
>
> [Rabbit-hearted, pork-belly, gorilla-nose,
> Incarnation of the most bitter Vishnu,

> Dubut de Laforest, de-eared by scabies,
> A doddering old fool, he shines among us.][17]

—as a model for Pound's diatribe or "blast" at the literary community in "Salutation the Third":

> You slut-bellied obstructionist,
> You sworn foe to free speech and good letters,
> You fungus, you continuous gangrene.
>
> (*P*, 75)

All in all, Taupin greatly extends Tailhade's important influence on Pound when he says, "*The Garden* montre les lignes d'un poème de Tailhade; de même *Les Millwin.*—Tels gestes, tels mouvements de *Vendredi Saint*, de *Place des Victoires* se sont imposés; ce sont aussi les mêmes sujets: portraits de vieilles femmes, les mal-mariés, les vices littéraires et autres de l'époque" ["The Garden" has the lines of a poem by Tailhade, as does "Les Millwin."—The gestures, the movements of "Vendredi Saint" or "Place des Victoires" are contained in these poems. They also treat the same subjects: portraits of elderly women, poor marriages, the literary and other vices of the era].[18] We can easily add to this list by including almost any of the satirical or epigrammatic portraits in *Lustra*. Pound esteems Tailhade because he "is painting contemporary Paris, with verve. His eye is on the thing itself" (*Inst*, 48). And insofar as Pound begins to address modern subjects in a predominantly satirical fashion, Tailhade is always lurking in the background and serves to legitimize Pound's choice of satire as a vehicle for the expression of a "modern" sensibility. Such poems as "The Temperaments," "The Bellaires," and "Moeurs Contemporaines" are not far removed from Tailhade's voyage "au pays du Mufle," where "Le vieux monsieur qu'on sait un magistrat farouche/ Tient des propos grivois aux filles de douze ans" [The old man, well known as a stern judge,/Extends lewd propositions to twelve-year-old girls].[19] Because of the preponderance of Tailhadian invective and imagery in *Lustra*, the satirical tone underlying Pound's "presentative method" comes to the fore in most critical examinations of the influential role of French verse in Pound's developing modernism.[20]

Unfortunately, however, such critical approaches tend to limit themselves to the isolation of local stylistic details linking Pound's poetry of the *Lustra* period with that of his French predecessors. Because Pound is a fundamentally imitative poet who can effortlessly adopt or adapt another poet's stylistic tics, such arguments tell us little about poetic influence (in the strong sense). It is precisely here that we must reevaluate the role of such poets as Corbière and Tailhade, for although Taupin is correct when he says that in following Tailhade

Pound seeks "non des émotions nouvelles, une sensibilité originale, mais l'articulation nette des sensations éprouvées par ses contemporains" [neither new emotions, nor an original sensibility, but the clear delineation of the sensations experienced by his contemporaries],[21] we encounter a problem when it comes to Pound's esteem for Tristan Corbière. When we look to Pound's critical accounts of Corbière, we can see that what he in fact discovers is Corbière's "original sensibility." While both Corbière and Tailhade certainly do function as exemplars of a particular trend in Pound's poetry, of a newfound "intensity" and "violence of invective and imagery," the role they played in Pound's development is much more illustrative of a fundamental contradiction contained in Pound's vision of the poet. If we turn to Pound's statement that Corbière "is more real than the 'realists' because he still recognises that force of romance that is a quite real and apparently ineradicable part of our life" (SP, 372–73), we can see that the fundamental concepts set forth in Pound's discussion of Corbière, his "realism" and "romance," have now become so intertwined that Taupin's attempt to distinguish between an impersonal rendering of "moeurs contemporaines" and a romantically oriented "original sensibility" breaks down once and for all.

·   ·   ·

> Since Gautier, Corbière has been hard, not with a glaze or
> parian finish, but hard like weather-bit granite.
> —(LE, 288)

For Pound, Corbière was the poet who "restored French verse to the vigour of Villon and to an intensity that no Frenchman had touched during the intervening four centuries" (LE, 33). Though by no means original,[22] Pound's claim that "it is Villon whom most by life and temperament [Corbière] must be said to resemble" (Inst, 28) reveals a great deal about his strong interest in Corbière. Just as Villon was in Pound's eyes the poet "of unvarnished, intimate speech" (SR, 167), the poet "whose gaze cannot be deflected from the actual fact before him" (SR, 168), so too Corbière was the poet of "swift mordant speech" who "looked the thing in the eye and was no more minded to be a 'stand-pat-er' or to soothe the world or the world-of-letters with flattery than he would have been to deceive himself about the state of the Channel off his native village" (SP, 371–72). Just as Villon had "no care whatever for the flowery traditions of mediaeval art, and no anxiety to revive the massive rhetoric of the Romans" (SR, 167), so too Corbière was "the first . . . to hurl anything as apt and violent as 'garde nationale épique' or 'inventeur de la larme écrite' at the Romantico-rhetorico and the sentimento-romantico of Hugo and Lamartine" (*Inst*, 28). Having previously found "seeds or signs of a far more modern outbreak" (*SR*, 167) in Villon, Pound sets out to convince us that he has "found another poet to put on the little rack with Villon and Heine, with the poets whom one actually reads" (*SP*, 373). And if "there walked the gutters of Paris one François Montcorbier, poet and gaolbird" (*SR*, 167), "Corbière came also to 'Paris'" (*Inst*, 27):

> Bâtard de Créole et Breton,
> Il vint aussi là—fourmilière,
> Bazar où rien n'est en pierre,
> Où le soleil manque de ton.
>
> .   .   .   .
>
> Là, sa pauvre Muse pucelle
> Fit le trottoir en *demoiselle.*
> Ils disaient: Qu'est-ce qu'elle vend?
>
> —Rien.—Elle restait là, stupide,
> N'entendant pas sonner le vide
> Et regardant passer le vent . . .
>
> [Bastard Breton-Créole,
> he too to this anthill comes—
> this bazaar, not of stone at all,
> where there's no style to the sun.
>
> .   .   .   .
>
> Here, his poor virgin Muse
> made her start, a street *demoiselle.*
> They said: What's she got to sell?
>
> —Nothing.—She stood there, confused,
> not hearing the emptiness cry
> and watching the wind go by . . .][23]

Pound begins his 1913 essay with Corbière's "Parisian gasconadings," poems filled with (largely fabricated) references to his Villonesque life in the gutter and in police stations. As Pound would later put it, "Corbière had . . . but one level of poverty" (*Inst*, 29). But first and foremost in these Parisian poems, we discover the poet who demystifies "l'éternel féminin":

> Je voudrais être alors chien de fille publique,
> Lécher un peu d'amour qui ne soit pas payé;
> Ou déesse à tous crins sur la côte d'Afrique,
> Ou fou, mais réussi; fou, mais pas à moitié.

[So I'd like to be some prostitute's pet dog,
Lapping up love for which I needn't pay;
Or a fanatical goddess on the African coast,
Or insane, but successfully; truly mad, not just half-crazy.][24]

Pound quotes the first two lines of this quatrain from "Sous un portrait de Corbière" to illustrate his point that "it is precisely that a man should not speak at all until he has something (it matters very little what) to say" (*SP*, 371); these lines are, says Pound, but one example of Corbière's "constant emission of equally vigorous phrases" (*Inst*, 28) like "Fille de marbre, en rut!" or "Mannequin idéal, tête-de-turc du leurre" in "À L'Éternel madame." For Corbière, and increasingly for Pound as he begins to move away from the troubadour vision of the Lady possessing "mediumistic properties" set forth in *The Spirit of Romance*, there is the realization that the poet's openness to emotional currents must of necessity lead to his defensively cavalier and cynical response to any overture of love:

Ah! si j'étais un peu compris! Si, par pitié
Une femme pouvait me sourire à moitié,
Je lui dirais: oh! viens, ange qui me consoles! . . .
. . . .
. . . Et je la conduirais à l'hospice des folles.

[Ah! if I were a little understood! If, through pity
A woman could just smile at me,
I would say to her: oh! come, my comforting angel! . . .
. . . .
. . . And I would lead her to the insane asylum.][25]

Corbière's conjunction of madness and desire in this self-portrait—"Ou fou, mais réussi; fou, mais pas à moitié"—anticipates Pound's similar concern with the love-poet's potential madness in the face of a hostile world, his fascination with that "mad poseur Vidal" (*SR*, 178), for example, or with the "gaunt, grave councillor" in "La Fraisne": "She hath drawn me from mine old ways,/Till men say that I am mad" (*P*, 5). Whereas Pound was an unabashed "servant of Amor" (*SR*, 91) in his pre-*Lustra* poems, the double bind created by the potentially creative conjunction of cynical sophistication and sensitivity—"We were in especial bored with male stupidity./We went forth gathering delicate thoughts,/Our *"fantastikon"* delighted to serve us" (*P*, 84)[26]—now becomes threatening and spawns Pound's defensive posturing in *Lustra*.

Indeed, Pound's "Salutation the Third" might be counted as a direct response to both the theme of madness raised in "Sous un portrait de Corbière" and the fear of an early death raised in "Épitaphe" and

"Un Jeune qui s'en va (mourir)." Whereas this latter poem contains a quasi-ironic catalog of the poets that Corbière has *read* die ("J'en ai lu mourir!")

> —Décès: Rolla:—l'Académie,—
> Murger, Baudelaire:—hôpital,—[27]

Pound's "Salutation the Third" provides us with a romantic's-eye view of the poet's life in support of Corbière's assertion that writing poetry is a "métier de mourir":

> It has been your habit for long
> to do away with good writers,
> You either drive them mad, or else you blink at their suicides,
> Or else you condone their drugs,
> and talk of insanity and genius.

But instead of flattering his reader with what Kenner calls "the immolation of auctorial personality,"[28] Pound adopts Corbière's role of "le poète contumace" in an attempt to underscore his living presence (and, here, his almost sadistic authority) by means of his envenomed sallies on the "hypocrite lecteur":

> But I will not go mad to please you,
> I will not flatter you with an early death,
> Oh, no, I will stick it out,
> Feel your hates wriggling about my feet
> As a pleasant tickle,
> to be observed with derision,
> Though many move with suspicion,
> Afraid to say that they hate you;
> The taste of my boot?
> Here is the taste of my boot,
> Caress it,
> lick off the blacking.
>
> (*P*, 75–76)

Corbière's Parisian poems, and "Un Jeune qui s'en va (mourir)" in particular, become touchstones for Pound because they present a poet who discovers his own voice by flaunting and parodying poetic convention and the literary tradition—a poet, as Michel Dansel has argued, for whom "La parodie . . . correspond à un besoin de désacraliser tout ce qui symbolise pour lui l'autorité, la loi, la tradition, le modèle, l'archétype" [Corbière's parody corresponds to a need to profane everything that symbolizes for him authority, law, tradition, the model, the archetype].[29] He is, in other words, a poet who "made it new." And yet, there are in fact two quite distinct Corbières in Pound's

pantheon, each of whom will have a significantly different impact on
Pound as both his vision of Corbière and his own poetic evolve.

Despite Pound's initial emphasis on Corbière's satirical Parisian
poems in this early essay, Corbière "'stands',," according to Pound, "by
his songs of the Breton coast" (*SP*, 372). What catches Pound's eye, or
ear, is the realism of Corbière's *Armor* and his *Gens de Mer*.[30] Pound
praises Corbière's "Au Vieux Roscoff" for the "note of the sea" (*SP*,
372) in the lines,

> Trou de flibustiers, vieux nid
> À corsaires! . . .
>
> .   .   .   .   .   .
> Dors: tu peux fermer ton Oeil borgne
> Ouvert sur le large, et qui lorgne
> Les Anglais, depuis trois cent ans . . .
>
> [Den of buccaneers, old nest
> of corsairs! . . .
>
> .   .   .   .   .   .
> —Sleep: you can close your Cyclops' eye
> long open on the main to spy
> on the English, these three centuries.][31]

But perhaps more than the poem Pound quotes, Corbière's "Le Bossu
Bitor" contains a veritable catalog of sailor's slang and riotous descrip-
tions of debauchery; this poem is an application of le mot juste, as it
were, that exceeds the limits of a proper decorum. Once a year, Bitor,
the hunchback ship's boy, "s'ensauvait à terre/Comme un rat dont on
a cacheté le derrière" [he'd escape to land,/ wild as a rat with a stop-
pered-up rear end . . .].[32] After Bitor has been humiliated by prosti-
tutes on his last shore leave and has committed suicide,

> l'eau soulevait une masse vaseuse
> Dans le dock. On trouva des plaques de vareuse . . .
> Un cadavre bossu, ballonné, démasqué
> Par les crabes. Et ça fut jeté sur le quai,
> Tout comme l'autre soir, sur une couverture.
> Restant de crabes, encore il servit de pâture
> Au rire du public; et les gamins d'enfants
> Jouant au bord de l'eau noire sous le beau temps,
> Sur sa bosse tapaient comme sur un tambour
> Crevé . . .
>   —Le pauvre corps avait connu l'amour.
>
> [a slimy mass was cast by the water
> onto the dock. A sailor's jacket in tatters . . .

a hunchback's carcass, swollen, face gnawed away
by crabs. And that had been tossed on the quay,
just as the other night, on a bedspread.
Left by the crabs, he still served as Turk's-head
for the public's joke. And the gutter-brats, together
playing along the black water, in the nice weather,
beat on his hump, like the cracked parchment of
a drum . . .
                —This wretched body had known love.][33]

With its painful account of a sailor's shore leave, this poem provides
a precedent for Pound's similarly bawdy story of the "pore honest
sailor, a heavy drinker" (12/56) who enters a hospital and is tricked
into believing that he himself gave birth to the son of a prostitute, and
who, on his deathbed, reveals the "truth" to his "son":

> "You called me your father, and I ain't.
> "I ain't your dad, no,
> "I am not your fader but your moder," quod he,
> "Your fader was a rich merchant in Stambouli."

                                                        (12/57)

The ribald twist to the end of the story, with its uncharacteristic
rhymed couplet, develops the Corbièrian strategy of a quick, ironic
exit that concludes a fairly straightforward narrative. As with
Corbière's "Le Bossu Bitor," we feel a certain compassion for the hon-
est sailor despite, or perhaps because of, the supposedly perverse ad-
mission. If Corbière frequently "se révèle comme l'annonciateur
d'une poésie réaliste qui oscille entre le viscéral et le morbide par le
biais d'un langage anatomique" [is the harbinger of a realist poetry
that oscillates between the visceral and the morbid along the bias of an
anatomical language],[34] so too will Pound begin to add this anatomical
bias to the "realism" in poems like "Fratres Minores."

Moreover, Corbière's spoken idiom and argot provide an additional
precedent for Pound's incorporation of phonetic spelling—"I am not
your fader but your moder"—and of spoken dialect, and French argot
in particular, into the fabric of the Cantos:

> Et les boches, tout ce que vous voulez,
>   militarisme, et cætera, et cætera.
> Tout ça, mais, MAIS,
>   l'français, i s'bat quand y a mangé.
> Mais ces pauvres types
> A la fin y s'attaquaient pour manger,
>   Sans ordres, les bêtes sauvages,

[And the Jerries, you can say anything you want,
militarism, etc. . . . etc. . . .
All that, but, BUT,
        the Frenchman, he fights when he has eaten.
But those poor guys
at the end they attacked each other so they could eat,
Without orders, wild animals.]

$(16/73)^{35}$

Although this passage derives from Ferdinand Leger's account of his war experience,[36] its literary ancestry can be traced back to Corbière's antiwar poem, "La Pastorale de Conlie," which had a direct influence on Wilfred Owen's "Dulce et Decorum Est," as Enid Starkie has suggested,[37] and, in all likelihood, on Pound's war poems in *Mauberley*. Describing the harsh reality of war and replete with spoken idiom and argot, the message and tone of "La Pastorale" can hardly be distinguished from the passage quoted above:

—Soldats tant qu'on voudra! . . . soldat est donc un être
    Fait pour perdre le goût du pain? . . .
        .   .   .   .
—S'il vous plaît: quelque chose à mettre dans nos bouches? . . .
        —Héros et bêtes à moitié!—
        .   .   .   .
—Allons donc: l'abattoir—Bestiaux galeux qu'on rosse,
    On nous fournit aux Prussiens;
Et, nous voyant rouler plat sous les coups de crosse,
    Des Français aboyaient—Bons chiens!

[Soldiers as long as they want us! . . . Is a soldier thus a being
    Created to lose his taste for bread? . . .
        .   .   .   .
—If you please: a little something to put in our mouths? . . .
        —Half heroes and half beasts!—
        .   .   .   .
—Let's go then: to the slaughterhouse—Brutish, mangy dogs they beat,
    They furnish us to the Prussians;
And, seeing us fall down beneath blows from rifle-butts,
    The French bayed—Good dogs!][38]

Given Pound's predilection for Villon, for whom "death is death, war is war . . . filth is filth, crime is crime" (*SR*, 173), it is not hard to comprehend his fondness for Corbière's Breton poems, filled as they are with vivid and unsentimentalized descriptions of the hard lot of the sailor. In his "Matelots" and "La Fin," to name just two characteristic poems from his *Gens de Mer*, Corbière pokes fun at the "marins de quinquets à l'Opéra . . . comique" [sailors in the footlights at the comic opera][39] and at Hugo's romantic vision of the sea in *Oceano Nox:*

> Eh bien, tous ces marins—matelots, capitaines,
> Dans leur grand Océan à jamais engloutis . . .
>
> . . . .
>
> Allons! c'est leur métier; ils sont morts dans leurs bottes!
>
> . . . .
>
> . . . Votre *mort* est bien pâle
> Et pas grand'chose à bord, sous la lourde rafale . . .
> Pas grand-chose devant le grand sourire amer
> Du matelot qui lutte.
>
> [Well, all these seamen—sailors and skippers—they,
> are swallowed forever in their mighty Sea
>
> . . . .
>
> What the hell! it's their business! they died in their boots!
>
> . . . .
>
> . . . Your *death* is pale
> and no great shakes on board, in a heavy gale . . .
> small stuff compared with the bitter irony
> of a struggling sailor's grin.][40]

Corbière's unsentimentalized appraisal of death leads to a further, and for Pound very attractive, realization. If Corbière's fellow Bretons are able to accept their lot unflinchingly and with dignity, it must be because their piety and folk superstitions provide a strong bulwark against their hardships and their ultimate fate; Corbière's high regard for the stoicism of his comrades lends credibility to the supernatural world of Celtic folklore described in these "songs of the Breton coast." In "Paysage mauvais," for example, Corbière evokes a mysterious landscape filled with the funereal nightsounds of *Ankou* or Death:[41]

> Sables de vieux os—Le flot râle
> Des glas: crevant bruit sur bruit . . .
> —Palud pâle, où la lune avale
> De gros vers pour passer la nuit.
>
> —Calme de peste, où la fièvre
> Cuit . . . Le follet damné languit.
> —Herbe puante où le lièvre
> Est un sourcier poltron qui fuit . . .
>
> —La Lavandière blanche étale
> Des trépassés le linge sale,
> Au *soleil des loups* . . . —Les crapauds,

Petits chantres mélancoliques,
Empoissonnent de leurs coliques
Les champignons, leurs escabeaux.

[Sands of old bones—The wave gasps
knells: breaking sound on sound . . .
—Pale salt-marsh, where the moon downs
fat worms to make the night pass.

—Calm of pestilence, where
fever cooks . . . The curs'd marsh-light
dies.—Stinking grass where the hare
is a scared warlock in flight . . .

—The White Laundress spreads
the dirty clothes of the dead,
to the *sun of the wolves* . . . —The toads,

little precentors of gloom,
poison with their bellies' loads
their round stools, the mushrooms.][42]

Instead of the jaundiced vision and witty "mélange adultère du tout"[43] of the Parisian poems, Corbière here expresses his reverence for the simple traditions of his native Brittany. The haunting image of the bone-strewn beach—"Sables de vieux os"—provides unimpeachable testimony to the hardships and dangers to which these seafaring Bretons have long and stoically subjected themselves. Corbière's description of this Breton landscape certainly has literary affiliations with Virgil's Stygian Marsh peopled by the drowned sailors whose bones lie unburied upon the shore, but it is perhaps comparable in intensity only to the bone-strewn landscapes of a Tanguy or a Dali. Corbière achieves this surreal effect through a cumulative imagery (Pound's imagisme) instead of the paradox and antithesis (Pound's logopoeia) of his Parisian poems and through his personification of the sea and moon.[44] The half-illuminating moonlight creates a magically self-contained world wherein all intellectually-based dualisms dissolve. The heavenly moon feeds upon the earth and the dead (*De gros vers*) but, in turn, controls the tide, whose last-gasp death knell monotonously repeats itself to form this malarial salt marsh. Corbière depicts a world given over to death, but because death is part of the human condition it must be stoically accepted.

Although Corbière is often faulted for being a *poète naïf*, his prosody is also perfectly suited to his uncompromising portrayal of the harsh life of his fellow Bretons. One can hear, as would Pound, the death rattle of the sea in Corbière's "Le flot râle/Des glas: crevant bruit sur bruit . . ."[45] This cacaphonous little phrase captures the struggles of a drowning man in a turbulent sea; the distinctive features of each successive phoneme are in opposition at so many different levels that the tongue trips as it tries to articulate each word. For example, *Glas* (glα) is comprised of a voiced, high-back, stopped consonant, a front unstopped sonorant, and a low, mid-back vowel; in other words, one's tongue makes a wavelike motion in order to pronounce it. Because this happens with every phoneme, one has to slow down, and each phrase is thus foregrounded and crystallized into a jumble of fragmented images or word-things linked only by the assonance, consonance, and internal rhymes (os-flot-gros vers; râle-Palud pâle-avale; bruit-nuit-cuit-languit-fuit) that Corbière uses so effectively to lend subtle connotations and coloring to these seemingly heterogeneous elements.

Given Pound's own penchant for a spatialized, visual rendering of sound, his "sound ply over ply," we can see why he would have been attracted to Corbière's music, to his "hardness" and his vigorously "masculine" melopoeia. And although it would be imprudent to isolate a single impetus behind Pound's poetic development, we can catch a glimpse of Corbière's influence by examining Pound's reworking in "The Coming of War: Actaeon" (1915) of the *nekeuia* theme set forth earlier in "Δώρια" (1912):

Δώρια

Be in me as the eternal moods
    of the bleak wind, and not
As transient things are—
    gaiety of flowers.
Have me in the strong loneliness
    of sunless cliffs
And of grey waters.
    Let the gods speak softly of us
In days hereafter,
    The shadowy flowers of Orcus
Remember thee.

(*P*, 64)

"Δώρια" is another one of Pound's attempts in *Ripostes* to modernize his idiom; although he invokes an otherworldly realm when he asks his beloved to "be in me as the eternal moods," that transcendent realm includes the harsh reality of daily life because it is a world "of the bleak wind." Moreover, the poem depends upon an abrupt juxtaposition of images—each injunction ends with a quasi-mysterious image that "presents" but does not "comment": the "gaiety of flowers," the "sunless cliffs," "grey waters," and "The shadowy flowers of Orcus." Despite these technical advances, however, "Δώρια" nonetheless remains a proto-imagist poem because it is predominantly discursive and because these images have not yet been completely freed from their role as poetic ornamentation. Pound's "shadowy flowers of Orcus" are more symbolic than they are "natural objects" (*LE*, 5).

"The Coming of War: Actaeon," on the other hand, although it adopts this same "image of Lethe" and gray seascape, presents us with a swirling dance of images that gain form and substance through Pound's masterful scoring and choreography:

> An image of Lethe,
>   and the fields
> Full of faint light
>   but golden,
> Gray cliffs,
>   and beneath them
> A sea
> Harsher than granite,
>   unstill, never ceasing;
> High forms
>   with the movement of gods,
> Perilous aspect;
>   And one said:
> "This is Actaeon."
>   Actaeon of golden greaves!
> Over fair meadows,
> Over the cool face of that field,
> Unstill, ever moving
> Hosts of an ancient people,
> The silent cortège.
>
> (*P*, 109–10)

The poem's short lines mime Pound's deepening perception and, in turn, pull the reader's own vision downward to an essential world of Hellenic myth. Pound's use of enjambed short lines and proleptic syntax gives the poem a kinetic energy checked only by the musicality of his verse, the assonance and consonance characteristic of his lyrical moments: "fields / Full of faint light / but golden, / Gray cliffs / and beneath them / A sea." This passage contains three distinct images—fields, cliffs, sea—but they blend together in the gold-grey atmosphere in the same way that Corbière's seascape dissolves beneath the pale moonlight.[46]

Pound's "sea / Harsher than granite" should remind us that he once described Corbière's poetry as "weather-bit granite" (LE, 288), but we should also note another suggestive parallel between "Paysage mauvais" and "The Coming of War: Actaeon": Whereas Corbière's poem recalls the "incertam lunam sub luce maligna" of Virgil's Underworld,[47] Pound has crossed the Stygian marsh and has entered the realm of the blessed with its pleasant fields and otherworldly light. And although Virgil's light is purple and Pound's is "faint but golden," Pound's peculiar invocation of Actaeon in this underworld scene raises the specter of Diana-Hecate-Artemis and, thus, of Corbière's moonlit world governed by chance or, in Pound's words, *forsitan*: "above the Moon there is order, / beneath the Moon, forsitan" (97/ 691). Actaeon was punished not because he willfully transgressed, but, like Pound's dead soldiers and Corbière's drowned sailors, because he was ill-fated and unlucky. Once again, Pound's assessment of Villon is equally true of Corbière and, in this instance, himself: "Villon makes excuses neither for God nor for himself; he does not rail at providence because its laws are not adjusted to punish all weaknesses except his own" (SR, 172). But as compensation, both Corbière's and Pound's unsentimentalized acknowledgment of death legitimizes their wholly unsceptical belief in a supernatural world of Celtic or Hellenic origins.

This quasi-religious attitude is perhaps nowhere more evident than in Corbière's "La Rapsode foraine et le pardon de Sainte Anne." This poem is without doubt one of Corbière's masterpieces and captures the religious, folk atmosphere of Brittany. A long poem in four parts, the opening section describes the worn, wooden figures of Saint Anne, Mary, and Joseph in "la chapelle sauvage / De Sainte-Anne-de-la-Palud" [the rugged chapel/of Saint Anne of La Palud], where all the surrounding parishes come to celebrate the Pardon. The second section, which Pound singled out as the "proper introduction" (SP, 372) to Corbière and which we will later consider in greater detail, contains the spiritual canticle to Saint Anne celebrating her role in the Nativity and asking her to intercede on behalf of the poor here on earth : "Prête ta douce et chaste flamme / Aux chrétiens qui sont ici" [Lend your chaste flame/to all Christians here below].[48] The third part contains what C. F. MacIntyre aptly describes as "a fine vigorous sketch of the visiting pilgrims and a catalog of the sick and infirm, more in the manner of Goya than of Chaucer."[49] Here we see the faithful—the rachitics, epileptics, lepers, the mentally retarded, and those afflicted with various and sundry ulcers and abscesses—who come to "boivent l'eau miraculeuse / Où les Job teigneux ont lavé / Leur nudité contagieuse . . ." [drink the miraculous water/where these Jobs with scurvy have had a bath,/washing their contagious flesh . . .].[50] Although their suffering becomes proof in the Church's eyes that these lamentable pilgrims are the chosen, sanctified ones, this sentimentalized piety is thoroughly undercut by Corbière's backhanded paeon to an apparently malevolent God. Corbière, provoked by his vision of these pilgrims, permits himself a bitter condemnation of society and the church:

> Parmi les autres, après vêpre,
> Qui sont d'eau bénite arrosés,
> Un cadavre, vivant de lèpre,
> Fleurit,—souvenir des croisés . . .
>
> Puis tous ceux que les Rois de France
> Guérissaient d'un toucher de doigts . . .
> —Mais la France n'a plus de rois,
> Et leur dieu suspend sa clémence.
>
> . . . .
>
> —Nous, taisons-nous! . . . Ils sont sacrés.
> C'est la faute d'Adam punie
> Le doigt d'En-haut les a marqués:
> —La droite d'En-haut soit bénie!
>
> Du grand troupeau, boucs émissaires
> Chargés des forfaits d'ici-bas,
> Sur eux Dieu purge ses colères! . . .
> —Le pasteur de Sainte-Anne est gras.—
>
> [After vespers, among the others—
> with holy water they've all been sprayed—
> blossoms a leper, a living cadaver,—
> a souvenir of the Crusades . . .
>
> Next, all those the Kings of France
> used to heal by the touch of a finger . . .
> —but their God has suspended his clemency,
> and there are no French kings any longer.
>
> . . . .
>
> —Let us be silent! . . . They are sacred.
> Adam's sin paid its penalty.
> The finger from On High has marked them:
> —Blest be the hand of the Most High!
>
> As for the big flock, scapegoats laden
> with all the sins we're busy at,
> on them the wrath of God is vented! . . .
> —The pastor of Saint Anne's he's fat.—][51]

Finally, the fourth section presents *La Rapsode foraine*, or wandering singer, of the title. Moaning her simple, unpolished ballads, she is herself a poet and, like Saint Anne, reveals to us the true meaning of Christian charity:

> —Si tu la rencontres, Poète,
> Avec son vieux sac de soldat:
> C'est notre sœur . . . donne—c'est fête—
> Pour sa pipe, un peu de tabac! . . .
>
> Tu verras dans sa face creuse
> Se creuser, comme dans du bois,
> Un sourire; et sa main galeuse
> Te faire un vrai signe de croix.
>
> [If you happen to come across her, Poet,
> with her old army haversack, oh,
> She's our sister . . .—it's a holy day—
> give her a pinch of pipe tobacco! . . .
>
> You'll see then, as if dug in wood,
> scooped deeper in her furrowed face,
> a smile; and with her mangy hand
> she'll make you a true sign of the cross.][52]

Although Pound does not provide any direct evidence, the poem would surely appeal to him because of the Villonesque expression of resentment of the disease and suffering inflicted on these pilgrims, and on humanity in general, by a malevolent God. As C. F. MacIntyre rightly observes, "Truly, after Villon and Baudelaire, Corbière shows, without sentimentality, more real sympathy with the disinherited than any other French poet. He often appears to scoff and jibe because he is suffering a tragic catharsis and refuses to confess it openly."[53] Curiously, however, Pound's 1913 discussion of the "Cantique spirituel" suggests, albeit indirectly, that his overriding interest is not in the religious subject and tonality of the poem, but in the stylistic and prosodic aspects of Corbière's poetry. Although Pound warns us that "one garbles it so in quotation and it is much too long to give in full" (*SP*, 372), Pound's quotation itself misleads in that it silently elides much of the hymn:[54]

> Mère taillée à coups de hache. (1)
>
> Bâton des aveugles! Béquille (17)
> Des Vieilles! Bras des nouveau-nés!

Mère de madame ta fille!
Parente des abandonnés!

Des croix profondes sont tes rides, (37)
Tes cheveux sont blancs comme fils . . .

Fais venir et conserve en joie (41)
Ceux à naître et ceux qui sont nés.
Et verse, sans que Dieu te voie,
L'eau de tes yeux sur les damnés!

[Mother hacked out with blows of the hatchet
. . . .
—Staff of blindmen! Crutch to prop
old women! Arms for the new swaddling!
Mother of Our Lady your daughter!
Foster-parent of the foundling!
. . . .
Your wrinkles are crosses of deep affliction,
Your hair is white as linen threads . . .
. . . .
The new-born and the yet unborn
summon, and make glad their years.
Without God's ever seeing you,
sprinkle on the damned your tears!][55]

Pound eliminates much of the poignant religious sentiment of the hymn in favor of the "hard-bit," constative lines like those in the second stanza that depend heavily on alliteration: "Bâton des aveugles! Béquille / Des Vieilles! Bras des nouveau-nés!" Gone in Pound's version are the central stanzas containing the more lyrical prayer addressed to Saint Anne. In essence, Pound has created through his selective quotation an imagist poem consisting largely of juxtaposed images couched in syntactically incomplete noun clauses.

As we can see, Pound's early consideration of Corbière is thoroughly bound up with his own imagist program. Although he makes passing mention of Corbière's Parisian poems, these interest him because of their "realistic" portrayals of Parisian life and because their disregard for literary convention suggests a means to "make it new." Surprisingly, Pound takes no notice of Corbière's incessant logopoeia and self-irony in these poems and focuses instead on the Gautieresque hard-bit lines whereby "Corbière conveys [his content] by ejaculation, as if the words were wrenched and knocked out of him by fatality" (*Inst*, 29). Moreover, his principal interest is in Corbière's "songs of the Breton coast," which rely on the heaping of nouns and images rather than a logopoetic dissociation achieved through punning, paradox, and antithesis.[56] It is in these poems, Pound argues, that Corbière "is more real than the 'realists' because he still recognises that force of romance that is a quite real and apparently ineradicable part of our life" (*SP*, 372). Pound here assimilates Corbière's realism and romance, and, thus, what he elsewhere describes as "the cult of ugliness" and "the cult of beauty" (*LE*, 45), creating a poetic ancestry for his own imagistic attempts to "bust thru from quotidian into 'divine or permanent world'" (*SL*, 210).

When Pound returns to Corbière in his 1918 "Study of French Poets," however, we see a radically new Corbière, one who now seems to Pound "the greatest poet of the period" (*Inst*, 19). Although Pound begins by quoting "La Rapsode" in full, saying that it is "beyond all comment" (*Inst*, 19), he quickly shifts his attention to the Parisian poems: "People, at least some of them, think more highly of his Breton subjects than of the Parisian, but I can not see that he loses force on leaving the seaboard; for example, his 'Frère et Soeur Jumeaux' seems to me 'by the same hand' and rather better than his 'Roscoff'" (*Inst*, 28). Instead of idealizing this rugged Breton spirit capable of magically synthesizing both "realism" and "romance," he now emphasizes the "vigorous phrases" and the violence of Corbière's Parisian satires.

This shift in emphasis is carried over to Pound's own postwar poetry, and to *Mauberley* in particular. Although the ironic rhyming in *Mauberley* has always been attributed to the influence of Laforgue, we can see that it owes just as much to this newly discovered satirical Corbière who deflates the well-intended piety of "Le Pardon":

> C'est le *Pardon.*—Liesse et mystères—
> Déjà l'herbe rase a des poux . . .
> —*Sainte Anne, onguent des belles-mères!*
> *Consolation des époux!* . . .
>
> . . . .
>
> Trois jours, trois nuits, la palud grogne,
> Selon l'antique rituel,
> —Choeur séraphique et chant d'ivrogne—
> Le CANTIQUE SPIRITUEL.
>
> [It's the Pardon,—Gaiety and mysteries—
> there are lice already in the straw . . .
> —*Sainte Anne, balm of young wives' mothers!*
> *consolation of sons-in-law!* . . .
>
> . . . .
>
> Three days, three nights, the salt-marsh grunts,

faithful to ancient ritual,
—seraphic choir and songs of the drunks—
The CANTIQUE SPIRITUEL.][57]

Here, Corbière's ironic rhyming of "mystères/belles-mères" and
"poux/époux," as well as his ironic juxtaposition of the "choeur
séraphique" and the "chant d'ivrogne," undercuts the reverence con-
tained in the prayer to Saint Anne in exactly the same manner that
Pound will use to deflate Christian sentimentality in what is described
as his Laforguian and Gautieresque *Mauberley:*

> Christ follows Dionysus
> Phallic and ambrosial
> Made way for macerations;
> Caliban casts out Ariel.
>
>   (*P*, 186)

Similarly, Corbière's self-deprecating irony at the conclusion of the
hymn implicates the speaker himself in the drama much as does
Pound's "E. P. Ode Pour l'Election de Son Sépulchre":

> —A l'an prochain!—Voici ton cierge:
> (C'est deux livres qu'il a coûté)
> . . . Respects à Madame la Vierge
> Sans oublier la Trinité.
>
> [—*Now till next year!—Here's your candle:*
> *(two good francs they got of me)*
> . . . *my respects to Our Lady the Virgin,*
> *not forgetting the Trinity.*][58]

And Corbière's "Épitaphe," with its dialectical realization that a pref-
ace is actually a postface ("Égale une épitaphe égale une préface et
réciproquement"),[59] serves as a model for Pound's "E. P. Ode Pour
L'Election," a poem describing E. P.'s "pass[ing] from men's memory
in *l'an trentuniesme / De son eage*" (*P*, 185).

Corbière's ironic and satirical poems will now become central to
Pound's developing poetic. Pound's "To a Friend Writing on Cabaret
Dancers," for example, a poem which Pound considered his best since
"Ballad of the Goodly Fere" (*P/J*, 284), is a self-conscious parody of
standard poetic attempts to idealize dancers and adheres to the princi-
ple of an unsentimentalized realism that Pound had discovered in
Corbière:[60]

> "Poète, writ me a poème!"
> Spanish and Paris, love of the arts part of your geisha-culture!
> Euhenia, in short skirts, slaps her wide stomach,

Pulls up a roll of fat for the pianist,
"Pauvre femme maigre!" she says.

. . . .

Euhenia will have a *fonda* in Orbajosa.
The amorous nerves will give way to digestive;
"Delight thy soul in fatness," saith the preacher.
We can't preserve the elusive "*mica salis*,"

(*P*, 159–60)

Pound's comic conflation of Isaiah and Catullus (and Gautier via the *mica salis*),[61] of spiritual and carnal love, undermines completely, as Pound fully intends it to do, any moral categories by which the dancers can be judged: "I treat the dancers as human beings, not as 'symbols of sin'" (*SL*, 82). More importantly, although "To a Friend Writing" pays homage to Gautier's "Carmen," because of its many allusions, clichés, pastiches of foreign languages, and nonsensical "bribes de parole," this poem is much closer in spirit and in texture to a poem like Corbière's "Veder Napoli poi mori":

Voir *Naples et* . . . —Fort bien, merci, j'en viens.—Patrie
D'Anglais en vrai, mal peints sur fond bleu—perruquier!
Dans l'indigo l'artiste en tous genres oublie
Ce *Ne-m'oubliez-pas* d'outremer: le douanier.
—O Corinne! . . . ils sont là déclamant sur ma malle . . .
Lasciate speranza, mes cigares dedans!
—O Mignon! . . . ils ont tout éclos mon linge sale
Pour le passer au bleu de l'éternel printemps!

[See *Naples and* . . . —Thanks much, I just came from there.—In truth a nation
Of Englishmen, badly painted on a blue background—Hey! wig maker!
Enraptured by the indigo, every artist forgets to mention
This ultramarine *Forget-me-not* of overseas trade: the customs inspector.
—O Corinna! . . . He's sitting on my trunk, declaiming . . .
Abandon all hope, and with my cigars so poorly hidden!
—O Dear Mignon! . . . He's hatched all my dirty linen
To let it fly off into the blue of eternal spring.][62]

As in Pound's "To a Friend," we have a similar conflation of the sacred and the profane, of Dante and Ovid, as well as the witty shading (*bleu, indigo, outremer*) which manifests a *logopoetic* sensibility similar to the one exemplified by Pound's allusion to "the elusive 'mica salis.'" The intensity of such a poem, says Michel Dansel, "réside principale-ment dans la juxtaposition, l'assemblage, l'alternance ou la chute de vocables tirés de milieux, de mondes, d'époques, voire de langues, les plus divers. Le brassage s'opère sous le signe d'un baroque jamais gra-

tuit qui se réfère à des 'niveaux' culturels, hétéroclites et dont la mani-
festation la plus saillante est le *jeu*" [consists for the most part in the
juxtaposition, the combination, the alternation, the downpour of
words drawn from diverse milieus, worlds, epochs, and languages.
This baroque assemblage is never gratuitous, but refers to heteroge-
neous cultural levels and is most conspicuous in Corbière's word-
play][63]; Corbière's "langage syncopé, haché, fouetté, disloqué, rebelle,
n'a d'autre correspondance esthétique que dans le collage, qui est
l'une des techniques d'expression que préconisa et appliqua Dada"
[syncopated, cut-up, dislocated, rebellious, and over-heated language
has no other aesthetic correspondence than the collage method advo-
cated by the dadaists].[64] This description of Corbière's poetic is nota-
ble because it is as relevant to Pound's poetry (perhaps more so) as it
is to Corbière's, suggesting that Pound's poetry, his baroque assem-
blage of heterogeneous cultures, epochs, and languages, has much in
common with a collage poetry originating with Corbière and leading
to dada.

At the same time, and despite the obvious parallels between
Corbière and Pound, there is a very important distinction to be made.
Returning to the concept of the *jeu* at the heart of Corbière's poetry,
we cannot but be struck by the element of free association in
Corbière's verse, a technique that is at odds with Pound's neoclassical
outlook. Perhaps the best illustration of Corbière's poetic method is
contained in this brief excerpt from "Litanies du sommeil" where
image follows upon image in an almost random fashion:

> SOMMEIL—Loup-Garou gris! Sommeil! Noir de fumée!
> SOMMEIL!—Loup de velours, de dentelle embaumée!
> Baiser de l'Inconnue, et Baiser de l'Aimée!
> —SOMMEIL! Voleur de nuit! Folle-brise pâmée!
> Parfum qui monte au ciel des tombes parfumées!
> *Carrosse à Cendrillon* ramassant *les Traînées*!
> Obscène Confesseur des dévotes mort-nées!
>
> TOI qui viens, comme un chien, lécher la vieille plaie
> Du martyr que la mort tiraille sur sa claie!
> O sourire forcé de la crise tuée!
> SOMMEIL! Brise alizée! Aurorale buée!
>
> [SLEEP!—Grey werewolf! Black smoke!
> SLEEP!—Wolfish velvet, scented lace!
> Kiss of the Unknown Woman, Kiss of the Beloved!
> —SLEEP! Thief of night! Mad breeze swooning!
> Fragrance climbing from tombs to the sky!

Cinderella's coach gathering *the prostitutes!*
Obscene Confessor of the still-born devotees!

You who come, like a dog, to lick the old wound
Of the martyr whom death pulls over the hurdle!
O forced smile of the murdered crisis!
SLEEP! Trade-wind! Dawn's mist!][65]

The constraints imposed upon Corbière by the monorhyme obviously generate a certain attitude of playfulness, but the prevalence of unnecessary internal rhymes suggests, in addition, an attitude of wilfullness, which is, as Albert Sonnenfeld remarks, "un défi à toutes les techniques traditionnelles." In Corbière, "intellectual rigour" is replaced by what amounts to "une sorte d'intoxication verbale, de technique par association, dans laquelle le pouvoir de suggestion d'un son mène le poète d'une image à la suivante" [an assault on all traditional verse techniques. . . . a kind of verbal intoxication, an associative technique in which the suggestive power of a sound leads the poet from one image to the next].[66]

Now consider a poem by Pound on a similar theme, "Before Sleep":

1

The lateral vibrations caress me,
They leap and caress me,
They work pathetically in my favour,
They seek my financial good.

She of the spear stands present.
The gods of the underworld attend me, O Annubis,
These are they of thy company.
With a pathetic solicitude they attend me;
Undulant,
Their realm is the lateral courses.

2

Light!
I am up to follow thee, Pallas.
Up and out of their caresses.
You were gone up as a rocket,
Bending your passages from right to left and from left to right
In the flat projection of a spiral.
The gods of drugged sleep attend me,
Wishing me well;
I am up to follow thee, Pallas.

(*P*, 77)

Where Corbière is content to see himself as a bundle of contradictions, as a "jeune philosophe en dérive" possessing a playful willingness to leave suspended his "mélange adultère de tout," Pound's vorticist dream remains subject to the geometric constraints of Pound's "planes in relation." Pound's lapse into the unconscious state of sleep is made innocuous by his *passéiste* invocation of another world inhabited by pagan deities. Corbière's collage method, then, when it becomes unhinged, leads ultimately to "the royal road" to the unconscious traversed by the surrealists in their *écriture automatique*, whereas Pound recoils from this unconstrained outpouring of words and images in much the same way he later rejects the Joyce of *Finnegans Wake*.

Finally, Pound's satirical attacks on l'éternel féminin become more and more remote from Corbière's in proportion to his simplification of the complex emotional register underlying Corbière's response to a thwarted love. Although Corbière insists on treating ironically the "Mannequin idéal, tête-de-turc du leurre, / Eternel Féminin,"[67] he is much more playful and involved, or even implicated, in the drama. The woman is the butt of his delusion but is nonetheless granted a wider range of emotions and actions: "Damne-toi, pure idole! et ris! et chante! et pleure, / Amante!" [Figmental mannequin, Turk's-head for the trap, / Eternal Feminine! . . . Damn yourself, pure idol! laugh! sing! cry! / belov'd!].[68] Moreover, the poet mocks himself for creating such a Muse:

> Sois femelle de l'homme, et sers de Muse, ô femme,
> Quand le poète brame en *Ame*, en *Lame*, en *Flamme*!
> Puis—quand il ronflera—viens baiser ton Vainqueur!

> [Be female to the male, his Muse, and when
> the poet bells: *Ame*! *Lame*! *Flamme*! ah, then—
> when he snores—come kiss your conqueror!][69]

As Robert Mitchell rightly observes, "It is not a question, with Corbière, of a metaphysical misogyny (cf. Laforgue, Schopenhauer), but rather of another literary pose: the frustration and failure of his amorous attempts are hidden behind a mask of frivolity or irony."[70]

Following Corbière, so too does Pound adopt a similar, though less effective, strategy. But where Pound's poetry through *Ripostes* left room for a vision of the Beloved that corroborated his arguments in *The Spirit of Romance*, in *Lustra* it tends, for the time being at least, toward a simple denunciation of l'éternel féminin. In "Passing," for example, Pound paints an unflattering and extremely simplistic portrait of a woman who is "Thoroughly beautiful"—she is, in fact, as "Flawless as Aphrodite"—and therefore "Brainless." Given such a crude sketch, it is not surprising that she has little or no impact on the poet:

> The faint odour of your patchouli,
> Faint, almost, as the lines of cruelty about your chin,
> Assails me, and concerns me almost as little.

(P, 105)

In this instance, at least, Wyndham Lewis was not entirely wrong when he argued that Pound "never seems to have *seen* the individual at all. . . . People are seen by him only as types. There is the 'museum official,' the 'norman cocotte,' and so on."[71] Most remarkably, Pound can not discern in Corbière that poignant self-irony that he celebrated in Villon: "Villon's abuse finds precedent in the lower type of sirvente, with this distinction, that Villon at times says of himself what the Provençals said only of one another" (*SR*, 167).

Although Pound discovers in Corbière another example of a vigorous realism; of a spoken language augmenting that of Browning; of a language less susceptible to domination by abstract reason because it is all the more kaleidoscopic,[72] there is ultimately a world of difference between Corbière's ironic image of himself as "Le Crapaud" and Pound's self-aggrandizingly phallic persona. While Pound's poetry does approach Corbière's collage method, it nonetheless remains contained by a need to fix the relationship between objects to establish an overarching moral framework guaranteed by the bald assertion of his own superiority. Pound transforms Corbière's "both . . . and" into an "either . . . or," with the explicit assumption that he can, especially in the domain of ethics, distinguish and arbitrate between the true and the false. Whereas Corbière's "Épitaphe" maintains a comically harmless dialectic between naïveté and cynicism—"Trop naïf, étant trop cynique;/Ne croyant à rien, croyant tout"—Pound closes off the limitless possibilities contained in the act of negation by choosing only one of the variables. Although Pound's satirical stance in *Lustra* suggests a liberating vision, we can see how alien to his sensibility it really is when we consider "The Commission" in the context of his later Confucian ethics:

> Go to those who have delicate lust,
> Go to those whose delicate desires are thwarted,
> Go like a blight upon the dulness of the world;
>
> . . . .
>
> Go to the adolescent who are smothered in family—
> Oh how hideous it is
> To see three generations of one house gathered together!

It is like an old tree with shoots,
And with some branches rotted and falling.

Go out and defy opinion,
Go against this vegetable bondage of the blood.
Be against all sorts of mortmain.

(P, 89–90)

While this and many other poems in *Lustra* amount to a playful nose-thumbing at the bourgeoisie, at heart we know that such pronouncements are extremely limited and contain no room for a more sophisticated understanding. The problem here is not that Pound is wrong, but that when he changes his mind, as he does later in his career, his new opinion is merely a simple negation of the old one and is just as limiting. As Peter Makin rightly describes Pound's middle cantos: "There is the mutual moral surveillance of the early New England communities . . . the ubiquitous internalised father . . . the worship of fixity . . . the dread of religious and social elaboration in all forms, of sumptuousness, of sensuality (incense, incantation). . . . One is far distant from the Pound of 'Commission.'"[73]

Because of his singular emphasis on Corbière's satirical representation of "externals," Pound is compelled to ignore the self-implicating irony grounding Corbière's representation of his own subjectivity, of his world, and of l'éternel féminin. Thus, while many of Pound's subsequent poetic strategies are anticipated in his early discussions of Corbière, it is only intermittently, and with the help of Laforgue's "delicate irony," that Pound will be able to mount the assault on "the citadel of the intelligent" (*LE*, 281) that Corbière had so swiftly and effortlessly accomplished. And in poems where he does (most strikingly in *Mauberley*), Pound's difficulties tell us as much about his poetic as do his successes.

Chapter Three

THE CITADEL OF THE INTELLIGENT: POUND'S LAFORGUE

We make out of the quarrel with others, rhetoric, but
of the quarrel with ourselves, poetry.
—William Butler Yeats

C'est l'homme qui déclare son amour et qui est dépité
si on l'écoute, qui fuit la société et se lamente qu'on le
laisse seul. L'enfant gâté qui ne sait ce qu'il veut, re-
fuse sa soupe parce qu'on la lui prêche et pleurniche
dès qu'on la lui enlève.
—Jules Laforgue, "Une Étude Sur Corbière"

POUND discovered Laforgue surprisingly late, considering his famili-
arity with modern French poetry and his interest in Eliot's poetry be-
ginning in late 1914. He first mentions Laforgue in two letters dated
August 1916, where he compares him to an eighth-century Chinese
poet, Wang Wei, and he writes his first of a series of articles on him in
November of 1917.[1] This time lag is all the more remarkable given his
esteem for Corbière, whose *Les Amours jaunes* was seen by many to have
anticipated Laforgue's own innovations, so much so that the latter felt
compelled to attack Corbière in his angry and defensive "Étude sur
Corbière." Moreover, Laforgue was well represented in Van Bever's
and Léautaud's *Poètes d'aujourd'hui*, and Remy de Gourmont included
an appreciative discussion of his work in *Livre des masques*, as did
Arthur Symons in *The Symbolist Movement in Literature*.[2]

Yet despite the belatedness of Pound's discovery, Laforgue's influ-
ence on him seems to be a seminal one. Whereas Eliot became disen-
chanted with his early Laforguian persona and soon adopted a more
centrally symbolist outlook,[3] Pound continued throughout his career
to acknowledge Laforgue's preeminence. In his famous letter of May
1928 to René Taupin, for example, we find Pound's assessment of La-
forgue's influence on both himself and Eliot: "Je crois que Eliot, dont
les premiers poésies ont montré influence de Laforgue, a moins de
respect pour Laf. que le respect que j'ai pour Laf" [I believe that Eliot,
whose early poetry was influenced by Laforgue, has less respect for

Laforgue than I have] (*SL*, 218). And in his last canto, we find this
poignant homage to Laforgue:

> Disney against the metaphysicals,
> and Laforgue more than they thought in him,
> Spire thanked me in propositio
> And I have learned more from Jules
> > > (Jules Laforgue) since then
> deeps in him,
> > and Linnaeus.

> > > > > (116/810)[4]

Indeed, Laforgue's importance to Pound becomes readily evident
when we follow the course of Pound's poetic output between the
years 1915 and 1925. Not only did Laforgue have a direct impact on
Propertius and *Mauberley*, but, as John Porter Houston suggests, he
also played a crucial role in the radical transformation of the *Three
Cantos'* Browningesque persona: "Pound ... insisted even more in
the original form of the first cantos than in the ultimate version on the
role of Browning as inspirer of his monologue, but the monologue in
its elliptic final form resembles to a greater extent passages in La-
forgue or James Joyce, if anything."[5] With its complex play of often
heterogeneous levels of diction, literary poses, and clichés, this
Laforguian voice becomes, according to Pound, "a vehicle for the ex-
pression of his own very personal emotions, of his own unperturbed
sincerity" (*LE*, 282).

Pound begins his discussion of Laforgue by characteristically mis-
representing the biographical details of his life: "He was born in 1860,
died in 1887 of *la misère*, of consumption and abject poverty in Paris.
The vaunted sensitiveness of French perception, and the fact that he
knew a reasonable number of wealthy and influential people, did
nothing to prevent this" (*LE*, 281). As with Corbière, and somewhat
against the biographical grain, Pound insists on mythologizing La-
forgue as another *poète maudit*. Pound tends to emphasize Laforgue's
Pierrot poems, treating as they do the isolation engendered by the
poet's ironic, self-conscious stance. We can certainly understand why
Pound would be attracted to this picture of the artist *raté* whose defen-
sive irony enables him to overcome an uncomprehending public, but
given Pound's more far-reaching appreciation of Laforgue as ex-
pressed to René Taupin, we would be hard-pressed to advance
Pound's sympathetic attitude toward the figure of the poète maudit as
the sole explanation for his interest in Laforgue.

Characteristic of Laforgue, and more particularly the Laforgue of
Les Complaintes, is the overwhelming fragmentation of the poetic voice
into a multiplicity of voices. Representative of the diverse occasional

and philosophical poems subsumed under the generic *complainte*, "Complainte des grands pins dans une villa abandonnée," for example, sets forth a dual perspective without specifying the spatiotemporal relationship between the various speakers and interlocutors:

> Tout hier, le soleil a boudé dans ses brumes,
> Le vent jusqu'au matin n'a pas décoléré,
> Mais, nous point des coteaux là-bas, un oeil sacré
> Qui va vous bousculer ces paquets de bitume!
>
>> —Ah! vous m'avez trop, trop vanné,
>> Bals de diamants, hanches roses;
>> Et, bien sûr, je n'étais pas né
>>> Pour ces choses.
>
> —Le vent jusqu'au matin n'a pas décoléré.
> Oh! ces quintes de toux d'un chaos bien posthume,
>
>> —Prés et bois vendus! Que de gens,
>> Qui me tanaient mes gants, serviles,
>> A cette heure, de mes argents,
>>> Font de piles!
>
> —Délayant en ciels bas ces paquets de bitume
> Qui grimpaient talonnés de noirs Misérérés!
>
> [All yesterday in mists the sun was sulking then.
> The wind, till morning, never let its anger die,
> But from the hillsides lights on us a blessed eye
> Designed to tumble on you sacks of bitumen!
>
>> —Ah, but you've fleeced me much too much,
>> Diamond balls and thighs of roses;
>> Indeed, I wasn't born for such
>>> Things as those.
>
> The wind, till morning, never let its anger die.
> Oh, these coughs of good and posthumous chaos, phlegm,
>
>> —Woods and fields all sold. How many
>> Menials who held my gloves out once
>> Now make themselves a pretty penny
>>> Out of my funds.
>
> —Dilute, in louring skies those sacks of bitumen
> That, chased by blackest Misereres, climb on high.][6]

As David Arkell remarks, "Those 'many different voices'—the multiple selves of Laforgue and others—today seem to produce a magical synthesis, but then they seemed a mere cacophony."[7] Pound, of course, emphasizes this "cacophony" in his first article on Laforgue, for it gives him ammunition for his mounting attack on bourgeois philistines, although Pound's more or less condescending estimation of this poem's effect on the average bourgeois seems a trifle overstated:

> What in heaven's name is the man in the street to make of ["Complainte sur certains ennuis"], or of the *Complainte des Bons Ménages!* . . . The red-blood has turned away, like the soldier in one of Plato's dialogues. Delicate irony, the citadel of the intelligent, has a curious effect on these people. They wish always to be exhorted, at all times no matter how incongruous and unsuitable, to do those things which almost anyone will and does do whenever suitable opportunity is presented. . . . The ironist is one who suggests that the reader should think, and this process being unnatural to the majority of mankind, the way of the ironical is beset with snares and with furze-bushes. (*LE*, 281)

The two poems that Pound mentions concern themselves directly with the poet's ennui and his relationship with women. In "Complainte des bons ménages," Laforgue's speaker ironically relates the difficulties facing the creative artist, as well as the need for quotidian distractions that are themselves trivialized:

> L'Art sans poitrine m'a trop longtemps bercé dupe.
> Si ses labours sont fiers, que ses blés décevants!
> Tiens, laisse-moi bêler tout aux plis de ta jupe
>   Qui fleure le couvent.
>
> Le Génie avec moi, serf, a fait des manières;
> Toi, jupe, fais frou-frou, sans t'inquiéter pourquoi,
> Sous l'oeillet bleu de ciel de l'unique théière,
>   Sois toi-même, à part moi.
>
> Je veux être pendu, si tu n'es pas discrète
> Et *comme il faut*, vraiment! Et d'ailleurs tu m'es tout.
> Tiens, j'aimerais les plissés de ta collerette
>   Sans en venir à bout.
>
> Mais l'Art, c'est l'Inconnu! qu'on y dorme et s'y vautre,
> On peut ne pas l'avoir constamment sur les bras!
> Eh bien, ménage au vent! Soyons Lui, Elle et l'Autre.
>   Et puis, n'insistons pas.
>
> [Breastless, Art's suckered me too long inert.
> If her tillage is fine, how disappointing the wheat.

Now let me bellow at the pleats of your skirt
    Which smells of the convent, sweet.

Genius with me, slave, has put on its air.
You, skirt, rustle unworried at your part.
Under the sky-blue pink of the teapot's stare
    You be yourself in my heart.

I'll be hanged if you're not totally discreet
And *as one should be*, truly. You're otherwise all.
Goodness, I'd love the folds of your collar, sweet,
    And that would never pall.

But Art's the Stranger. It's sleep in it, smother,
But can't be on our hands each turn and twist.
Well, goodbye, bliss. Let's be Him, Her, the Other
    And then let's not insist.][8]

This poem does, of course, set forth a number of startlingly incongru-
ous images and comparisons, the most striking being the surreal
image of "l'oeillet bleu de ciel de l'unique théière." The speaker rejects
the artist's *via dura*, initiating a parodic carpe diem in which haughty
Genius is contrasted with the unaffected, rustling skirt of the woman,
but he then inexplicably reaffirms his initial topos in the offhand con-
clusion to the poem: "Eh bien, ménage au vent! Soyons Lui, Elle et
l'Autre./Et puis, n'insistons pas." The light touch of Laforgue's irony
is the result of a strange flattening of perspective whereby these two
opposed worlds—the world of Art and the quotidian world—are
brought into contact and transmuted, with each world losing and gain-
ing something in the process. While the poem does present local dif-
ficulties—the imagery, the incongruous admixture of high and low
diction that deflates a romantic vision of the artist, the peculiar objec-
tification of the various personae in the poem ("Lui, Elle et l'Autre")—
it does nonetheless lend itself to at least a rudimentary understanding,
even on the part, we must suppose, of the "man in the street . . . the
red-blood."

Similarly, Laforgue's "Complainte sur certains ennuis," another of
the poems Pound cites as an affront to the average man, contains a
perfectly comprehensible, though perhaps intolerable, message.
Pound quotes only the initial stanza, as though to suggest that an ab-
stract philosophical consideration of a quotidian ennui is the heart of
the matter in this poem:

        Un couchant des Cosmogonies!
        Ah! que la Vie est quotidienne . . .

> Et, du plus vrai qu'on se souvienne,
> Comme on fut piètre et sans génie . . .
>
> [A sunset of Cosmogonies!
> How mundane Life is. And of all
> The truest things we may recall
> How paltry we were, no geniuses.][9]

Laforgue's "sunset of Cosmogonies"—speculative thought's failure to provide a convincing teleological account of human existence—admittedly brings with it the stark realization that life is merely quotidian, a realization that might present "snares and furze-bushes" to the common reader. At the same time, such theories were gaining in popularity during Laforgue's lifetime and were certainly familiar during Pound's.[10] Indeed, the popularity of didactic poetry during the Victorian era would tend to undermine Pound's condescending argument about the "man in the street's" inability to understand or appreciate such poetry. Moreover, we must remember that Pound is writing in 1917 in the wake of Eliot's "Lovesong of J. Alfred Prufrock," a poem which uses such ironic effects and, like Laforgue's Pierrot poems, might even have begun to seem a little precious at the time Pound is writing this article.

However, what *is* radical about Laforgue's irony, as with Eliot's, is the manner in which he ironically redirects his hyper-intelligence against himself:

> On voudrait saigner le Silence,
> Secouer l'exil des causeries;
> Et non! ces dames sont aigries
> Par des questions de préséance.
>
> Elles boudent là, l'air capable.
> Et sous le ciel, plus d'un s'explique,
> Par quels gâchis suresthétiques
> Ces êtres-là sont adorables.
>
> Justement, une nous appelle,
> Pour l'aider à chercher sa bague,
> Perdue (où dans ce terrain vague?)
> Un souvenir *d'AMOUR*, dit-elle!
>
> Ces êtres-là sont adorables!
>
> [We'd like to confess to some things
> Which would astound us as we go,

And once for all would make it so
We'd hear ourselves through posturings.

We'd like to bleed the Silence white,
Shake off the exile of small-talk,
But no, the ladies sour and balk
On points of precedence and right.

They sulk with their superior air,
And, under heaven, the men make guesses
On what superaesthetic messes
Such creatures are adorable there.

Quite rightly then one gives a call
For us to find her missing ring,
Lost (where in this waste's the thing?)
—Keepsake of LOVE, she tells us all.

Such creatures are adorable there!][11]

The irony in "Complainte sur certains ennuis" is not directed against the man in the street, but against the superaesthetic consciousness who always manages to succumb to these "adorable creatures." Pound, on the other hand, shifts the ironic burden away from the poet and idealizes a manner of thinking which he considers an attribute of the artistic elite and which he hopes will become the basis of a cross-cultural *resorgimento*.

Although Pound constantly runs the risk of transforming Laforgue into another Walter Villerant, Pound's supercilious aesthete in his *Imaginary Letters*,[12] there is of course a great deal of truth to his claim regarding Laforgue's preeminence: "He writes not the popular language of any country but an international tongue common to the excessively cultivated, and to those more or less familiar with French literature of the first three-fourths of the nineteenth century" (*LE*, 283). Not only does Laforgue extend the realm of his poetry by including technical, scientific, and philosophical terminology,[13] but, unlike Baudelaire, he can incorporate successfully a modern backdrop into his works without having to resort to a transcendental framework. As Raymond Poggenburg suggests, "Laforgue's ironical position called for some sort of systematic bridge back to effective action. . . . Laforgue appears occasionally to be trying to find an order that will make life amenable to art, while Baudelaire insists upon making order of his life through art."[14] According to Poggenburg, while both Laforgue and Baudelaire share a vision of an omnipresent evil, Laforgue always suggests a movement toward a more optimistic possibility; nature, for Laforgue, although it is potentially dangerous, is not to be cursed in the manner of a Baudelaire. Laforgue's optimism and ironic stance toward any transcendental vision help explain Pound's fondness for the poetry of Laforgue, and his subsequent adherence to those post-Symbolist poets who largely derive from Laforgue.

N. Christophe de Nagy, in his "Place of Laforgue in Ezra Pound's Literary Criticism,"[15] emphasizes the important role Laforgue played in Pound's attempt to renovate his poetic. Discussing Pound's criticism of Laforgue, de Nagy observes that Pound's interest in Laforgue's *logopoeia* over his use of *vers libre* and colloquialism leads him to define logopoeia as a "dance of the intellect among words" (*LE*, 25). Defined as such, logopoeia is not necessarily an ironic strategy, but rather a disengaging of the word, a recognition of its semantic determination, that enables the poet to represent the complexity of the modern world by joining together discourses from diverse, often divergent, worldly fields. This notion of a nonironic disengagement of the word is applicable not only to *Mauberley*, but to the *Cantos* as a whole, particularly in view of Pound's fascination with philology, and suggests a link to what Hugh Kenner sees as "certain symbolist premises—the willingness to lift a word out of 'usage.'"[16] In addition, Warren Ramsey suggests that both Laforgue and Pound share a similar plastic imagination, a tendency to think in "rather bare, conceptual terms, to assimilate refractory materials into verse that tore loose from traditional prosodic moorings, a *vers libre* founded on the autonomy of the rhythmic unit," and that Laforgue's poetry contains "a fusion of legendary figures in just such a continuous present as Pound's."[17]

In *Salomé*, Laforgue satirically fuses his contemporary world with one of ancient grandeur in a manner that will be echoed by Joyce, Eliot, and Pound. Moreover, Laforgue's portrait of Salomé in his *Moralités légendaires* enables Pound to see the limitations of a Flaubertian realism: "Laforgue was a purge and a critic. He laughed out the errors of Flaubert, i.e., the clogging and cumbrous historical detail. . . . His, Laforgue's, *Salomé* makes game of the rest" (*LE*, 282). As Herbert Schneidau argues, "The general effect of Laforgue on Pound seems to have been the opening up of new visions of continuities. . . . [H]e saw a new relationship between composition and criticism in the Laforgian practice of *logopoeia*."[18] This "new relationship" was, of course, Pound's "criticism by translation" in his *Homage to Sextus Propertius*, a poem which results directly from Pound's not entirely unfounded claim "that sometime after his first 'book' S. P. ceased to be the dupe of magniloquence and began to touch words somewhat as

Laforgue did" (*SL*, 178). But because Pound's criticism by translation in *Propertius* is intended to demonstrate Propertius's logopoeia, we are compelled to examine this poem for its "delicate irony, the citadel of the intelligent" (*LE*, 281).

. . .

As the debate between Pound and W. G. Hale following the publication of Pund's *Homage to Sextus Propertius* demonstrates, the question of critical translation is very much an issue here. Hale charges that *Propertius* is replete with impossible blunders and that Pound creates a Propertius who did not really exist.[19] Fortunately, this debate has been laid to rest by J. P. Sullivan, who asserts with good reason that "were Pound as 'incredibly ignorant of Latin' (in Hale's words) as to make *unintentionally* the bloomers Hale accuses him of, he would not have been able to read Propertius at all or get anything like the sense out of his elegies that he actually does."[20] Against what appear to be only rudimentary errors—"Io mooed the first years with averted head / And now drinks Nile water like a god" for "Io versa caput primos mugiverat annos: / Nunc dea, quae Nili flumina vacca bibit"[21]—we must oppose Pound's claim that "all [his] revisions were made *away* from and not *toward* a literal rendering."[22]

Pound's conclusion to section 8 of *Propertius*, for example, is a classic example of Pound's disdain for a literal rendering:

> Now you may bear fate's stroke unperturbed,
> Or Jove, harsh as he is, may turn aside your ultimate day.
> Old lecher, let not Juno get wind of the matter,
> Or perhaps Juno herself will go under,
>   If the young lady is taken?
>
> There will be, in any case, a stir on Olympus.
>
> (P, 218)

We must of course acknowledge, with Adrian Collins, that "the effective ending of No. 8 is Mr. Pound's own invention, Propertius saying the exact opposite";[23] but a closer examination of the text will support Pound's claim that *Propertius* was "never intended to be an *ad verbum* translation"[24] and will reveal that Pound will almost always exploit secondary meanings for ironic purposes. Whereas the Latin reads—

> nunc, utcumque potes, fato gere saucia morem:
>   et deus et durus vertitur ipse dies.

hoc tibi vel poterit coniunx ignoscere Iuno:
frangitur et Iuno, si qua puella perit.

[Now as best thou may, bear thyself reverently towards destiny on thy couch of pain; heaven and the cruel hour alike may change. Even Juno, the jealous wife, will forgive thee for thy beauty; even Juno is touched with pity for a maiden's death.][25]

—Pound has substituted *ignoro* ("not to know," "to be unacquainted," or "to be ignorant"), whether inadvertently or not, for *ignoscere* ("pardon" or "forgive"), allowing him to address Jove and to plead with him to keep Cynthia's transgressions a secret from Juno; he has opted for the primary sense of *frangere* ("shatter," "dash to pieces," "to suffer a shipwreck") for the seemingly more appropriate figurative sense of "soften" or "weaken" in order to implicate Juno herself in Cynthia's trespasses; and, finally, in order to consolidate this new theomachy, Pound himself assures us that "there will be, in any case, a stir on Olympus."

In addition to the passage quoted above, Pound begins section 5 with the line, "Now if ever it is time to cleanse Helicon" (Sed tempus lustrare aliis Helicona choreis), substituting the primary "to light up," "illuminate," "to make bright" for the secondary and more appropriate "wander over" or "traverse."[26] Similarly, in section 12, Pound translates *testudo* as "tortoise" instead of the expected "lyre," substituting for Propertius's more decorous *recusatio* what Sullivan singles out as a bitter jibe instigated by Pound's own dislike of Virgil: "Like a trained and performing tortoise,/I would make verse in your fashion, if she should/command it" (tale facis carmen docta testudine quale/Cynthius impositis temperat articulis).[27] Moreover, there is the pastiche created from lines drawn from the poetry of both Pound and Yeats, the Laforguian use of clichés and latinate polysyllables to deflate a potentially sentimentalized reading ("For I am swelled up with inane pleasurabilities"); Latinisms ("formal girls," "the ornamental goddess"); bilingual puns ("My vote [votum—wish, vow] coming from the temple of Phoebus"); legal jargon and journalese ("Small talk O Ilion . . . If Homer had not stated your case!"; "Happy who are mentioned in my pamphlets"); archaisms ("Have you contempted Juno's Pelasgian temples"); foreign languages ("Cypris is his cicerone"); and, most important, the Laforguian tactic of conflating past and present for ironic effect:[28]

> Nor are my caverns stuffed stiff with a Marcian vintage,
> My cellar does not date from Numa Pompilius,
> Nor bristle with wine jars,

> Nor is it equipped with a frigidaire patent;
> Yet the companions of the Muses
>   will keep their collective nose in my books,
> And weary with historical data, they will turn to my
>   dance tune.
>
> (*P*, 206)

Pound's "collages of sense" result, as Kenner notes, in a radical flattening of perspective whereby language contains no depth:

> There is no "point of view" that will relate these idioms: neither a modern voice ("bristle"; "frigidaire patent"; "collective nose") nor an ancient one ("Phaeacia"; "Marcian") can be assigned this long sentence. . . . In transparent overlay, two times have become as one, and we are meant to be equally aware of both dictions (and yet they seem the same diction). The words lie flat like the forms on a Cubist surface.[29]

All of this bespeaks a refashioning of Propertius's Latin into an almost artificial language which begins to approximate Laforgue's "international tongue common to the excessively cultivated" (*LE*, 283). Like Laforgue's "sexciproques" or his "cou qui, raide, émerge/D'une fraise empesée idem,/Une face imberbe au cold-cream" [There, on a neck emerging, spare,/Out of a ruff that's starched *idem*,/A face with cold-cream bearded hem],[30] Pound's "collages of sense" extend to the words themselves, and their often improbable connotations, without much concern for their probable grammatical meaning.[31] In other words, Pound's rendering of "Gaudeat in solito tacta puella sono" ("And the devirginated young ladies will enjoy [my songs]/when they have got over the strangeness" [*P*, 206]) depends on a word ordering possible only in an inflected language; Pound's translation of this line is determined wholly by his belief that "the division of *in* and *tacta* is [not] wholly accidental."[32] Thus, according to Kenner, Pound's translation of this line "is a scepticism directed at Latin professors, who take *tacta* not as the opposite of *intacta* but as meaning that the ladies were touched by poetry."[33]

This flattening of perspective and emerging *binarisme* enables Pound to recreate *Propertius* in his own fashion. Propoundius, as Ruthven aptly dubs him, is a forceful voice arguing for artistic freedom in an age of bureaucratic contraints. Indeed, Pound's rendering of Propertius, like Propertius's of Callimachus, serves to confirm Nietzsche's insights about the nature of Roman poetry itself: "They did not know the delights of the historical sense; what was past and alien was an embarrassment for them; and being Romans, they saw it as an incentive for a Roman conquest. . . . Not only did one omit what was historical; one also added allusions to the present and, above all, struck out the name of the poet and replaced it with one's own."[34] As May Sinclair remarked, "Ezra Pound has never found a mask that fitted him better than his Propertius. In all his adventures he goes out to the encounter with himself; he maintains himself, a salient, abrupt, unmistakable entity, through all his transformations."[35] Although there was no real theory of or justification for "free translation," the artistic license that Sinclair is arguing for would surely be Pound's own bedrock defense against the approved attitude of reverence and fidelity to the classics which affected the whole modernist rethinking and appropriation of the tradition.

This abrupt and unmistakable entity to which Sinclair refers can be explained to some extent by the forceful prosody that emerges in *Propertius*, the asyntactical line which Ronald Bush suggests is the cornerstone of Pound's attempt to integrate "the movements of an antecedent consciousness" into the poem.[36] By a happy coincidence, what emerges is a new Poundian voice and "certain qualities in this poem," which, as Ruthven remarks, "more than compensate for the desecration of the *Elegies*."[37] The opening invocation anticipates Pound's many subsequent descents in the *Cantos* and presents a forceful argument for his "creating in English verse a verse reincarnation, as it were, of Propertius."[38] Pound's approximation of the Latin elegiac pentameter provides him with a strongly cadenced spoken idiom based not on verse patterns but on sense patterns;[39] at every juncture we find Pound striving for an active syntax to accentuate the apparent rapidity of his translation:

> The time is come, the air heaves in torridity,
> The dry earth pants against the canicular heat,
>
> (P, 217)
>
> venit enim tempus, quo torridus aestuat aer,
> incipit et sicco fervere terra Cane.[40]

Once again, Pound searches for a secondary meaning with stronger connotations, translating *aestuat* with "heaves," referring to the sea, instead of the primary "rage" or "burn."

In addition, Propertius's mythological machinery enables Pound, when he is bored with it, to attain the compression characteristic of his later verse wherein logical connectives are eliminated so that image follows upon image in an almost elliptical fashion:

> Oh, oh, and enough of this,
>   by dew-spread caverns,
> The Muses clinging to the mossy ridges;
>   to the ledge of the rocks:

Zeus' clever rapes, in the old days,
                    combusted Semele's, of Io strayed.

                                                    (*P*, 222)

Armed with what can be seen as an emerging scepticism on Propertius's part, Pound adopts a cynical pose which becomes the motive force in the poem, with the resulting newfound strength derived from the articulation of Pound's voice against the voice of another.

As Ruthven argues, however, "In creating lines like this, Pound deliberately ignored the fact that Propertius's words have a grammatical relationship to one another. Instead, he treated them as if they were purely separate elements capable of meaning whatever one wants them to mean."[41] Similarly, Sullivan suggests that "Pound, as always when he is infusing the verse with his deepest convictions, departs radically from the sense of the original."[42] Pound tones down considerably Propertius's elegiac love poetry and prefers to emphasize his arguments for artistic freedom in an age demanding civic propaganda. In essence, Pound's version of the "mythical method" is deceptively subjective, enabling him both to discover a contemporaneousness which is curiously ahistorical and to ignore those temporal and historical traces embedded in language that permit a speaking people to reflect its subjectivity.

Whereas logopoeia as Pound defines it should be a liberating possibility, "a vehicle for the expression of his own very personal emotions" (*LE*, 282), here we find it somewhat limiting in that it depends solely upon a simple inversion of terms. In this respect, the criticism of Pound's *Homage* as schoolboy humor is partially warranted because it is so patently bound by the perusal of a dictionary. What is lost is the unexpectedness of the joke, the *Witz*, and, with it, the sense that language has a life of its own and is capable of teaching us something new. While the Pound who meets Professor Lévy in Canto 20 will powerfully evoke the liberating aspects of philology, and will make manifest his own ability to read himself into the landscape at the behest of a word—

> "Noigandres, eh, *noi*gandres,
> "Now what the DEFFIL can that mean!"
> Wind over the olive trees, ranunculae ordered,
> By the clear edge of the rocks
> The water runs, and the wind scented with pine
> And with hay-fields under sun-swath.
>
>   (20/90)

—the logopoetic Pound of *Propertius* eliminates Propertius's intentionality by substituting his own. Although he was largely responsible for making it possible to admit that Propertius was an ironist, unconscious or otherwise, Pound himself will not accept anything other than a rationalist position, and he transforms Propertius into what Ronald Bush describes as "a characteristically Poundian cross between Pierrot and the intelligence of Voltaire."[43]

Moreover, Bush's emphasis on the subjective element in Pound's postimagist poetry, as opposed to his social satires which are limited by the realism of his third-person descriptions, raises an interesting problem given Pound's new interest in Laforgue and Propertius. While the prosody in *Propertius* does help Pound to incorporate the energies of perception into the poem, the subjective element noted by Bush complicates our understanding of the more fundamental satirical ground of the poem. In his defense of *Propertius*, Pound continually returns to "Ride to Lanuvium" as an instance supporting his discovery of the logopoetic Propertius. Satire thus becomes an extremely important concept for Pound in that it in some way permits him to mediate between the more objective prose tradition and the subjective lyricism that he now apparently wants to escape.

As Pound argues in his essay on Henry James, "Most good prose arises, perhaps, from an instinct of negation; is the detailed, convincing analysis of something detestable; of something which one wants to eliminate. Poetry is the assertion of a positive, i.e. of desire, and endures for a longer period. Poetic satire is only an assertion of this positive, inversely, i.e. as an opposite hatred" (*LE*, 324). Pound's early poetry, especially of the period of *The Spirit of Romance*, is certainly "the assertion of a positive, i.e of desire," but, as I have noted, it increasingly comes to be seen by Pound as maudlin sentimentality. As the above quotation suggests, Pound needs a modern backdrop for his poetry in order to approximate the "prose method," but at the same time we can sense that he hates this modern backdrop and must seek a "positive" to differentiate poetry from "an instinct of negation." Pound's early attempts in *Lustra* to modernize his verse foundered because the classical types introduced into his epigrammatic renderings of contemporary London are not realistic but literary. In *Propertius*, however, and later in the *Cantos*, the flattening of perspective allows the rifts in Pound's presentation to become all the more forceful because they are the more restrained. Whereas an unchecked aestheticism becomes a critical trap in *Mauberley*, the tough cynicism in *Propertius* harbors an intermittently imagistic sentimentalism which, more often than not, escapes detection. As a result of the objective backdrop granted by his projected *Homage*, Pound permits himself to indulge occasionally in imagist verse: "'Bright tips reach up from twin towers, / Anienan spring water falls into flat-spread pools'" (*P*, 209).

Such moments become important not because they are lyrical, but because they are indications of an enunciative presence welding together what appears to be a broken surface. Discussing this passage, Sullivan argues that "the *Homage* makes violent use of this emotional linkage, this abrupt juxtaposition of different feelings and tones."[44] It is precisely this violence that gives the poem its modern texture and simultaneously permits Pound to continue his quest for the beautiful image which might otherwise appear to be too precious or maudlin. The distance implicit in the idea of a persona permits Pound to rediscover his subjective lyricism within the framework of Propertius's text.

In theory, Pound is able to assert the existence of an unbroken surface because he rebels against the idea of a dualistic separation between subject and object. However, this rejection of a dualistic framework merely reasserts it at another level. Although Pound defines this "positive" found in poetic satire as an "opposite hatred," there is no indication that this dialectic is seen as an ambivalence in the psychoanalytic sense. Rather, Pound in his satire becomes ambivalent about the concept of ambivalence itself and maintains the simple dualism between love and hate through projective mechanisms. For Pound, Hell remains outside as a place for others, and the Self is not implicated in this Hell except insofar as it is incapable of distinguishing between Good and Evil because of its own inherent ignorance. As long as one remains within this framework, within Pound's canon, there is a self-assured unity. The central focus of Pound's *Homage* is not Propertius's complexly rendered tale of his love for Cynthia, but Pound's own denunciation of the stupidity of the populace. As a consummate satirist, Pound's Propertius is clearly superior to everyone around him, and, thus, he manages to escape some of the perplexities that beset the real Propertius.

While Pound constantly returns to Propertius's line, "Ingenium nobis ipsa puella facit" ("My genius is no more than a girl"), comparing it to the mystical practices of the troubadour poets, and while Pound echoes Propertius's horror of death in section 9, he empties these themes of their content and, as Sullivan argues, "utiliz[es] Propertius's horror of death (which Pound himself does not have) to symbolize the artistic death for which he wrote in *Mauberley* the impressive poem—'E. P. Ode pour l'election de son sepulchre.'"[45] It is as though Pound's "collages of sense" render him incapable of feeling in depth. In many respects, Pound's control over his homage is as remarkable for the elements which Pound rejects as it is for Pound's ability to capture aspects of Propertius overlooked by the philologists Pound is attacking. Because Pound views Propertius's "Ride to Lanuvium" as the core of the entire poem, he tends to ignore aspects of the poem which are central to a more standard academic interpretation. Propertius's frightening dream of Cynthia's death—

> In that night, my love,
>   I dreamed a broken keel,
>   your tired arms splashing
>   in Ionian spindrift,
>   and heard your duplicity confessed,
> yet you couldn't raise up your head,
>   long hair heavy in the sea,

—or her visitation—

> Spirits float in that night
>   liberated by death,
>   that illusion of finality.
> The shadowing ghost rises lurid
>   from the smoking fire;
> Cynthia, just buried in the murmur
>   of her last road,
>   came in the dark,
>   a wraith at my bed, when sleep hovered
>   in the wake of love's funeral,
>   and I mourned in the cold-couched realm.[46]

—are widely removed from Pound's casual, epigrammatic rendering of this theme in his "Homage to Quintus Septimius Florentis Christianus":

> Woman? Oh, woman is a consummate rage,
>   but dead, or asleep, she pleases.
> Take her. She has two excellent seasons.
>
> <div align="right">(<i>P</i>, 162)</div>

By ignoring Propertius's concern with death, Pound in essence also denies the reality of his love for Cynthia; as a corollary, I think one can argue that Pound's fascination with Propertius's "My genius is no more than a girl," despite his arguments to the contrary, does not suggest a subjective involvement in any very real sense and makes suspect Pound's idealization of the tension he sees in the Provençal poets: "What is the difference between Provence and Hellas? There is, let us grant, a line in Propertius about *ingenium nobis fecit*. But the subject is not greatly developed. I mean that Propertius remains mostly inside the classic world and the classic aesthetic, plastic to coitus. Plastic plus immediate satisfaction" (*LE*, 151). Even the most cursory reading of Propertius will belie this idea that Propertius is fortunate enough to live in a world of "immediate satisfaction." Pound tends to discount what seems to be a legitimate love interest on the part of Propertius by arguing that love poetry was in the process of becoming irrelevant, or even impossible and inherently parodic, and that it was ultimately emptied of any real significance by Ovid. But as Sullivan argues with regard to Pound's emphasis on Propertius's ironic, and therefore more "sophisticated," tone, "the continued use of this tone makes us lose sight of the passion that makes itself felt in Propertius' style—even at its most ironic and when it is working through stock themes and images. Pound seems to assimilate Propertius to Ovid."[47] Put simply, Pound's discovery of irony in Propertius should not lead us to accept the portrait Pound has given us. Indeed, Pound's argument advancing the notion of Propertius's logopoeia enables us to see in Propertius a "modern" sensibility capable of Laforguian self-mockery, one capable of a "delicate irony" far different from Pound's satirical attack on his audience. In lieu of the Laforguian self-consciousness and irony he sees as "the citadel of the intelligent," Pound adopts in his first presentation of a logopoetic sensibility the extremely Corbièrean *persona* of *le poète contumace*.

. . .

Given Pound's concurrent interest in Laforgue, another way of supporting my argument that Pound surreptitiously redefines Laforgue's "delicate irony" would be to look at Pound's 1918 translation of Laforgue's "Salomé." As is the case with his *Propertius*, Pound's omissions in "Our Tetrarchal Précieuse" provide a striking indication of his real interests, or lack thereof. Whereas Laforgue himself alters the central focus of Flaubert's story by eliminating the perverse relationship between Herod and Herodias and transforming sexual desire into mysticism, Pound goes one step further by toning down any sexual mysticism and eliminating altogether any mention of Laforgue's Unconscious, which, as every critic of Laforgue has remarked, is central to an understanding and appreciation of Laforgue.

"Salomé" is a central work in Laforgue's oeuvre because it contains precisely those elements of Laforgue's philosophy which Pound ignores. "The most adverse critics of Laforgue," says Ramsey, "could hardly deny the interest of the elements held in suspension by this none too limpid prose. At the fatal feast are the clowns of the Idea, the Will, and the Unconscious, characterizing clearly if summarily the Absolute according to the Hegelian, Schopenhauerian, and Hartmannian philosophies."[48] Laforgue's poetic application of Hartmann's Unconscious lends his verse a paradoxical combination of both philo-

sophical pessimism and a meliorist vision. In the first case, the bond-
age of Ideas to the Will leads to a teleological movement wherein the
subject must seek total ascesis and a relegation of the Will to the noth-
ingness of nirvana. As Ramsey describes it:

> At the Fall the two elements of the Unconscious became separated, Rea-
> son was cut off from Will. The latter rules the world as we know it. In
> order to encourage men to perpetuate themselves, to obstruct progress
> toward nirvana, Will fosters three illusions: (a) that happiness is actually
> attainable at a given stage of the world's development, is within the grasp
> of the individual during his earthly life; (b) that men will be happy in a
> hereafter; (c) that the race will some day be happy in this world.[49]

At the same time, says Ramsey, this pessimistic tradition contains
within it a potentially optimistic vision because "awaiting nirvana, men
go about improving the lot of their fellows."[50] There is a sense of *be-
coming*, of a purposiveness of the particulars within this world. Hence,
we can begin to understand the striking particularity of Laforgue's
verse and his movement toward a more optimistic vision in his *Derniers
Vers*. Because the Unconscious has an instinctive, physiological basis,
there is the further possibility of a collective vitalism at odds with a
Darwinian approach, which would have appealed to the later Pound.[51]

Although it is much more likely that Pound either mistook La-
forgue's idea of the Unconscious for the Freudian unconscious that
would later influence the surrealists, or simply didn't understand the
romantic philosophy behind it, we might be able to understand
Pound's refusal to mention the Unconscious if we consider Laforgue's
descriptions of this realm:

> A l'aquarium de Berlin—devant le regard atone, gavé, sage, boud-
> dhique des crocodiles, des pithons (les ophites) etc.—comme je com-
> prends ces vieilles races d'orient qui avaient épuisé tous les sens, tous les
> tempéraments, toutes les métaphysiques—et qui finissaient par adorer,
> béatifier comme symbole du Nirvâna promis ces regards nuls dont on ne
> peut dire s'ils sont plus infinis qu'immuables—
> Mais l'idéal c'est ces éponges, ces astéries, ces plasmas dans le silence
> opaque et frais, tout au rêve, de l'eau—
> Et les mystères obscènes de Cybèle—
>
> [In the Berlin aquarium—in front of the dull, stuffed, sage, buddhist
> look of the crocodiles, the pythons (the ophites) etc.—as I understand
> these old oriental races who have exhausted all the meanings, all the tem-
> peraments, all the metaphysics—and who finished by worshiping, beati-
> fying as a symbol of the promised Nirvana these vacant looks of which it's
> hard to say whether they're more infinite than unchanging—

But the ideal is represented by these sponges, these starfish, these plas-
mas, all of them dreaming in the opaque and cool water—
And the obscene mysteries of Cybele—][52]

While such a realm would become more and more appealing to Pound
in the *Pisan* and later cantos, at this juncture he was still under the
spell of his vorticist program which was attempting to drive his poetry
or, as Pound puts, "any new idea into the great passive vulva of Lon-
don, a sensation analogous to the male feeling in copulation" (*P&D*,
204).

Thus, Pound finds himself compelled to avoid any mention of La-
forgue's Unconscious. He reduces Salomé's very explicit and not en-
tirely dismissable oration to the following catalog of amusing philo-
sophical epithets:

"Canaan, excellent nothingness; nothingness-latent, circumambient,
about to be the day after to-morrow, incipient, estimable, absolving, coex-
istent. . . ."
The princes were puzzled. "Concessions by the five senses to an all-
inscribing affective insanity; latitudes, altitudes, nebulae, Medusae of
gentle water, affinities of the ineradicable, passages over earth so emi-
nently identical with incalculably numerous duplicates, alone in indefi-
nite infinite. Do you take me? I mean that the pragmatic essence attracted
self-ward dynamically but more or less in its own volition, whistling in the
bagpipes of the soul without termination.—But to be natural passives, to
enter into the cosmos of harmonics.—Hydrocephalic theosophies, act it,
aromas of populace, phenomena without stable order, contaminated
with prudence.—Fatal Jordans, abysmal Ganges—to an end with 'em—
insubmersible sidereal currents—nurse-maid cosmogonies." (*P&D*, 196)

Similarly, where Laforgue incorporates a discourse on the Uncon-
scious into his description of the Aquarium on the White Isle, Pound
reduces Laforgue's peroration to the flat statement: "The keeper of
the aquarium moralized for an hour upon the calm life of his fishes"
(*P&D*, 192–93).[53] Whereas Laforgue was fascinated with the Berlin
Aquarium and saw the submarine world as an analogue for Nirvana,
Pound's rendering of Laforgue, despite the fact that he himself echoes
such sentiments in his "Sub Mare," should force us to question the
disinterestedness of Pound's reading of Laforgue.

Discussing Pound's translation, William Jay Smith suggests that
Pound "catches the spirit of the original," but that "he also omits one
of the main points of Laforgue's story, which is that Iaokanann pays
with his head for having taken Salome's virginity."[54] Smith's last claim
is an important one and supports Ramsey's contention that "not with-

standing all the whimsical appearances, the theme of 'Salomé' is the
rather serious one central to Laforgue's work: purity and how it shall
be retained."[55] Where Pound plays down Salomé's loss of virginity—
"But she was no more the 'little' Salomé, this night brought a change
of relations, exorcised from her virginity of tissue she felt peer to these
matrices, fecund as they in gyratory evolutions" (P&D, 199)—La-
forgue is less reticent about the motives behind Salomé's request for
the head of John the Baptist:

> Ah! chères compagnes des prairies stellaires, Salomé n'était plus la pe-
> tite Salomé! et cette nuit allait inaugurer une ère nouvelle de relations et
> d'étiquette!
>
> D'abord, exorcisée de sa virginité de tissus, elle se sentait maintenant,
> vis-à-vis de ces nébuleuses-matrices, fécondée tout comme elles d'évolu-
> tions giratoires.

> [Ah, dear companions of stellar meadows, Salomé was no longer just
> little Salomé—tonight she planned to launch a new era in relations and
> etiquette!
>
> In the first place, exorcised of the virginity of her tissue, she felt now,
> in relation to these nebulous matrices, fecundated like them by gyratory
> evolutions.][56]

In Laforgue's more explicit version, Salomé has been exorcised of her
virginity, "fecundated" or impregnated by—not simply "fecund" or
rich from—these "gyratory evolutions."

Thus, while critics have pointed to the subaquatic motifs in Pound's
own poetry as proof that he was influenced by Laforgue, it is crucial to
point out that certain Laforguian themes are not at all important to
Pound at this point. Not only is Pound's translation much more com-
pressed and elliptical (or garbled) than the original, Pound tends to
ignore the mystical aspects of Laforgue's tale as well as the desire for
a transcendent world which functions as the motive force in "Salomé."
As I have indicated before, Pound eliminates all mention of the Un-
conscious, as well as the fact that Iaokanaan had been kept alive "grâce
aux inexplicables intercessions de . . . Salomé" [thanks to the inexpli-
cable intercessions of Salome].[57] Ramsey suggests that such omissions
arise because "Pound apparently wished to preserve Laforgue's name
from any stain of sentimentality"; unfortunately, continues Ramsey,
"if we do not know about Salomé's tender sentiments we cannot un-
derstand why Jao kept his head as long as he did or why he finally lost
it. Moreover, we cannot understand Salomé, for whom such emotions
were momentous."[58]

Whereas Laforgue provides a deliberately skewed moral to the tale
("Ainsi connut le trépas, Salomé, du moins celle des Iles Blanches

Esotériques; moins victime des hasards illettrés que d'avoir voulu vivre dans le factice et non à la bonne franquette à l'instar de chacun de nous" [So that was how Salome met her death—Salome of the White Esoteric Islands, that is; less a victim of illiterate chance than of the desire to live in a world of artifice and not in a simpie, wholesome one like the rest of us]),[59] Pound effectively turns the tale into a "parodie sociale," diminishing the central focus of the story by emphasizing trivial social distinctions: "Thus died Salome of the Isles . . . less from uncultured misventure than from trying to fabricate some distinction between herself and every one else; like the rest of us" (P&D, 200). Laforgue posits a "simple" or "wholesome" community of readers, the existence of which provides us with both an element of comfort and an explanation as to why Salomé behaves as she does; Pound, on the other hand, minimizes Salomé's ritual sacrifice by suggesting that she is merely attempting to fabricate for herself trivial distinctions in the manner of the petty denizens of the everyday world. Once again, we find Pound transforming irony into satire as he did in *Propertius*. At bottom, what Pound seems to gain from his study of Laforgue is primarily a more vigorous voice and a new poetic stance buttressed by the projective mechanisms inherent in satire. But with this transformation of irony into satire, we must ask ourselves whether Pound ever does manage to approximate Laforgue's "delicate irony."

• • •

While Pound's interest in the *Moralités* is only of secondary importance to his developing poetic, his general interest in Laforgue does shed some light on Pound's subsequent poetry, and on *Mauberley* in particular. Both Warren Ramsey and John Espey have made strong cases for Laforgue's influence on *Mauberley* at both the thematic and formal levels by pointing to the Pierrot-like Mauberley and to Pound's use of cliché ("march of events," etc.), scientific terminology (seismograph, half-watt rays, etc.), international rhymes (*trentuniesme*/diadem), Latinate polysyllables, and literary allusions (including an allusion to Laforgue's "Complainte des pianos qu'on entend dans les quartiers aisés").[60] Although Espey goes on to argue that "Laforgue's essential tone occurs rarely in *Mauberley* after the *Ode*" and that "Pound's white remains Gautier's 'blanc d'albâtre' rather than Laforgue's 'blanc de cold-cream,'" he does nonetheless maintain that "the contrasts, the musical pattern of development and variation, do stand in close relation to Laforgue and are early evidence of Pound's application of the Laforguian techniques."[61] And as Espey has rightly observed, "just as Laforgue's Pierrots advance and withdraw in their sophistication, viewing the human scene with a double sense of desire and detachment, so Mauberley, disarmed by his own sensibility, gelded by his own perceptions, withdraws altogether."[62] Espey's characterization of the poem thus raises the extremely important question as to whether Laforgue's "double sense of desire and detachment" is operative in Pound's poem; in short, the central question is whether Pound has endowed Mauberley with his own preoccupations and self-criticisms in the same way that Laforgue presents his Pierrots in a self-ironizing fashion.

Unfortunately, although it is commonly agreed that both Pound and Mauberley speak in the poem, there are a variety of critical arguments, some of them diametrically opposed, attempting to locate Pound's voice in the poem. Seemingly trapped in a dialectic of its own, criticism of *Mauberley* has more or less contented itself with three possible variations on the relationship between E. P. and Mauberley: (1) Pound identifies with Mauberley so that the poem itself becomes an admission of failure; (2) Pound speaks intermittently or ironically in response to the critics (or Mauberley) who "bury" him in the "Ode," but never identifies with Mauberley; (3) Pound differentiates himself from Mauberley insofar as the subject of the poem is an aestheticized sensibility, but he sympathizes and identifies with Mauberley's criticism of society.[63]

What all such arguments attempting to locate and identify the speaker in the poem accomplish is the complete elimination of the Laforguian strategy of intertwined and self-implicated voices; such readings remove all of the doubt and hesitation that would align Pound's most Laforguian poem with Laforgue's self-ironizing Pierrots. In other words, critical arguments attempting to separate E. P. and Mauberley need to ask why Pound would bother to write about someone, fictional or not, who is irrelevant to Pound himself. Indeed, Pound's presentation of Mauberley's mind in "Mauberley 1920"—

> drifted . . . drifted precipitate,
> Asking time to be rid of . . .
> Of his bewilderment; to designate
> His new found orchid. . . .
>
> To be certain . . . certain . . .
> (Amid aerial flowers) . . . time for arrangements—
> Drifted on
> To the final estrangement;
>
> *(P*, 197)

—suggests that Mauberley's aestheticism is very close to that of the early Pound, who upholds such "driftings":

Once there was a woman . . .
. . . but I forget . . . she was . .
. . . I hope she will not come again.

. . . I do not remember. . . . .

I think she hurt me once, but
That was very long ago.

("La Fraisne," P, 5–6)

While it is certainly possible to see "E. P. Ode pour l'election de son sepulchre" as being spoken, or mis-spoken, by Mauberley, the misguided though representative critic of Pound's age, such a reading effectively removes the Laforguian overtones identified by Warren Ramsey.[64] What we have to remember is that from the beginning of his career Pound has been searching for a form of beauty that would vie with earlier manifestations of divinity.[65] In this respect, Hugh Witemeyer's characterization of Mauberley's dilemma seems to me essentially correct:

> Mauberley begins as a proto-Imagist, an imitator of Gautier, a lesser poet of *emaux et camées*. He moves, during his three creative years, amid "phantasmagoria," a word that Pound had explicitly associated with Imagisme and *phanopoeia*. Thus far he pursues a worthy goal. But he becomes confused, and proves unable to designate or arrange the "aerial flowers" of his phantasmagoric Arcadia. In other words he lacks the Vorticist *virtù*, the ability to "produce 'order-giving vibrations'" which can "departmentalise such part of the life-force as flows through him."[66] (*SP*, 376)

And Pound himself as early as 1915 had described the nature of the artist in a manner that can only remind us of Mauberley's predicament: "The good artist is perhaps a good seismograph, but the difference between man and a machine is that man can in some degree 'start his machinery going'. He can, within limits, not only record but create" (*SP*, 376).

In effect, then, Pound's characterization of Hugh Selwyn Mauberley is a rendering of the artist raté so familiar to us from Laforgue's similar portraits. But this characterization also raises the question of how distant Pound himself is from this vision of the artist raté. The simplest response to this question would be to underscore the likelihood of Pound's expression of doubt regarding his early poetry given his characterization of these poems as "stale creampuffs." His early poetry is undeniably "bent resolutely on wringing lilies from the acorn" (*P*, 185); and although it would be correct to assert that Pound, in 1920, rejects a Decadent program, Pound could, in retrospect, "patronizingly note the futility"[67] of his earlier poetic program as easily as Mauberley could.

However, while Pound seems to condemn Mauberley's inability to transcend his impressionism and thereby make an "immediate application/Of this to relation of the state/To the individual" (*P*, 199), the publication history of the poem indicates that Pound himself had still not settled upon a form that would permit him to resolve this very problem. After its initial publication in a limited edition by John Rodker's Ovid Press, *Hugh Selwyn Mauberley* was published in *Poems 1918–1921*, a volume containing "Three Portraits and Four Cantos" (*Homage to Sextus Propertius*, "Langue d'Oc" and "Moeurs contemporaines," *Mauberley*, and cantos 4–7). According to Noel Stock, "Worrying still about the form his work was taking [Pound] hoped perhaps to give some shape or direction to it by bringing these four groups of poems together under a single heading."[68] What underlies Pound's concern for form at this juncture is his disconcerting realization that, despite his increasing interest in Major Douglas's social-credit theories, he had still not found a form that would permit him to escape his "antiquarian" interests. While Berryman's discussion of the "Ode" makes it clear that Pound dissociates himself from the critical opinion that sees E. P. "pass[ing] from men's memory in *l'an trentuniesme / De son eage*," it in no way precludes the possibility that Pound himself is searching for a new poetic voice that would enable him to escape the Mauberleyisms of his early verse.

An even more telling indication of Pound's dilemma at this point is provided by the critical response to this volume. Turning to Pound's "Four Cantos" after discussing *Mauberley*, Maxwell Bodenheim offers this not entirely erroneous description of Pound's method:

> The upheavals and gambles of the present world form a jest to him, and he seeks to escape them by analysing the perfections and ardours of past centuries and by turning his eyes inward upon himself—'the obscure reveries of the inward gaze.' This latter aim is the driving-power of the four Cantos that close his volume. . . . They contain the subconscious matter deposited by years of reading and observation in one man's mind, and in their residence in this sub-conscious state they have blended into the man's mental and emotional prejudices and undergone a metamorphosis, in which they became his visualization and interpretation of past men and events.[69]

What is striking about Bodenheim's discussion is the explicit comparison between Pound and Mauberley provided by the problematic "inward gaze" containing "the subconscious matter deposited by years of reading and observation in one man's mind."

Bodenheim is referring, of course, to one of the more ambiguous poems in the suite, a poem that serves as a prime example of the difficulties in determining who is speaking throughout *Mauberley:*

II

The age demanded an image
Of its accelerated grimace,
Something for the modern stage,
Not, at any rate, an Attic grace;

Not, not certainly, the obscure reveries
Of the inward gaze;
Better mendacities
Than the classics in paraphrase!

The "age demanded" chiefly a mould in plaster
Made with no loss of time,
A prose kinema, not, not assuredly, alabaster
Or the "sculpture" of rhyme.

(*P*, 186)

We can never be certain whether the speaker here is a neutral, objective one, or whether he has succumbed to current aesthetic cant; in short, it would be difficult to say whether E. P. or Mauberley is speaking in this poem. The phrase, "The age demanded," for example, can be read in two diametrically opposed ways: (1) prescriptively, i.e., contemporary aesthetic fashions dictate that artists provide a "false" (futuristic?) image of the times; or (2) descriptively, i.e., adherence to mimetic realism necessitates a "true," though perhaps unpleasant, representation of modern life.

The problem of interpretation is further compounded by Pound's use of polarized, although seemingly stable, values in his criticism of the modern arts. We can easily trace a chain of aesthetic and emotional values that are counterposed to the tawdriness of "modern" life; a grimace on the modern stage is contrasted with "an Attic grace," and a quickly fashioned "mould in plaster" or "prose kinema" is set against Gautier's "alabaster / Or the 'sculpture' of rhyme." Unfortunately, a number of problems arise as a result of this parallelism. First, as we saw in Chapter 2, Pound left behind his quest for "an Attic grace" in *Lustra* and was now working in the Latin satirical tradition. Second, the identical phrasing of his various disclaimers ("Not, not certainly,") forces us to posit an equivalence between a seemingly exemplary "Attic grace" and "the obscure reveries / Of the inward gaze," the valence of which is extremely difficult to determine, particularly when it is used negatively to describe Mauberley later in the poem:

The coral isle, the lion-coloured sand
Burst in upon the porcelain revery:
Impetuous troubling
Of his imagery.

(P, 199)

Finally, the logic of the poem demands that we lend a positive valence
to the chain of aesthetic values composed of "Attic grace," "the ob-
scure reveries," and "the classics in paraphrase" and that we contrast
these with the obviously negative "mendacities." However, the very
mention of "classics in paraphrase" is troubling, and given Pound's
spirited defense of his *Homage to Sextus Propertius*, it is hard to dismiss
the speaker's implicit criticism of the poem as Laforguian self-irony.
This relatively transparent confusion should lead us to ask ourselves
how much control Pound has over his multiple ironies and is, I think,
indicative of a much more profound tension at the heart of *Mauberley*.

Although Pound directs his criticism at the passive impressionism
which makes it impossible for Mauberley to comprehend the "relation
of the state / To the individual" (*P*, 199), a similar charge can be lev-
eled against Pound's own poetic. Indeed, the poem's opening epi-
graph from Nemesianus's "Eclogue 4" suggests, as Pound indicates in
his note to the American edition of *Personae*, that Pound himself has
begun his own pastoral withdrawal from the political realities of Lon-
don life, an act not entirely dissimilar to Mauberley's retreat to "the
coral isle."[70] Indeed, A. R. Orage was more than a little dismayed
by Pound's departure, as can be seen by his comments in the *New Age*
of January 1921: "I can perfectly well understand, even if I find it
difficult to approve"[71]—this disapproval stemming from his belief that
it is in London "that the most advanced trenches of the spirit are to
be found; and it is here . . . that the enemy will have to be defeated."[72]
Orage goes on to make the further interesting claim that "even with
Mr. Pound in it, [he expects] nothing from Paris for the next quar-
ter of a century": "Psychology—I mean psycho-analysis precisely—
has not yet learned to speak French, and least of all the French of
Paris. And without psychology what is left for Paris but to permute
and combine, in ingenious ways but with no essentially fresh results,
the pre-war European ideas."[73] Continuing in this vein, Orage main-
tains that the opening statement of Pound's "Axiomata"—"The inti-
mate essence of the universe is *not* of the same nature as our own
consciousness" (*SP*, 49)—is "confined in effect to self-consciousness,
waking consciousness, in short, to our normal everyday rational
consciousness."[74]

Orage's criticism of Pound for his "lack of psychological depth,"[75]
for his having ignored those interior landscapes discovered by psycho-

analysis, can also be extended to Pound's disregard for a similar sub-
ject matter in *Mauberley*. As I have suggested throughout the course of
my discussion, Pound has a tendency to ignore or suppress what is in
fact closest to him. In the case of Régnier, for example, Pound empha-
sizes his stylistic advances while imitating the mythological vision he
had just criticized. Similarly, Pound represses the psychological core
of Propertius's work, the close relationship between love and death,
while ostensibly paying homage to Latin love poetry; moreover, lan-
guage in *Propertius* becomes, as we have seen, a mere surface without
depth or intentionality. Finally, Pound eliminates all reference to the
Unconscious in "Our Tetrachal Précieuse" and mocks the mystical at-
titudes for which he once had such great sympathy. Pound's choice of
this tale is indeed a strategic one, for it enables him to make light of
and dismiss this "silly little girl" in a way that he couldn't Laforgue's
Hamlet, a tale much more relevant to Eliot and Joyce; indeed, Pound's
dislike of the Hamlet reference in "Prufrock" is indicative of his dis-
tance from an Eliotic or Laforguian introspection.[76]

Pound's reluctance to endorse Laforgue's Unconscious in "Salomé"
begins to help us fathom his characterization of an aestheticized Nir-
vana in *Mauberley*. Mauberley's impressionistic aestheticism contains
the murkiness of fluid, undifferentiated or unclear boundaries which
permit the dark sexuality of Circe to be mistaken for that of Penelope,
and, if we extend the ramifications of Mauberley's assumption of Elpe-
nor's role instead of Odysseus's, we can see that the unconscious forces
evident in Mauberley become, in Pound's view, tantamount to death.

The similarity between Mauberley and Laforgue's Pierrots has be-
come a commonplace, and critics have continued to seize upon
Mauberley's passive impressionism and to belittle him for being a Dec-
adent whose

> desire for survival,
> Faint in the most strenuous moods,
> Became an Olympian *apathein*
> In the presence of selected perceptions.
>
> (*P*, 200)

The resolution to Pound's troubling representation of this "conscious-
ness disjunct" is ultimately provided by Mauberley's death, which be-
comes, in William V. Spanos's apt phrase, an "exorcism by externaliza-
tion."[77] Most critics have welcomed Mauberley's self-condemnatory
epitaph—"'I was / And I no more exist; / Here drifted / An hedon-
ist'" (*P*, 201)—which, like Corbière's "Épitaphe," announces the
death of the poet as well as his rebirth in another guise. According to
these critics, it is only through this satirical portrait of Mauberley that

Pound is able to criticize, and ultimately to rid himself of, his own propensity to cultivate "selected perceptions." In other words, Pound condemns Mauberley for his (own) passive impressionism and adherence to the notion of l'art pour l'art, both of which lead to his "anaethesis" and his one missed opportunity:

> He had passed, inconscient, full gaze,
> The wide-banded irides
> And botticellian sprays implied
> In their diastasis;
>
> Which anaethesis, noted a year late,
> And weighed, revealed his great affect,
> (Orchid), mandate
> Of Eros, a retrospect.

(P, 198)

But if Pound is here upholding the possibility of "(Orchid), mandate / Of Eros," *Mauberley* then constitutes a radical revision of Laforgue which either belies Pound's contention that "Laforgue is incontrovertible" *(Inst, 19)* or provides an indication that Pound too sees the more optimistic possibility in Laforgue's philosophical stance that begins to emerge in his *Derniers Vers* (and, I will argue, in Pound's later cantos). Significantly, Pound reverses the characteristically Laforguian (and Eliotic) scenario by having Mauberley deliver the rebuff usually reserved in Laforgue's poems for "l'inconsciente femme." In Laforgue's "Complainte des consolations," for example, a poem which Pound quotes in his *Instigations*, the woman simply "overlooks" the speaker and buries him with one gesture:

> Ses yeux ne me voient pas, son corps serait jaloux;
> Elle m'a dit: «monsieur . . .» en m'enterrant d'un geste;
> . . . .
> Sans chercher à me consoler vers les étoiles,
> Ah! je trouverai bien deux yeux aussi sans clés,
>   Au Louvre, en quelque toile!
>
> [Her eyes don't see me; her body would be jealous.
> She just said, 'Sir . . .' and buried me with one gesture.
> . . . .
> No hunt for consolation in the stars that trail,
> Oh, I'll find a pair of eyes, all right, without the hooks,
>   In the Louvre, bit of a canvas tale!][78]

This is precisely that Laforguian attitude or *apathein* for which Pound and most critics attack Mauberley. Thus, given Pound's revision of

Laforgue, we need to ask which Laforgue it is that Pound envisions as the "angel with whom our modern poetic Jacob must struggle" (*Inst*, 11).

Because Pound is so ready to quote "Pierrot (Scène courte mais typique)" in contexts which suggest that it exemplifies a Laforguian "personality," we can only assume that he does in fact consider the following lines to be a "revelation" of Laforgue's "personal emotions, of his unperturbed sincerity" (*Inst*, 17):

> Je ne suis point ni Le Superbe!
> Mais mon âme, qu'un cri un peu cru exacerbe,
> Est au fond distinguée et franche comme une herbe.
>
> [I'm not at all 'that strapping fellow' nor The Superb!
> And yet my soul—that somewhat coarse cries can perturb—
> Is underneath it all distinguished, frank as a herb.][79]

Unfortunately, despite this profession of a radical innocence, Laforgue can only ironically undercut his plaintive longing for what from his theoretical perspective is an impossibility, because the self can only know itself and cannot know or be known by the others it desires to know. Laforgue's irony is not simply the elitist attempt to *épater le bourgeois* that Pound so admired and wanted to emulate, but the result of a radical solipsism. Instead of creating what Pound defines as "the citadel of the intelligent," Laforgue's "imaginative isolationism," argues Michael Collie, "allows him to believe in his own 'exquisite intelligence' at the expense of supposing that other intelligences are not, cannot be 'exquisite'."[80] In addition, says Collie, as a result of his deterministic and mechanistic vision of man, Laforgue views "the human body . . . not [as] an active agency, but a passive one, capable of sensitive response but not capable of any activity that is not ultimately arbitrary."[81] In short, Laforgue had created both a poetic and a philosophical position diametrically opposed to Pound's own.

Similarly, Pound's adaptation of Laforgue's eye imagery complicates his and our attempts to condemn Mauberley for being oblivious to the "mandate of Eros" contained in "the wide-banded irides." For Laforgue, the eye is the chief means by which sense impressions are gathered and people relate to one another, but it can only register surface phenomenona seen from a distance.[82] Although the many eyes in Laforgue's poems sometimes hold forth a promise of recognition, most often they are "sans clés" (as in "Complainte des consolations") and betray no depth or interiority: "Oui, divins, ces yeux! mais rien n'existe / Derrière! Son âme est affaire d'oculiste" [yes, eyes divine, but nothing much exists / Behind. Her soul is something from

the oculist's].[83] As Collie observes, "English readers will have no
difficulty in identifying these eyes in pre-Raphaelite and late Victorian
painting. They are the large, doleful eyes of the draped, essentially
inaccessible figure of a Burne-Jones or a Rossetti."[84] Thus, although
the Laforguian echoes in *Mauberley* prepare us for "the large, doleful
eyes" in the "Yeux Glauques" section, we need to know who is describ-
ing these eyes and how they relate to Pound's supposed exorcism of
Mauberley's passive impressionism:

> The Burne-Jones cartons
> Have preserved her eyes;
> Still, at the Tate, they teach
> Cophetua to rhapsodize;
>
> Thin like brook-water,
> With a vacant gaze.

(P, 189)

Attempting to answer precisely these questions, Ian F. A. Bell ac-
cepts Pound's proposition that "Mauberley is a mere surface" (*SL*, 180)
and argues that it is Pound himself who "undermines any illusion of
depth—that is to say: surface alone is the main feature we have to deal
with, dissociated from, to appropriate a Jamesian axiom, any myth of
'going behind'."[85] This "modernist" emphasis on surface in both
Pound and Wyndham Lewis is intended, continues Bell, "to demolish
that most pervasive of bourgeois myths of representation—the cen-
trality of the 'subject' or ego."[86] Thus, if Bell is right, we should not be
too surprised that the translucence described in "Yeux Glauques" is
far removed from the crystalline world of Pound's medieval vision in,
say, "Canzon: The Spear," where subject and object, lover and be-
loved, are bound together by this self-generating "light of love" and
where the "deep waters" provide a locus for "man's soul":

> 'Tis the clear light of love I praise
> That steadfast gloweth o'er deep waters,
> A clarity that gleams always.
> Though man's soul pass through troubled waters,
> Strange ways to him are openèd.
> To shore the beaten ship is sped
> If only love of light give aid.

(CEP, 134–35)

In 1920, however, this depth in "Canzon" can only be "medieval" or
retrograde when compared to *Mauberley* with its archetypally modern-
ist "plane geometry," with its "thin brook-water" and "vacant gaze"

emptied of any subjective content,[87] for *Mauberley* has now become Pound's "modern" version of Laforgue's retort to his Beloved: "La somme des angles d'un triangle, chère âme, / Est égale à deux droits" ['The angles of a triangle, dear soul, equate / With two right angles as a rule'].[88]

But before accepting such claims for a modernism of mere surfaces, we need to examine the other mask donned by Pound in *Mauberley*, for such notions as "surface" and "exorcism by externalization" will undoubtedly bring to mind Gautier's similar "angoisse provoquée par la profondeur métaphysique"[89] and thus may help us understand why so much of *Mauberley* is written under the sign of Gautier.

· · ·

John Espey has, of course, provided us with the strongest case for Gautier's influence on Pound by detailing the frequent references to Gautier in *Mauberley*, and Pound himself points to *Émaux et Camées* as a necessary corrective to the verbal prolixity that resulted from the Anglo-American adaptation of French *vers libre*. Beginning with his reference to Gautier's "alabaster / Or the 'sculpture' of rhyme" (*P*, 186), Pound makes numerous allusions to the poems in *Émaux et Camées*. In the third poem, Pound invokes both "À une robe rose" and "La Rose-thé"[90] with his mention of "The tea-rose tea-gown," "Coquetterie posthume" with his reference to "mousseline" (*P*, 186),[91] and, with his "Christ follows Dionysus," Gautier's "Bûchers et Tombeaux":

> Des dieux que l'art toujours révère
> Trônaient au ciel marmoréen;
> Mais l'Olympe cède au Calvaire,
> Jupiter au Nazaréen;
>
> [The gods, long revered through poetry,
> Sat enthroned in the marmoreal heaven;
> But Olympus yields to Calvary,
> And Jupiter to The Nazarene;][92]

The title of the sixth poem of the suite, "Yeux Glauques" (*P*, 189), derives from the "femme mystérieuse" in Gautier's "Cærulei Oculi" whose "yeux, où le ciel reflète . . . Les teintes glauques de la mer" [eyes in which the sky reflects . . . The blue-green tints of the sea].[93] In the tenth poem, Pound's description of the stylist's "sagging roof" (*P*, 192) alludes to Gautier's "Fumée": "Là-bas, sous les arbres s'abrite / Une chaumière au dos bossu; / Le toit penche, le mur s'effrite" [There beneath the trees takes shelter/A thatched cottage with a hunched back; /The roof sags, the wall crumbles].[94] And in the twelfth poem, Pound translates two lines from Gautier's "Le Château du souvenir"[95] to which I will return later in my discussion: "'Daphne with her thighs in bark/Stretches toward me her leafy hands'" (P, 193). Finally, because we must assume that Pound is borrowing the title of the closing poem from Gautier's programmatic statement that "Chaque pièce devait être un médaillon à enchâsser sur le couvercle d'un coffret, un cachet à porter au doigt, serti dans une bague, quelque chose qui rappelât les empreintes des médailles antiques qu'on voit chez les peintres et les sculpteurs" [Each work ought to be a medallion to mount on the lid of a jewel case, a seal to be set in a jeweled ring and worn on the finger, something which brings to mind the imprints of antique medals collected by painters and sculptors],[96] it would seem that we are forced to lend a positive valence to "Medallion." And if we accept this parallel between Gautier's *médaillons* and Pound's would-be "Medallion," we are almost compelled to argue that the final poem of *Mauberley* embodies the imagistic principles advocated by Pound since 1912.

Curiously, while such emphasis on the technical aspects of Gautier's influence does not seem at all controversial, these readings do in the end become problematic because they tend to overlook what Donald Davie describes as an almost psychological necessity on Pound's part to emulate Gautier: "It was emulating Gautier that purified and raised to a new power attitudes that in life were callow and unresolved; for, in learning the measure of Gautier's cadence and the dynamic shape of Gautier's stanzas, Pound by that very token became, for as long as he was writing the poem, as intelligent as Gautier and as civilized."[97] "Medallion," and the manifest presence of Gautier's influence in that poem, has in fact become the central crux of *Mauberley* because it has become allied with the problem of determining whether E. P. (Pound) or Mauberley is the poem's author; the problem of interpretation hinges upon the fact that "Medallion" sets forth a hard-edged "modernist surface," which, as we have been led to believe, is beyond the reach of the "impressionistic" Mauberley. This emphasis on a "modernist surface" has led Jo Brantley Berryman, for example, to suggest the seemingly plausible argument that both "Medallion" and "Envoi" are in fact Pound's poems and differ only in the media, music or sculpture, upon which they are based.[98]

What is surprising, however, is the reluctance on the part of critical opinion to even entertain such a possibility. Because "Medallion" seems to lack poetic depth and instances none of the active engagement of some of Pound's other attempts to capture another subject or subjectivity, most critics have tended to see the poem as being the somewhat feeble product of Mauberley's limited poetic talent. Thus, the argument goes, even if "Medallion" contains a vision of Aphrodite, this vision becomes in the end a sterile one because it does not escape the frame, so to speak, and as a consequence fails to engage either the reader or the external world. "Envoi," on the other hand, because of its active verbs and present participles, has an immediacy absent in "Medallion" and contains, as well, a complex layering of literary allusions and echoes which become the basis for Pound's poetry in the *Cantos*. The sinuosity of "Envoi," its complex syntax, provides movement, the arabesque, lacking in the flat statements in "Medallion."

Unfortunately, both interpretations contain some serious flaws. In order to uphold the argument identifying "Medallion" with Mauberley, we are required to deny the manifest influence of Gautier and to argue that Pound is at this point moving away from his imagist aesthetic. In addition, once we buttress our argument with reference to "Envoi" as Pound's poem, we must also acknowledge that "Envoi" is very alien to what emerges in Pound's poetry during the next twenty-five years. Only in the *Pisan Cantos* does Pound's nostalgic recreation of Elizabethan verse return as a ground bass for his poetry.

Berryman's argument associating both "Envoi" and "Medallion" with Pound, on the other hand, while very forceful and impressively documented, poses some interesting problems of its own. Berryman bases her interpretation on Pound's reference to Reinach's art history, *Apollo*, in the second stanza of "Medallion":

> The sleek head emerges
> From the gold-yellow frock
> As Anadyomene in the opening
> Pages of Reinach.

> (P, 202)

"The allusion to Anadyomene," says Berryman, is indubitably "to the head of Aphrodite in Lord Leconfield's Collection, London, pictured in S. Reinach's *Apollo*, fig. 83."[99] Indeed, Reinach's description of Praxiteles's *Head of Aphrodite* is entirely relevant to our discussion:

> The characteristics of the feminine ideal as conceived by this great and fascinating genius are all clearly defined in this head. The form of the face, hitherto round, has become oval; the eyes, instead of being fully opened, are half closed, and have that particular expression which the ancients described as "liquid," the eye-brows are but slightly marked, and the attenuation of the eyelids is such, that they melt, by almost insensible gradations, into the adjoining planes. The hair, like that of the Hermes, is freely modelled; and finally, the whole reveals a preoccupation with

effects of chiaroscuro, of a subdued play of light and shadow, which pre-
cludes any lingering vestiges of harshness and angularity. It is here that
we note the influence of painting upon sculpture.[100]

While Berryman rightly points to the lines in "Mcdallion" suggested
by Reinach's description ("The face-oval beneath the glaze"), she
tends to downplay, indeed ignore, the characteristically unmodern
(and therefore perhaps un-Poundian) softness described by Reinach:
"the attenuation of the eyelids . . . melt[ing], by almost insensible gra-
dations"; the "chiaroscuro . . . preclud[ing] any lingering vestiges of
harshness and angularity."[101] More interesting still, Reinach argues in
the next paragraph that "the suavity of a head like Lord Leconfield's
Aphrodite does, as a fact, recall Correggio; we recognise in it that essen-
tially pictorial quality which the Italian critics call *sfumato*, meaning a
vaporous gradation of tones, a melting of one tint into another."[102]
Ironically, therefore, not only does "Lord Leconfield's *Aphrodite* . . .
recall Correggio," but it also recalls the Aphrodite described *à la Cor-
reggio* in Gautier's "La Nue":

> A l'horizon monte une nue,
> Sculptant sa forme dans l'azur:
> On dirait une vierge nue
> Émergeant d'un lac au flot pur.
>
> Debout dans sa conque nacrée,
> Elle vogue sur le bleu clair,
> Comme une Aphrodite éthérée,
> Faite de l'écume de l'air.
>
> On voit onder en molle poses
> Son torse au contour incertain,
> Et l'aurore répand des roses
> Sur son épaule de satin.
>
> Ses blancheurs de marbre et de neige
> Se fondent amoureusement
> Comme, au clair-obscur du Corrège,
> Le corps d'Antiope dormant.
>
> Elle plane dans la lumière
> Plus haut que l'Alpe ou l'Apennin;
> Reflet de la beauté première,
> Soeur de "l'éternel féminin."
>
> [A cloud on the horizon
> Is sculpting its form in the azure:

Or should we say a naked virgin
Emerging from a lake that's pure?

Standing in her nacre shell,
She sails upon the blue clear
Like an Aphrodite become ethereal,
Made from the spray of the air.

Uncertain still her body's contour,
We see her soft and undulant poses,
And on her satin shoulder
Dawn scatters a thousand roses.

Her doubled whiteness of marble and snow
Embrace and blend together lovingly,
A Correggian chiaroscuro
Of the body of the sleeping Antiope.

She soars in all her radiance
Higher than the Alps or Apennines;
Reflection of primordial beauty,
Sister of "The Eternal Feminine."][103]

Such an allusion should indeed force us to qualify our account of Pound's vortex, his "planes in relation," for it reintroduces a troubling depth, a beneath or beyond, as well as a certain chiaroscuro softness to the "modernist surface," especially when Reinach's reference to Apelles as a precursor to Correggio points us directly to Gautier's "Le Poëme de la femme" and its mention of Apelles's Venus Anadyomene:

Pour Apelle ou pour Cléomène,
Elle semblait, marbre de chair,
En Vénus Anadyomène
Poser nue au bord de la mer.

[To Apelles or to Cleomenes,
She seemed, posing statuesquely,
A Venus Anadyomene
Nude at the edge of the sea.][104]

Because Pound's extensive references to poems in *Émaux et Camées* suggest a real familiarity with this volume, I think we are justified in assimilating this particular poem to the myriad allusions that come together in and make up "Medallion." But this and other of Gautier's representations of Venus Anadyomene are marked by their insistence on the power of infinite reflection contained in the eye of Venus, a power that Nietzsche once described as *"the magic of the extreme,* the seduction that everything extreme exercises."[105] In "Le Poëme de la femme," for example, we cannot help but be struck by the depth, "la nacre dc l'infini," contained in these divine eyes:

> Ses paupières battent des ailes
> Sur leurs globes d'argent bruni,
> Et l'on voit monter ses prunelles
> Dans la nacre de l'infini.

> [Her eyelids, like beating wings, open
> And close upon her eyes of burnished silver,
> And her pupils are glimpsed all of a sudden
> In that mother-of-pearl forever.][106]

And an even more characteristic representation of this depth, this "eye-deep" (*P*, 188), to borrow Pound's phrase, is contained in Gautier's "Caerulei Oculi," the poem from which Pound borrows the title for his "Yeux Glauques":

> Une femme mystérieuse,
> Dont la beauté trouble mes sens,
> Se tient debout, silencieuse,
> Au bord des flots retentissants.

> Ses yeux, où le ciel se reflète,
> Mêlent à leur azur amer,
> Qu'étoile une humide paillette,
> Les teintes glauques de la mer.

>   .   .   .   .
> Et leurs cils comme des mouettes
> Qui rasent le flot aplani,
> Palpitent, ailes inquiètes,
> Sur leur azur indéfini.

> [A mysterious woman,
> Whose beauty troubles my senses,
> Is silently standing,
> At the edge of the resounding waves.

> Her eyes, reflecting the heavens,
> Add to their bitter azure, smartly
> Spangled with watery sequins,
> The blue-green tints of the sea.

>   .   .   .   .
> And her lashes, like sea-gulls

> Skimming the calm of the seas,
> With fluttering wings, restless,
> Graze the vague azure of her eyes.][107]

Although the emphasis on depth, indefiniteness, and reflection in such a poem seems to provide a strong contrast to the topaz eyes seen "Beneath half-watt rays" in Pound's "Medallion," the "troubling of the senses" precipitated by this infinite power of reflection in "Caerulei Oculi" is strongly echoed in the "Impetuous troubling / Of [Mauberley's] imagery" (P, 199). Furthermore, this threatening "magic of the extreme" compels Gautier to explore a sinister undercurrent, the relationship between death and desire, that runs throughout the Decadent tradition and also subtends Mauberley's "hedonism" (P, 201). In "Caerulei Oculi," the spell cast by the eye of Venus is described as "Un pouvoir magique" which leads the speaker to the abyss:

> Un pouvoir magique m'entraîne
> Vers l'abîme de ce regard,
> Comme au sein des eaux la sirène
> Attirait Harald Harfagar.
>
> Mon âme, avec la violence
> D'un irrésistible désir,
> Au milieu du gouffre s'élance
> Vers l'ombre impossible à saisir.
>
> [A magic power leads me
> Toward the abyss of her regard,
> Just as to the bottom of the sea
> The siren drew Harald Harfagar.
>
> My soul, led by the violence
> Of an irresistable desire, vainly
> Leaps into the whirlpool's current
> Toward the shadow that cannot be seized.][108]

And like Prufrock, like Mauberley, or like Pound-Drake with his vision of Queen Elizabeth in Canto 91, Gautier succumbs to this vision of female beauty, "de ce regard céruléen," and risks his own immolation: "Et mon coeur, sous l'onde perfide, / Se noie et consomme l'hymen" [And my heart, beneath the perfidious wave / Drowns itself and consummates the marriage].[109] This vision of union, of atasal, is certainly not that of the "factive personality" Pound champions, but that of the poet as self-consuming *artifex;* it makes little difference whether "Medallion" is Mauberley's or Pound's poem, because poet and mask begin to converge in the Gautieresque aspects of Mauberley's persona and his art.

We can, of course, argue that Pound in fact rejects Gautier in *Mauberley* and that he is at this point moving away from his imagist principles, but this approach seems only to lead to an infinite regress. Even if we are able to localize the play of mask and voice by means of attributing "Envoi" and "Medallion" to a particular speaker, whatever interpretative stability generated by such a strategy soon dissolves in what appears to be a legitimate and unresolvable crux of the poem. If we want to differentiate Pound from Mauberley, the lesser poet, we must, as Donald Davie suggests, believe "that the exactness this poem achieves is in Pound's opinion bought at too great a cost, in view of the metallic inertness with which the imagery endows the subject."[110] But looking at Walter Villerant's (Pound's alter-ego) salient characterization of "high modernism" as "metal finish," "Joyce's hardness," and "Pound's sterilized surgery,"[111] Davie goes on to make this reasonable claim:

> Are we to believe that Villerant admires Joyce for the wrong reasons . . . ? We must believe this if we are to take "Medallion," with its conspicuously "metal finish," as Mauberley's poem rather than Pound's. In any case it looks more than ever as if Walter Villerant and Hugh Selwyn Mauberley are the same person. If so, then Pound's relation to the one fiction, Villerant, illuminates his relation to the other, Mauberley. . . . Villerant, so largely assembled of components from men whom Pound admired (James, Ford, Gourmont), appears to differ from Pound not as a limited person whom Pound will surpass but, much of the time, as an ideally civilized person whom Pound aspires to emulate. Pound surpasses Villerant in only one particular, in the barbaric virtue of energy. And this seems true of Pound's relation to Mauberley also.[112]

Thus, if Pound does manage to emulate Laforgue's "delicate irony" in *Mauberley*, this Pierrotesque quality only occurs in the unintentionally ironic conflation of poet and mask, of E. P. and Mauberley, and in the tension between poet and model, between Pound and Gautier, which in turn leads to the surreptitious introduction of a hidden depth running counter to Bell's emphasis on a modernism of "mere surface."

Another way of illustrating this point would be to return once more to Pound's allusion to "Le Château du souvenir" in Poem 12, an allusion which is, I think, extremely significant in the context of *Mauberley*, but one which has gone unremarked. Not only does Gautier's "château du souvenir" contain the tapestry depicting Apollo and Daphne, but it also contains the "Pastels blafards" and "sombres peintures" of "Jeunes beautés et vieux amis" who "quittent la muraille" and come to life [pale pastels and gloomy paintings of young beauties and old friends who leave the high wall]. "Le Château du souvenir" is purely autobiographical, an almost nightmarish walk down memory lane where Gautier encounters his long dead friends and mistresses. Indeed, these various portraits provide a model for Pound's own suite of poems commemorating his friends, especially if we assume, like Berryman, that "Medallion" celebrates the singer Raymonde Collignon.[113] And particularly relevant here is Gautier's uncanny confrontation with his past romantic self:

> Dans son cadre, que l'ombre moire,
> Au lieu de réfléchir mes traits,
> La glace ébauche de mémoire
> Le plus ancien de mes portraits.
>
> Spectre rétrospectif qui double
> Un type à jamais effacé,
> Il sort du fond du miroir trouble
> Et des ténèbres du passé.
> . . . .
> Terreur du bourgeois glabre et chauve,
> Une chevelure à tous crins
> De roi franc ou de lion fauve
> Roule en torrent jusqu'à ses reins.
>
> Tel, romantique opiniâtre,
> Soldat de l'art qui lutte encore,
> Il se ruait vers le théatre
> Quand d'Hernani sonnait le cor.
>
> [In its dark frame, glistening moistly,
> Instead of reflecting my traits,
> The mirror sketches from memory
> The oldest of my portraits.
>
> Retrospective specter doubling for
> A character never effaced,
> He exits the troubled mirror
> And the darkness of the past.
> . . . .
> Terror of the bald bourgeois shaved clean,
> The hair of a fanatic
> Frankish King or wild lion
> Falls in a torrent down his back.

> Opinionated Romantic,
> Soldier of art who still fights,
> He hurled himself toward the theater
> On *Hernani*'s opening night.][114]

Pound's allusion to this poem is a particularly rich one. In addition to the Daphne theme, the poem contains a typical Gautieresque reference to Venus—"Cette Vénus, mauvais mère, / Souvent a battu Cupidon" [This Venus, terrible mother, often battled Cupid]—which is echoed in Pound's portrait of Lady Valentine in Poem 12. Moreover, we can see that Pound, with his own "chevelure à tous crins," wants to adopt Gautier's compelling portrait of himself as a "romantique opiniâtre, / Soldat de l'art qui lutte encore." But Gautier is also arguing in this poem for an inescapable continuity between past and present selves, and if Pound has exorcised himself completely of his Mauberley-like traits, if he has bid good-bye to both London and his past self, and, most important, if *Mauberley* is not an autobiographical poem as Pound went to great pains to explain, "Le Château du souvenir" is a very bizarre poem to invoke in this context. What Pound's allusion suggests, whether inadvertently or not, is an extremely powerful doubling of conflicted selves, a "Spectre rétrospectif qui double / Un type à jamais effacé," and not the unambiguous resolve that most readings of *Mauberley* as pure satire would imply. Against Pound's claim that *Mauberley* is "distinctly a farewell to London,"[115] we might well oppose the concluding lines of "Le Château du souvenir": "Le présent entre dans ma chambre / Et me dit en vain d'oublier" [The present enters my room / And tells me in vain to forget].

Although the satirical aspect of *Mauberley* parallels the double-edged nature of Gautier's sketches of nineteenth-century bourgeois society, Pound inadvertently preserves some of the romantic idealization so central to Gautier's poetry. Indeed, it would seem that *Mauberley* contains the seeds of another poetic somewhat at variance with the one voiced in the more programmatic vorticist manifestos. The tension between the Parnassian and satirical aspects in *Mauberley* will come to haunt the *Cantos* where, as we shall see, Pound's poetic becomes even more complexly textured as a result of the collage-like juxtapositions of irreconcilable poetic modes and mutually exclusive *epistèmes*.

Chapter Four

THE WOBBLING PIVOT: SURFACE AND DEPTH
IN THE EARLY CANTOS

> Very shaggy, and lacking in Gautier's
> perfection of neatness.
> —(*P/J*, 112)

WE HAVE traced up to this point a clear progression from Pound's Parnassian *Ripostes*, to the satirical realism of *Lustra*, to the quasi-irony of *Propertius* and *Mauberley*, the last of which founders, as we saw, in the illicit return of Gautier's romanticism. Unfortunately, as a result of this strange turn, it might seem that this teleological account has prepared us somewhat inadequately for a study of Pound's "long poem including history," for, given that the *Cantos* have been variously considered "the only kind of long poem that the Symbolist aesthetic will admit,"[1] a vorticist or a cubist collage,[2] and a modern verse epic,[3] the extent of Gautier's or Laforgue's influence on Pound's early cantos indeed becomes a vexing question. Even as early as *Three Cantos*, for example, Pound contrasts Gautier's "intaglio method" with Browning's "semi-epic story" (*P*, 231)[4] in order to foreground the problems attending his attempts to recall past history:

> Say that I dump my catch, shiny and silvery
> As fresh sardines flapping and slipping on the marginal cobbles?
> (I stand before the booth, the speech; but the truth
> Is inside this discourse—this booth is full of the marrow of
>   wisdom.)
> Give up th'intaglio method.
>
> (P, 230)

Pound's suggestion that he might have to "Give up th'intaglio method" betrays his suspicion that his imagism will not be able to represent historical truth as effectively, if at all, as Browning's "rag-bag" and its admittedly historiographical bias: "You had some basis, had some set belief" (*P*, 230).

And despite the fact that Pound's final revision of the poem in 1924 makes incontestable the historico-epic foundations of the *Cantos*,[5] Pound's reluctance to forsake his imagistic principles can be seen in his affirmation of the "intaglio method" at the end of ur-Canto 1—"If for a year man write to paint, and not to music" (*P*, 234)—and in his approbatory mention of Wyndham Lewis and Picasso. Pound's parenthetical remarks in the opening of the canto suggest that there is a large gap between objective speech (i.e., Browning's "showman's booth" in which history will unfold) and an interiority or wisdom held suspended within that discourse. Moreover, there is no guarantee that such originary speech or interior wisdom will appear, precisely because it is predicated on the poet's subjective intervention:

> Oh, we have worlds enough, and brave *décors*,
> And from these like we guess a soul for man
> And build him full of aery populations.

> (*P*, 234)

As the above quotation suggests, there is no surety in guessing and no solidity in such "aery populations." Although Browning's example provided Pound with a sufficiently flexible method to incorporate historical particulars into his poem, Pound's revisions attest to his realization that Browning also led him to engage in a largely unproductive dialogue with the ghosts of the past. The continual intrusion of Pound's own voice makes the "drama wholly subjective" and short-circuits his attempt to represent generalized historical truths; thus, the poem is not far removed from "Near Perigord," a poem in which Pound sets out to discover the real Bertrand de Born only to find that the project is largely a subjective interpretation or reconstruction of the Book and can only disintegrate into fragments.

In addition to this unresolved tension between a Gautieresque and a Browningesque poetic, there is also the question of Laforgue's importance to Pound's early attempts at writing his epic. As John Porter Houston has argued, "the monologue in its elliptic final form resembles to a greater extent passages in Laforgue or James Joyce, if anything."[6] In this same vein, Warren Ramsey points to the similarity between Pound's and Laforgue's "fusion of legendary figures in . . . a 'continuous present.'"[7] For Ramsey, Pound's ideogramic method is only successful when it manages to achieve the symbolist fusion of *forma*[8] occuring in Canto 4 with Pound's ideogramic juxtaposition of Greece and Provence, Helen and Eleanor, or Itys and Cabestan.[9] This argument on behalf of Pound's symbolist formalism has been greatly extended by Christine Froula who, remarking that Canto 4 was the first of the early cantos to be published in its current form, argues that it signals "a beginning of beginnings" for both the *Cantos* and modernist poetry in general,[10] a beginning whereby Pound evolves an abstract, paradisal language capable of representing visionary experience in purely formal terms. Discussing Pound's reworking of the Itys/Cabestan parallel, Froula writes, "The stories, indeed, are all but erased as the true subject becomes the pattern itself. . . . Pound's allusive mode blurs and partly erases the individual narrative lines of the stories, giving the expressive powers of sound and rhythm precedence over the representation of the object."[11] Pound's interest in Fenellosa's rough translations of the Chinese, speculates Froula, "was only increased by the syntactic obscurity of the text he confronted," leading to "a poetics based not on words as signs but on their powers of suggestion."[12]

Against these Laforguian readings emphasizing a symbolist underpinning to the *Cantos*, however, we can argue that Pound was not particularly interested at this point in Laforgue's vers libre and that it would be difficult to distinguish a voice or tone which we could characterize as being distinctly Laforguian.[13] Although a Laforguian emphasis on a failed intersubjectivity is manifest in Lorenzo de Medici's concern that Alessandro be cognizant of the cause of his own death, the problem of self-knowledge is not ironized and trivialized as it is in *Mauberley*, and Varchi's question, "*Se pia? / O empia?*" (5/19), though ultimately unanswerable because "Both sayings run in the wind" (5/20), raises the question of man's finitude much more profoundly than do Pound's various *nekuiai*. In lieu of the timeless realm of Pound's Homeric underworld with its omniscient ghosts, Pound's recreation of this event depicts three individuals—Lorenzo, Alessandro, and Varchi—attempting to understand and shape the historical circumstances in which they find themselves. Finally, because Pound is striving for a clear delineation of ethical positives, the instances of linguistic interpretation or philological divagations in *A Draft of XXX Cantos* betray none of the whimsicality of the Laforguian logopoeia of *Propertius* and *Mauberley*.[14] Pound's consideration of the etymology of *enoigandres* results, as we have seen, in a powerful lyric vision, and even the philological exercise of "ἥλιος, ἄλιος, ἄλιος = μάταιος / ('Derivation uncertain'. The idiot / Odysseus furrowed the sand)" (23/107) is motivated by an underlying seriousness of purpose, which, as Guy Davenport explains it, is Pound's belief that "Stesichorus felt the tension of opposing meanings in *alios*, as though it were a pun, and symbolized in his poem the double nature of the word, growing and ungrowing, light and dark, order and confusion."[15]

Once more, therefore, we have delineated a strongly articulated tension between a Symbolist and post-Symbolist aesthetic, between a poésie pure and an epic voicing a series of moral imperatives, a tension reminiscent of the oscillation between the Gautieresque and Laforguian vision that we uncovered in *Mauberley*. However, while that analysis suggested the undeniable relevance to the *Cantos* of Laforgue's depersonalized and fragmented first-person voice, his enlarged decorum and extension of poetic diction and themes, and, finally, the Laforguian strategy of conflating past and present into a uniform surface,[16] it would appear that the singular emphasis on Laforgue, on Browning, or on the Gautier of "the intaglio method," has an extremely limited force and has perhaps obscured an even more revealing confluence of influences.

In face of this seemingly insoluble and characteristically Poundian dialectic, I would like to begin by suggesting that critical discussions of Laforgue's influence, while largely reliable with regard to *Mauberley*, are somewhat suspect when it comes to the *Cantos*, because they disregard what seems to me an important disequilibrium in Pound's critical writings about French poetry. Pound began in 1913, as we saw, writing about Régnier, Corbière, Tailhade, Romains, Vildrac, and Jammes. Then, in 1916, Pound "discovered" Laforgue and wrote "Irony, Laforgue, and Some Satire" in 1917. Finally, in 1918, before he embarks on his brief career as a dadaist, Pound returns in "Hard and Soft in French Poetry" and "A Study in French Poets" to those poets he discussed in 1913. Taken as a whole, his essays of 1918, despite his expanded discussion of Laforgue in "A Study in French Poets," focus primarily on poets who are completely unrelated to the Laforguian poetic operative in *Mauberley*. More interesting still, despite his growing aversion to the "softness" in poets like Samain and Heredia, Pound qualifies, albeit with a few reservations, his "semetaphorical [sic]" (*LE*, 285) and entirely prescriptive terms when he considers the *unanimistes*: "Romains, Vildrac, Spire, Arcos, are not hard, any one of them, though Spire can be acid. These men have left the ambitions of Gautier; they have done so deliberately, or at least they have, in quest of something well worth seeking, made a new kind of French poetry" (*LE*, 288).[17]

Pound's "Study in French Poets" might provide us a clue in determining what that "new kind of French poetry" might consist of, for, while much of this essay merely preserves or expands his insights of four years previous in the *New Age*, his discussion of Romains is considerably revised. Whereas in 1913 Pound discussed only Romains's more recent *Un être en marche* (1910) and *Odes et prières* (1913), Pound focuses his discussion in 1918 entirely on Romains's important *La Vie unanime* (1908). As with the other poets in his pantheon, Pound is initially attracted to Romains's poetic itself, to what Michel Décaudin describes as "un vocabulaire simple, direct, 'immédiat' . . . un vocabulaire de la dénomination, qui frôle la prose, qui 'donne à voir'" [a simple, direct and "immediate" vocabulary . . . a vocabulary of designation which approaches that of prose, one that "plays to the visual"].[18] Consider, for example, this passage quoted by Pound to illustrate Romains's method:

> Les marchands sont assis aux portes des boutiques;
> Ils regardent. Les toits joignent la rue au ciel.
> Et les pavés semblent féconds sous le soleil
> Comme un champ de maïs.
>
> Les marchands ont laissé dormir près du comptoir
> Le désir de gagner qui travaille dès l'aube.
> On dirait que, malgré leur âme habituelle,
> Une autre âme s'avance et vient au seuil d'eux-mêmes,
> Comme ils viennent au seuil de leurs boutiques noires.
>
> [The merchants are seated at the doors of their shops;
> They watch. The roofs join the street to the sky.
> And the cobblestones out in the sun
> Seem as fruitful as a field of corn.
>
> The merchants have let nap at the counter
> Their desire to earn hard at work since dawn.
> One might say that, despite their habitual nature,
> Another soul has arrived at the threshold of their selves,
> Just as they come to the doorstep of their dark shops.][19]

This cityscape composed solely of unmodified, concrete nouns—*portes des boutiques*, *les toits*, *les pavés*, *la rue*—exemplifies the restrained diction that appeals to Pound, who "happen[s] to be tired of verses which are left full of blank spaces for interchangeable adjectives" (*AP*, 631–33). André Cuisenier, for example, has noted that Romains "se contente, pour évoquer la nature, d'une vingtaine de mots, les plus simples ou les plus généraux" [contents himself with twenty or so of the most simple or most general words in order to evoke the natural world].[20] Discussing another passage, Pound says that Romains's style "has the freshness of grass, not of new furniture polish. In his work many nouns meet their verbs for the first time" (*Inst*, 73):

> La grande ville s'évapore,
> Et pleut à verse sur la plaine
> Qu'elle sature;
> La campagne alentour n'est plus
> Que de la ville diluée
> Dans la nature.

[The great city evaporates
And pours down onto the plain,
      saturating it;
The surrounding countryside's no more
Than the city being distilled
      Into nature.][21]

Both of these passages are representative of what Pound defines as
Romains's "perfectly simple order of words . . . the simple statement
of a man saying things for the first time" (*Inst*, 72), and of what
Décaudin describes as "une dynamique fondée sur le phrasé, voire sur
la syntaxe" [a dynamic grounded on phrasing, indeed on syntax].[22]

In addition to these stylistic issues, Romains provides Pound with a
more contemporary model for representing the modern city, a model
that embodies the modernist "neo-primitivism" voiced in Pound's and
Gaudier's manifestos.[23] *La Vie unanime* was extremely significant be-
cause it contained a broad and well-defined expression of the collec-
tive spirit governing the enterprise undertaken at L'Abbaye de
Créteil.[24] The poem is a long, Whitmanesque "epic" comprised of a
series of interconnected "objective lyrics" describing life in the me-
tropolis in all its complexity. The poet walks down bustling city streets,
goes to the theater, and walks past military barracks, all the while real-
izing that he is participating in this vast collective existence and that he
cannot extricate himself from it in order to create an autonomous ego.
What attracts Pound is Romains's "general replunge of mind into in-
stinct, or this development of instinct to cope with a metropolis. . . .
[his] regaining for cities a little of what savage man has for the forest"
(*Inst*, 70). Pound quotes these lines to illustrate a modernist "growing,
or returning, or perhaps only newly-noticed, sensitization to crowd
feeling; to the metropolis and its peculiar sensations" (*Inst*, 71):

Je croyais les murs de ma chambre imperméables.
Or ils laissent passer une tiède bruine
Qui s'épaissit et qui m'empêche de me voir.
Le papier à fleurs bleues lui cède. Il fait le bruit
Du sable et du cresson qu'une source traverse.
L'air qui touche mes nerfs est extrêmement lourd.
Ce n'est pas comme avant le pur milieu de vie
Où montait de la solitude sublimée.

Voilà que par osmose
Toute l'immensité d'alentour le sature.

Il charge mes poumons, il empoisse les choses,
Il sépare mon corps des meubles familiers,

Et l'attache, là-bas, à des réalités
Que les murailles exilaient dans l'autre monde.

Les forces du dehors s'enroulent à mes mains.
Oh! comment faire avec ces guides inconnues?

[I thought the walls of my room impermeable.
But now they're letting in a tepid drizzle
Which becomes even denser and keeps me from seeing myself.
The blue flowered wallpaper withdraws before it. It sounds
Like a river flowing over sand and through cress.
The air touching my nerves is extremely heavy.
This is no longer that pure milieu
Where arose a sublimated solitude.

Voilà, as though by osmosis
The surrounding expanses saturate the air.

It makes my breathing heavy, it makes things viscous,
It separates my body from its familiar surroundings,
And attaches itself to those realities down there
That these walls had banished into another world.

These external forces flow in my veins.
Oh! what will I do with these unfamiliar reins?][25]

Although Romains is much more a poet of the immediate present than Pound, both possess a largely Bergsonian intuition of flux, and their poetry presupposes the existence of gods—the "bust thru from quotidian into 'divine or permanent world.' Gods, etc." (*LE*, 210)— who manifest themselves as creative energy beneath inert social matter not yet subject to the rigidity fostered by everyday perception and conventional authority.[26] And although the Williams of *Paterson* is much closer in spirit to Romains's "vie unanime," we can see a similar sense of a perpetual "present" and of the permeability of the physical environment in one of Pound's few attempts to represent the metropolis:

We also made ghostly visits, and the stair
That knew us, found us again on the turn of it,
Knocking at empty rooms, seeking for buried beauty;
. . . .
　　　　The Elysée carries a name on
And the bus behind me gives me a date for peg;
Low ceiling and the Erard and the silver,
These are in "time." Four chairs, the bow-front dresser,
The panier of the desk, cloth top sunk in.

> "Beer-bottle on the statue's pediment!
> "That, Fritz, is the era, to-day against the past,
> "Contemporary." And the passion endures.
> Against their action, aromas. Rooms, against chronicles.
> Smaragdos, chrysolithos; De Gama wore striped pants in Africa
>
> (7/25)

Finally, and perhaps most important, Romains's unanimisme provides Pound with another, more modern example of a poet who, like Laforgue, has "dipped his wings in the dye of scientific terminology" (*LE*, 283). According to Cuisenier, "Le nombre des termes scientifiques paraît supérieur; il exprime, à la fois, le rôle des sciences dans la société moderne, et quelques-unes des principales curiosités de Romains. La physique . . . lui révèle un monde de forces, d'atomes, de molécules en harmonie avec sa propre vision des multitudes humaines" [Scientific terms are more numerous; they express both the importance of science in modern society and some of Romains's principal interests. Physics reveals to him a world of forces, atoms, and molecules that harmonizes with his own vision of human multitudes].[27] Similarly, biology, sociology, and philosophy play important roles in Romains's poetry, and, given his own "sperm-essay,"[28] Pound could hardly overlook such lines by Romains as these:

> Il est très fort; il est le sperme d'une foule.
> D'immenses mouvements se compriment et bouillent
> En lui; toute une mer déferle dans ce dé;
> Et la Ville, qui vient d'assassiner le Groupe,
> A sentir le passant tressaille, fécondée.
>
> [He is very strong; he is the sperm of a crowd.
> Immense movements are compressed and then released
> In him; an entire ocean unfurls in this thimble;
> And the City, which had just assassinated the Group,
> Swoons at the touch of the passerby, and became pregnant.][29]

Pound is strongly aware that scientific and philosophical thought are central to the poetry of both Laforgue and Romains, and, remembering his own laments about not having an "Aquinas-map" for his long poem, we should, I think, be attuned to the respect Pound pays Romains in this passage:

> [Romains] has . . . tried to formulate this new consciousness, and in so far as such formulation is dogmatic, debatable, intellectual, hypothetical, he is open to argument and dispute; that is to say he is philosopher, and his

philosophy is definite and defined. . . . Romains has made a new kind of poetry. Since the scrapping of the Aquinian, Dantescan system, he is perhaps the first person who had dared put up so definite a philosophical frame-work for his emotions. (*Inst*, 71)

Though Pound's appreciative response to Romains's "system" and his emphasis on the "dogmatic, debatable, intellectual [and] hypothetical" is surprising given his frequent diatribes against didactic verse, against "ideas" dressed up with poetic ornament, he reiterates his belief in Romains in an April 1918 letter attempting to pursuade John Quinn that Romains should become French Editor of the *Little Review:* "Jules Romains is ideologue, and undoubtedly mars his work by riding an idea to death. If he didn't he probably wouldn't give himself the opportunity of getting out the really good part of his stuff. He seems to me about the only 'younger' man in France whose head works at all" (*SL*, 133). And Pound pays Romains perhaps his greatest possible compliment by comparing him to Wyndham Lewis:

> Among all the younger writers and groups in Paris, the group centering in Romains is the only one which seems to me to have an energy comparable to that of the Blast group in London. . . . As for those who will not have Lewis "at any price," there remains to them no other course than the acceptance of Romains, for these two men hold the two tenable positions: the Mountain and the Multitude. (*Inst*, 76–77)

The best "formulation of the Unanimiste Aesthetic, or 'Pathetique'" (*Inst*, 79), Pound argues, is contained in Romains's "Reflexions" in *Puissances de Paris*. Romains begins his essay by asserting "that there are in the world beings more real than man" (*Inst*, 79). This "being," says Romains, is that of the group, the crowd in the street, the metropolis:

> Where does la Place de la Trinité begin? The streets mingle their bodies. The squares isolate themselves with great difficulty. The crowd at the theatre takes on no contour until it has lived for some time, and with vigor. A being (*être*) has a centre, or centres in harmony, but a being is not compelled to have limits. He exists a great deal in one place, rather less in others, and, further on, a second being commences before the first has left off. Every being has, somewhere in space, its maximum. Only ancestored individuals possess affirmative contours, a skin which cuts them off from the infinite.
>
> Space is no one's possession. No being has succeeded in appropriating one scrap of space and saturating it with his own unique existence. Everything over-crosses, coincides, and cohabits. Every point is a perch for a

thousand birds. Paris, the rue Montmartre, a crowd, a man, a protoplasm are on the same spot of pavement. A thousand existences are concentric. We see a little of some of them. (*Inst*, 81–82)

Romains's unanimisme is based on the primacy of sense experience and emotions, not on abstract reason: "As spirals of smoke from village chimneys, the profound senses of each organ had mounted toward him; joy, sorrow, all the emotions are deeds more fully of consciousness than are the thoughts of man's reason. Reason makes a concept of man, but the heart perceives the flesh of his body" (*Inst*, 79–80). As Cyrena Pondrom puts it, Pound was attracted primarily to Jules Romains's "new definitions of *being* in which the poet played a major role as the intelligence which gave voice to a vision of order not part of the traditional way of viewing experience." Moreover, argues Pondrom, "It was such conceptions of multiple perspectives and of the continuous interpenetrating nature of matter . . . that lay behind such steps toward artistic abstraction as analytical cubism and futurism."[30]

This pantheistic fallacy, this interpenetration of beings fostered by a strong identificatory desire, becomes, according to Pound, "almost a religion," and, given his fervent discussion in *Gaudier-Brzeska* of "moods" and "emotional motifs" as the basis of imagism, we should not be too surprised that he praises Romains's "series of 'prayers'—to the God-one, the god-couple, the god-house, the god-street, and so on" (*LE*, 288), or that he continually quotes from passages like the following in order to illustrate Romains's *pathétique:*

> Je suis l'esclave heureux des hommes dont l'haleine
> Flotte ici. Leur vouloir s'écoule dans mes nerfs;
> Ce qui est moi commence à fondre. Je me perds.
> Ma pensée, à travers mon crâne, goutte à goutte,
> Filtre, et s'évaporant à mesure, s'ajoute
> Aux émanations des cerveaux fraternels
> Que l'heure épanouit dans les chambres d'hôtels,
> Sur la chaussée, au fond des arrière-boutiques.

> [I am the contented slave of these men whose breath
> Floats about me. Their will flows through my nerves.
> What was me begins to dissolve. I lose myself.
> My thought seeps, drop by drop, through my skull,
> And evaporating immediately, adds itself
> To the emanations of fraternal minds
> Blooming at this hour in hotels,
> In the roadway, and in rooms at the back of shops.][31]

Pound's interest in Romains attests to the fact that he was not wholly opposed to the incorporation of systematic or philosophical thought into verse, but his overly simplistic characterization of these two exclusive poetic positions—Lewis's Mountain and Romains's Multitude—inscribes poetry in an overt political ideology and anticipates Pound's subsequent political confusion regarding the nature of a "conservative revolution."[32] We can see the seeds of this political-philosophical confusion as early as 1913 when Pound suggests through his rhetoric that the unanimist Romains is an advance over the "pre-unanimist" Charles Vildrac: "Romains flows into his crowd, or at least he would have us believe so. The subject of M. Vildrac's poem is of the Nietzschean, pre-unanimist type. He tries to impress his personality on the crowd and is disillusioned" (*SP*, 363). In 1918, however, although Pound suggests that "Lewis on giants is nearer Romains than anything else in English" (*Inst*, 70), we can see that Pound's earlier qualifications ("at least he would have us believe so") and seemingly negative terms (the "Nietzschean, pre-unanimist" disillusionment) are given a positive valence and that Pound too becomes an ideologue of sorts by siding with Lewis over Romains, with the Mountain over the Multitude: "Quant à moi? Caveat! Beware of agglomerates."[33] Pound warns us, "There is in inferior minds a passion for unity, that is, for a confusion and melting together of things which a good mind will want kept distinct" (*Inst*, 70). And in a strange rhetorical ploy, Pound gives Romains's own very personalized terminology a Nietzschean slant in order to dissociate once and for all Lewis's Giant and Romains's "esclave heureux des hommes": "vorticism is, in the realm of biology, the hypothesis of the dominant cell" (*Inst*, 70).[34]

.   .   .

Pound's intriguing reference to "Lewis on giants" refers to a whole series of Lewis's quasi-Nietzschean articles appearing at Pound's instigation in the *Little Review* beginning in 1917.[35] Although Pound's "Study in French Poets" (Feb. 1918) preceded any actual mention by Pound of Lewis's "giants," we must suppose that Pound had access to his manuscripts, including a March letter, where Lewis talks about "twenty men . . . conglomerated into a giant,"[36] and, more particularly, his play, "The Ideal Giant," which appeared in the May 1918 *Little Review*.[37] In all of these pieces, Lewis adopts Nietzsche's vocabulary to describe his own intense disdain for the "gentleman-animal" who belongs "to a distinguished herd":[38] "I feel that we are obviously in the position of Ulysses' companions; and there is nothing I resent more than people settling down to become what is sensible for a swine. I will still stalk about with my stumpy legs, and hold my snout high, however absurd it may be."[39] Borrowing once more from Nietzsche, the philosopher of the Mountain,[40] Lewis urges us "to stick to the Code of the Mountain," to avoid "herd-hypnotism,"[41] and he warns us that "*There are very stringent regulations* about the herd keeping off the sides of the mountain."[42]

"The Ideal Giant" is in every sense a dramatization of Nietzsche's theory of the mask as set forth by Lewis in "The Code of the Herdsman," the central tenet of which is the schizophrenic quest for a multiple personality: "Cherish and develop, side by side, your six most constant indications of different personalities. . . . *Never* fall into the vulgarity of being or assuming yourself to be one ego. . . . Contradict yourself. In order to live, you must remain broken up."[43] The play revolves around writer-journalist John Porter Kemp, who prides himself on his newly discovered and hard-won ability to lie (badly, thereby conforming to the Herdsman's Code)[44] and, by so doing, to create a continuous series of disparate selves (or Masks): "The Ego's worst enemy is Truth. . . . Self. Self. One must rescue that sanity. Truth, duty—are insanity" (9). In his mysterious relation with Miss Rose Godd, Kemp continually calls for them to do "any wildly subversive action" to "escape from the machine in ourselves" (15), but his highly intellectualized "standards for *action* are so difficult" (17) that, in order to meet them, Miss Godd completely surprises Kemp by murdering her banker-father in a parodic (psychotic) reenactment of "the greatest recent event."[45] As the detective arrests Miss Godd, "Kemp sits with his white profile, and large eye distorted with shame and perplexity. He springs up, partly disappearing behind the table, where he is noticed to have seized the Detective by the collar" (18). Typically, Lewis reverses polarity here by having the coldly intellectual Kemp react with "shame and perplexity" and subsequently respond to the deeds of a woman who "feels that her intelligence is not quite good enough for her company: but [whose] pride in what she considers her latent power of action brings her into steadfastness" (14). Although Kemp espouses an abstract version of Egoism, Miss Godd lives the theory, following Stirner's dictum that "the self-willed egoist is necessarily a criminal, and his life is necessarily crime."[46]

The explicit contrast Pound draws between Lewis and Romains must refer, however, to this interesting passage where Kemp discusses the "opposition between the individual and the community" (9):

> KEMP. A hundred men is a giant. A giant is always rather lymphatic and inclined to be weak intellectually, we are told. He is also subject to violent rages. Just as legendary men were always at war with the giants, so are individuals with society.

That exceptional men can be spoilt by the world is a commonplace. But consider another thing. See how two or three distinguished people lose personal value in a mob—at a dinner, at a meeting. Their personalities deteriorate in a moment—for an hour or two. They hardly ever become the head and brain of the Giant.

FINGAL. That doesn't apply to all men. It is due to some weakness in the personality. Some shine most.

KEMP. Ah, yes. But examine those shiners by themselves, and look steadily at their words and acts. Theirs is a practical and relative success. The *solitary* test is the only searching one. The fine personality loses, in every case by association. *The problem in life is to maintain the Ideal Giant.*

The artist is the Ideal Giant or Many. The Crowd at its moments of heroism also is. But Art is never at its best without the assaults of Egotism and Life.

For the health of the Giant as much as for that of the individual this conflict and its alértes [sic] are necessary.

Revolution is the normal proper state of things. (10)

This extremely dense passage is typical of Lewis in that its seemingly conflicting threads maintain a precarious dialectic that is constantly redefining itself. The "crowd" or "multitude" is seen as an ever-present threat to the fine personality's potential for individuation and is defended against by Zarathustra's "solitude." But, as with Zarathustra ("I must go *under*"[47]), this "solitary test" is ultimately rejected and gives way to the problem of maintaining the Artist. (As Pound suggested in a discussion of Lewis, "The artist is the antidote for the multitude" [*SP*, 426].) The Artist becomes "the Ideal Giant," representing and subsuming the Many, because he listens to the daemonic Life-forces both within and without, and because his necessary Egotism renders him impervious to "herd-hypnotism." Lewis's Ideal Giant, i.e., the great man or artist, is therefore necessarily always in conflict with society because "revolution is the normal proper state of things."

Thus, judging from Pound's critical essays of this period and his unqualified support of Lewis, we have to assume that Pound is moving closer to a Nietzschean perspective. Not only does Pound adopt Nietzsche's dichotomy between the "Mountain" and the "Multitude" set forth in Section 343 of *The Gay Science*, a dichotomy which, as we saw, would have been available to him through Lewis, but when he says, "for those who will not have Lewis 'at any price,' there remains to them no other course than the acceptance of Romains," he is almost certainly quoting from Section 344 where Nietzsche discusses "truth at any price" ("'Wahrheit um jeden Preis'")[48] in connection with his anti-metaphysical reversal of Platonism:

For you only have to ask yourself carefully, "Why do you not want to deceive?" especially if it should seem—and it does seem!—as if life aimed at semblance, meaning error, deception, simulation, delusion, self-delusion, and when the great sweep of life has actually always shown itself to be on the side of the most unscrupulous *polytropoi*.[49]

Referring to Odysseus *polytropos*, "the man of many ways,"[50] this passage can be seen as a kind of locus classicus from which the Poundian hero begins to emerge in full force (Malatesta, like Odysseus, is "a bit too POLUMETIS" [9/36]). As a result of his reading of Lewis and, in all probability, Nietzsche, we can see that Pound was already predisposed in 1917–18 to the type of hero that comes to the fore in the Malatesta Cantos.[51]

As Pound described Lewis's work in 1917, the central "motif is the fury of intelligence baffled and shut in by circumjacent stupidity" (*GB*, 93), and we can begin to discern in Pound's subsequent poetry a similar emphasis on the Artist as Enemy. In *Propertius*, for example, we can see how the zeal with which "Propoundius" attacks the Imperial poets now amounts to a siege mentality:

> Out-weariers of Apollo will, as we know, continue their Martian
>   generalities,
>   We have kept our erasers in order.
>
> .   .   .   .
>
> Annalists will continue to record Roman reputations,
> Celebrities from the Trans-Caucasus will belaud Roman
>   celebrities
> And expound the distentions of Empire,
> But for something to read in normal circumstances?
>
> (*P*, 205)

As a consummate satirist, Pound's Propertius is clearly superior to everyone around him, especially when his deprecating transformation of poets into mere annalists serves to shift the onus away from himself and onto others. But while *Propertius* constitutes an advance over Pound's previous personae in terms of its sustained and coherent presentation of a "circumjacent stupidity," his portrait of this consummate satirist is nonetheless compromised by Propertius's ironic perspective on his position as a lyric poet in Imperial Rome and, ultimately, by his resigned acceptance of the prevailing hierarchy of poetic forms. Thus, when Pound happens upon Malatesta as a potential "hero" for his cantos, his concern is to capture that "*fury* of the intelligence baffled and shut in": "If I find he was TOO bloody quiet

and orderly it will ruin the canto. Which needs a certain boisterous-
ness and disorder to contrast with his constructive work."[52]

Because the Malatesta Cantos have been thoroughly discussed by
recent critics, we need only say that they are pivotal to Pound's subse-
quent revision of the entire sequence.[53] Malatesta as a historical figure
answers several of the theoretical problems posed in Pound's *Three
Cantos*. First, Malatesta was undeniably possessed of "a certain bois-
terousness and disorder to contrast with his constructive work." As
any history will tell us, Malatesta's constant political skirmishing begins
to look a little like dada theater in its almost senseless nihilism. But
despite the historical pandemonium surrounding this figure, "He, Si-
gismundo, *templum aedificavit*" (8/32). Pound celebrates Malatesta's
Tempio—"the apex of what one man has embodied in the last 1000
years of the occident" (*GK*, 159)—and his patronage of the arts in an
era of incessant political intrigue, treachery and violence: "He had a
little bit of the best there in Rimini. He had perhaps Zuan Bellin's best
bit of painting. He had all he cd. get of Pier della Francesca. Federigo
Urbino was his Amy Lowell, Federigo with more wealth got the sec-
onds. . . . All that a single man could, Malatesta managed *against* the
current of power" (*GK*, 159). With their emphasis on Malatesta as ar-
tifex, the Malatesta cantos become, as Pound subsequently argues,
"openly volitionist, establishing . . . the effect of the factive personal-
ity" (*GK*, 194). In sum, they present us with a renaissance version of
Lewis's Ideal Giant, for whom "Art is never at its best without the as-
saults of Egotism and Life."

Second, against wholesale condemnations of Malatesta by such his-
torians as Burckhardt and Symonds,[54] Pound's research enables him
to write a revisionist account of Malatesta's life (subsequently corrobo-
rated by modern historians like P. J. Jones)[55] and to show, as Michael
Harper has previously argued,[56] how history can be subject to care-
ful reconstruction according to a stylistic analysis of historical docu-
ments. Pound incorporates these documents into the fabric of his
poem, forcing the reader to distinguish between them according to
their different stylistic registers. Thus, he intends that we dismiss
"Trachulo's damn'd epistle" (10/42) as evidence for Sigismundo's
conspiracy against Siena because of Sigismundo's own disregard for
such pompous rhetoric: "Unfitting as it is that I should offer counsels
to Hannibal . . ." (9/40). Similarly, Pound makes certain that we recog-
nize the historiographical nature of the documents upon which the
history of Malatesta is based, that Pius's condemnation of Malatesta
may have more to do with his Sienese origins than with Malatesta's
crimes, and that we dismiss it on account of its bombast and, as Harper

describes it, its "lack of discrimination, the absence of an ordering moral intelligence and sensibility":[57]

> So that in the end that pot-scraping little runt Andreas
> >   Benzi, da Siena
> Got up to spout out the bunkum
> That that monstrous swollen, swelling s. o. b.
> >   Papa Pio Secundo
> >   AEneas Silvius Piccolomini
> >   da Siena
> Had told him to spout, in their best bear's-greased latinity;
>
> *Stupro, caede, adulter,*
> *homocidia, parricidia ac periurus,*
> *presbitericidia, audax, libidinosus,*
> wives, jew-girls, nuns, necrophiliast, *fornicarium ac sicarium,*
> *proditor, raptor, incestuosus, incendiarius, ac concubinarius,*

$$(10/44)^{58}$$

As numerous critics have argued, the stylistic and narrative shifts in the Malatesta Cantos lead to a radical transformation of Pound's subsequent poetic. They are rendered in what Peter D'Epiro terms a "deflated epic style" composed of prosaic and colloquial diction, humor, bathos, and irony, and, thus, mark a departure from the epic/vatic stance of Cantos 1–7.[59] This disjunctive, heterogeneous style provides the illusion that the objective "facts" of history, of the "real," have intruded into the realm of the poetic, leading many critics to view these cantos as cubist collage.[60] And to foster this illusion, Pound includes a number of narrative voices and an overwhelming amount of documentary evidence in order to assure us that his "revisionist" history of Sigismundo Malatesta is an objective one. Finally, adopting the strategy he discovered in *Propertius*, Pound lets his own imagistically rendered ruminations appear *ex profundis* upon the heavily annotated and well-documented page. Thus, in the Malatesta Cantos, Pound's imagistic descriptions of the terrain ("From the forked rocks of Penna and Billi" [8/30]) or his beloved monuments ("In the gloom, the gold gathers the light against it" [11/51]) are characteristically elegiac, the deepest expressions of Pound's sense of an Ideal Beauty, and yet they betray no mawkishness because they are embedded in "objective history."[61]

By extending this strategy to subsequent revisions of the entire sequence, Pound is able to balance his visionary moments against an objective history by having another person authorize or footnote his own subjective visions:

And the water is full of silvery almond-white swimmers,
The silvery water glazes the up-turned nipple.
How shall we start hence, how begin the progress?

(P, 232–33)

And in the water, the almond-white swimmers,
The silvery water glazes the upturned nipple,
        As Poggio has remarked.

(3/11)

Whereas *Three Cantos* continually foreground Pound's fundamental ambivalence about the relationship between truth and belief or truth and memory, Pound resolves this dilemma in his revisions by shifting the onus from memory to assertion. Although *Three Cantos* does contain glimpses of the poetic method toward which Pound is tentatively striving, the revised cantos depend upon Pound's ceasing his search for "another gate" to the divine world (P, 239) in order to concentrate on the literary texts themselves as objective facts or documents. Whereas Pound had maintained in *Three Cantos* that "now it's all but truth and memory,/Dimmed only by the attritions of long time" (P, 233), we have the sense in the *Cantos* that memory is no longer an issue because literature and language exist in the world and in a sense supersede individual consciousness. Literary texts become for Pound documents and specimens that possess an objective reality by virtue of their physical existence. The ideogrammic method presupposes an infinite number of fragments/texts that can be brought into conjunction by a discerning consciousness and can thus begin to embody an existent reality.

We can see how undeniably important the strategies developed in the Malatesta Cantos are for the *Cantos* as a whole, particularly in view of the middle cantos where the bulk of Pound's poetry concerns such subjects as Jefferson, Adams, and Chinese history, for these strategies permit the extended examination of exemplary figures in a temporalized, particularized milieu which, not surprisingly, serves to naturalize an extrinsic moral analysis: "IF moral analysis/be not the purpose of historical writing" (62/346). If Malatesta and his attempt to build the Tempio were the central focus and the culmination of *A Draft of XVI Cantos*, Cantos 17–30 provide a wide panorama of the cultural *resorgimento* in which, according to Pound, Malatesta played a central role. These cantos contain a series of colloquially rendered historical vignettes done in much broader strokes in the manner of the Malatesta Cantos. Larger blocks of cantos are devoted to only two eras (Renaissance Italy and Modern Europe/America), permitting each canto to have its own historical density, thematic development, and documentary flavor (decrees of the Council Major, newspaper articles, personal reminiscences, etc.). After having developed this documentary technique in the Malatesta Cantos, Pound seems concerned to provide a historical backdrop against which the Malatesta Cantos can be read; thus, we have the extended treatment of Este's Ferrara, Medici Florence, the Council Major and Venice, and the Borgias, with Malatesta himself making occasional appearances (as he does in Venice's attempt to preserve a balance of power by means of its duplicitous negotiations with both the Pope and the Malatestas). Pound intends the "doings" of Renaissance Italy to provide a strong contrast to the *abuleia* represented most effectively in the popular songs and literature ("Stretti," Jammes's *Clara d'Ellébeuse*, etc.) of Europe before the war. This contrast is all the more easily achieved since Pound is almost forced to provide a prosaic account of his times given that the names available to him have none of the epic grandeur and historical resonance of the Medicis or the Borgias:

> "So there was my ole man sitting,
> They were in arm-chairs, according to protocol,
> And next him his nephew Mr. Wurmsdorf,
> And old Ptierstoff, for purely family reasons,
> Personal reasons, was held in great esteem
>   by his relatives,
> And he had his despatches from St. Petersburg,
> And Wurmsdorf had his from Vienna,
> And he knew, and they knew, and each knew
> That the other knew that the other knew he knew,
> And Wurmsdorf was just reaching into his pocket,
> That was to start things, and then my ole man
> Said it:
>   Albert, and the rest of it.
> Those days are gone by for ever."

                                                        (19/87)

Even the industrialists and munitions makers, the root cause of modern evil in Pound's eyes, are seen as total incompetents: "War, one war after another, / Men start'em who couldn't put up a good hen-roost" (18/83). As in the Malatesta sequence, Pound lets the historical milieu criticize itself by speaking in its own voice. Instead of highlighting an epic hero, this ironic presentation now highlights a speaker in search of the "facts," although one who does not yet have the assurance voiced in the middle cantos: "Seventeen / Years on this case" (46/231). From this point on, the major key of the *Cantos* has been sounded; henceforth, in the middle cantos at least, Pound's lyrical gift is subordinated to the prosaic realism necessitated by the economic and historical issues that Pound sees as the basis for a modern renaissance. He presents us with an increasingly programmatic and didactic emphasis on distributive economics and government control of credit, and he continually contrasts the conspiracy of greedy men with "models of the properly directed will"[62] (Jefferson, Adams, Leopoldo, Jackson, Confucius, Mussolini, etc.) who epitomize Pound's notion of the "factive personality." Pound's very Emersonian vision of early America is one of an aristocracy of intelligent men who, like Pound, and, to his mind, unlike the European aristocracy, are students of (human) nature, whether through empirical observation or the study of literature and history. The American Revolution comes to stand for constructive change imposed by the will of men who are capable of building a new civilization because they are attuned to the organic rhythms of the natural world.

And with his discovery of the Monte dei Paschi in Siena, the "second episode" of the *Cantos* (*GK*, 194), Pound has an even firmer foundation—"a base, a fondo, a deep, a sure and a certain" (43/219)—for his visionary economics. Unlike the Bank of England with its reputed power to create money ex nihilo, the Mount is guaranteed by profits from grazing rights and is thus based on the abundance of nature. Pound is now able to incorporate into his poem a mythological vision based on a conservative agrarian ethos because the natural foundation of the Mount has all the appearances of a modern banking institution and yet avoids what are, to Pound's mind, usurious—because ungrounded and thus artificial—economic practices. In response to a predominant Keynesianism, Pound espouses a largely Physiocratic economic theory and cultivates the agrarian mythos voiced in Hesiod or the *Li Ki*, both of which emphasize a scrupulous attention to natural rhythms and work. Like the Physiocrats, Pound locates value in the fecundity of a nature which "habitually overproduces" (*SP*, 233). Whereas modern economic thought views nature in terms of continually escalating expenses necessary to support an ever-increasing population, classical thought maintains that "all wealth springs from the land; the value of things is linked with exchange; money has value as the representation of the wealth in circulation"[63]; objects have value because they come to represent the fulfillment of universal needs, not because they possess any intrinsic worth. Whereas modern economic thought bases its analysis of value on the time and labor embodied in the object, classical economics depends upon the notion of an established identity between the sign and the thing represented.[64] So too does Pound join the "money-as-sign" faction, arguing that money is not a commodity, but is valuable solely because of its form, its representational value as a sign: "The moment man realizes that the guinea stamp, not the metal, is the essential component of the coin, he has broken with all materialist philosophies" (*GK*, 188). Pound's theory of money is entirely representational, permitting an identity between the sign and the thing represented and, because value is grounded in nature, between word and world.

This contiguous relationship between nature and society set forth in the middle cantos leads to Pound's dream of a natural, holistic language whereby thought goes into action in an almost unmediated fashion. This language is predicated on the absolute transparency of the sign, so that, as in this sad example, the sign reflects without distortion the essence: "Mussolini a great man, demonstrably in his effects on events, unadvertisedly so in the swiftness of mind, in the speed with which his real emotion is shown in his face, so that only a crooked man cd. misinterpret his meaning and his basic intention" (*GK*, 105). Having begun the *Cantos* hesitatingly and in a mode that shares some of the same flaws for which he criticizes Yeats, Pound finally adopts in the Chinese Dynasty Cantos a Confucian historiography that allows him to link together word and world, the mythical and the historical, the personal and the social. This totalitarian view of history permitted Pound to think in terms of an earthly paradise created in one generation by the intelligent dictatorship of a prince surrounded by "savants and artists."[65]

·   ·   ·

Fortunately, history proved Pound wrong. But even without the benefit of hindsight, we can, I think, see that Pound's epic project would never have succeeded. In the first place, Pound's ideogramic method contains a fatal flaw that doomed from the outset his "objectivist" poetic. Based upon Ernest Fenollosa's *Chinese Written Character as a Medium for Poetry*, a treatise that Pound indefatigably championed as the basis for a new poetics, Pound's ideogramic method is an intriguing admixture of linguistic speculation that appears to contain at one and the same time the seeds of a modern reflection on language and a resurrection of a preclassical tropological space. Written as an attack on the syllogistic logic that Fenollosa claimed was prevalent in modern linguistic discussions, *The Chinese Written Character* privileges the verb over the noun and copula governing the logical proposition.[66] In its very foundation, then, Fenollosa's and Pound's emphasis on the verb recapitulates a similar emphasis on the verb occurring with the advent of comparative philology in the nineteenth century. Whereas a classical nominalism depended entirely on the copula linking the two terms of the proposition, Foucault has argued that comparative philologists succeeded in undermining classical representation through their analysis of verbal radicals and their inflectional endings:

> As a result, it is not the adjunction of the *to be* that transforms an epithet into a verb; the radical itself contains a verbal signification, to which derived inflectional endings of the conjugation *to be* add merely modifications of person and tense. Originally, therefore, the roots of verbs designate not 'things', but actions, processes, desires, wills. . . . Verbs (and personal pronouns) thus become the primordial element of language—the element from which it can develop.[67]

From this view, language is a language of action "'rooted' not in the things perceived, but in the active subject,"[68] a formulation not unlike Fenollosa's "Will is the foundation of our speech" (*CWC*, 29).

But where Pound and Fenollosa see this "activity" as proof that language intersects the external world, Foucault's discussion of nineteenth-century comparative philology suggests that language becomes an entity with its own history and internal mechanisms for generating itself. As a result, the temporality incorporated into the thinking about language can only parallel the historicity of man. Thus, we have come to view language as being completely and irreparably divorced from the external world. Because subjectivity is linked to a finite consciousness living in a material present and subject to death, a poetics that includes the *Will* of a speaker can no longer coincide with the circularity of a world composed of signatures that infinitely reflect themselves in their full presence.[69]

Given this modern account of language, Pound's adaptation of Fenollosa's linguistic theory raises two problems. First, the traces within language of a spoken history effaced by time bring with them, almost of necessity, a reflection on temporality and, ultimately, on death, which, as Foucault argues, is the ground for any understanding of the predicament of modern man. The linking of an epic discourse to such a temporally grounded, finite subjectivity vitiates both the objectivity and the universality of the *chêng ming*, the word made perfect, and undermines the thrust of Pound's intent to "tell the tale of the tribe." At this juncture, Pound is very much caught up in a discursive loop, for his "modern" theory of the verb has folded back onto a medieval worldview, and his "medieval" doctrine of signatures has generated an unwanted finitude. Second, even if Pound is able to ignore this subjective residuum and uphold Fenollosa's "doctrine of signatures," there arises within this simple system of resemblances an infinite sliding of signs that makes impossible the creation of what Hugh Kenner calls the "hierarchy of values" effected by Pound's "isolating either volitional dynamics or persistent emotional currents from hundreds of different material contexts."[70]

To put it in the context of Pound's poem, the central drama of the *Cantos* is not the historical conflict between good and evil men, but a tension between the immediate presence of the sign-as-signature and the absence inscribed in language with the passing of time. In other words, there is an unbridgeable chasm between a language system that includes its own mode of dispersion and an exegetical desire to impose a fixed and imperiously univocal signification, between Pound's doctrine of signatures and his ideogramic method, on the one hand, and his critical project of translation, commentary, and exegesis on the other. In the case of Pound's description of his meeting with Professor Lévy, we see how closely this poetic of translation and exegesis is intertwined with an actual present and with a manifest desire. Pound's/Lévy's attempt to determine the meaning of the Provençal *de noigandres* becomes possible as a result of his ability to situate or read himself into that Provençal environment and to construct a context for a specific utterance:

> Sound: as of the nightingale too far off to be heard.
> Sandro, and Boccata, and Jacopo Sellaio;
> The ranunculae, and almond,
> Boughs set in espalier,
> Duccio, Agostino; *e l'olors*—
> The smell of that place—*d'enoi ganres*.
> Air moving under the boughs,
> The cedars there in the sun,
> Hay new cut on hill slope,
> And the water there in the cut
> Between the two lower meadows; sound,
> The sound, as I have said, a nightingale
> Too far off to be heard.
> And the light falls, *remir*, [I gaze]
> from her breast to thighs.

(20/90)

Although, as Kenner notes, Pound ultimately adopts Professor Lévy's solution to this crux ("and wards off boredom"),[71] he only hints at it here, leaving the reader to discover it for himself and leaving Pound room to elaborate upon his vision. As we can see, Pound's philological enterprise is motivated by a desire to write poetry, and that poetry is itself a product of desire. Lyric visions arise from the play of differences, from the "sound . . . too far off to be heard," from the flickering of the lamplight, the play of presence and absence.

This scintillating and never wholly delimited play of binary differences (light and dark, sound and silence) characterizes the visionary moments of the *Cantos*, and it is here that Pound's poetry most closely approximates the energy and texture of a poésie pure. The energy unleashed with this play of differences becomes erotically charged, and brings with it a reflection on the passing of time and on mortality. Pound's use of the Provençal *remir* subsumes the present within a textual past that includes Pound's reading of the troubadour poets and reiterates, as well, his troubled account of the contemporary world in Canto 7. The movement from Este to Helen in Canto 20 is only an elaboration of this same movement from the Provençal *e quel remir* to Nicea in this passage from Canto 7:

> Lamplight at Buovilla, e quel remir,
> > And all that day
> Nicea moved before me
> And the cold grey air troubled her not
> For all her naked beauty, bit not the tropic skin,
> And the long slender feet lit on the curb's marge
> And her moving height went before me,
> > We alone having being.
> And all that day, another day:
> > Thin husks I had known as men,
> Dry casques of departed locusts
> > speaking a shell of speech . . .
> Propped between chairs and table . . .
> Words like the locust-shells, moved by no inner being;
> > A dryness calling for death;
>
> > > > > > (7/26)

Although Pound establishes a strong contrast between ideal beauty and the empty "husk of talk," his vision of Nicea is subverted by her suicide, an act which is perhaps the ultimate existential gesture and which merits more consideration than Pound's empty condemnation of the present:

> Square even shoulders and the satin skin,
> Gone cheeks of the dancing woman,
> > Still the old dead dry talk, gassed out—
> It is ten years gone, makes stiff about her a glass,
> A petrefaction of air.
>
> > > > > > (7/26)

Very characteristic of Pound's reflections on women, this passage wholly ignores any consideration of Nicea's internal psychology and places the blame for her death entirely on the "old dead dry talk." Pound cannot understand, countenance, or represent her mental suffering, and he reverts, as he does so often, to the intaglio method in order to aestheticize, or plaster over, a potentially dark vision.

Evident at the outset of Pound's career, this tendency became the foundation of his aesthetic in *Lustra*, as we saw, and it is certainly central to his revision of the *Cantos*. In the *Cantos*, Pound has Tiresias preempt the *Three Cantos'* "news of many faded women— / Tyro, Alcmena, Chloris" (*P*, 245), and, from this point until Tyro and Alcmena return in the *Pisan Cantos*, women become important only insofar as they are framed and controlled by an authoritative male voice. In the China Cantos, for example, the sheer abundance of his negative portraits of women—"and the hochang ran the old empress / the old bitch ruled by prescription" (54/287)—shows how far removed Pound is from his early "spirit of romance." Moreover, his attempts to silence women have an artistic correlative which, as in the Nicea episode, "makes stiff about her a glass,/ A petrefaction of air." In Canto 2, for example, Pound's mythical "Ileuthyria, fair Dafne of sea-bords" (2/9), is metamorphosed into coral while fleeing a band of tritons, and Tyro is seized and raped by Neptune:

> And by the beach-run, Tyro,
>   Twisted arms of the sea-god,
> Lithe sinews of water, gripping her, cross-hold,
> And the blue-gray glass of the wave tents them,
> Glare azure of water, cold-welter, close cover.
>
>   (2/6)

Here, we can see that Pound feels compelled to impose what amounts to an Apollonian form on a Dionysian energy or ecstasy (or *pain*) that is in the process of becoming more and more threatening to Pound.[72] Just as Pound in the Malatesta Cantos cavalierly dismisses "the row about that German-Burgundian female" (9/36), we are now asked to disregard the implicit violence in his mythological set pieces because they enable the poet to celebrate and make eternal the forma of hitherto subjective and thus transcient perceptions. Recalling Pound's allusion in *Mauberley* to Gautier's rendering of Daphne's plight ("'Daphne with her thighs in bark / Stretches toward me her leafy hands,'— / Subjectively" [*P*, 193]),[73] we could therefore conceivably adopt the critical commonplace that Pound is merely adhering to Gautier's programmatic intent to "sculpte, lime, cisèle":

> Sculpte, lime, cisèle;
> Que ton rêve flottant
>   Se scelle
> Dans le bloc résistant!

[Carve, file, chisel;
    So that your floating dream
        is fixed
    In the resistent block.][74]

But this petrifaction is due neither to an overly simplistic artistic agenda nor to simple misogyny on Pound's part. The tension is real, and it is implicit not only in his ideogramic method but also in the poetic tradition Pound celebrates and in which he himself is still firmly situated. I began this chapter with a discussion of Jules Romains's important influence as a poet who could realistically represent modern life in the modern city; I now want to suggest that this influence is still operative in Pound's poetic even though he has opted for Lewis's Mountain over Romains's Multitude and has set himself firmly down on the side of the artifex, on the side of the "factive personality" and Lewis's Ideal Giant. In short, I argue that there are two Romains in Pound's pantheon, the realist and the visionary, and that what drew him to Romains is precisely that bifurcated vision we find in Gautier. Indeed, we have already witnessed this visionary thrust in Pound's discussion of Romains's *pathétique* wherein, as André Cuisenier has described it, Romains "se fond dans le Nous" [dissolves in the We].[75] Transliterating instead of translating, we have a sound formulation for what Robert Duncan has described as Pound's movement toward the Empyrean realm of the *Nous* wherein Aphrodite appears as a manifestation of the "higher intellect in which Beauty has become a pure essence."[76]

Throughout this study, we have seen Pound wavering between a Flaubertian (Realist), a Mallarméan (Parnassian-Symbolist), and a Baudelairean (Romantic) Gautier. And although he praises only one aspect of Gautier's poetic—the hard statement—Pound's doubts, hesitations, and the symbolist play of sympathies contained in his "ghostly visits" and glimpses of paradise in Cantos 17–30 suggest that Pound is unwilling or unable to adopt his new prosaic mode. Pound's visionary moments consistently rely on a melopoeia governed by repetition and parallelism in such a way that the verse proceeds by incremental differences which begin to attain an autonomy over the supposed sense-pattern or idea contained in the image; in other words, such lyrical passages privilege language *as* language in a manner that undermines the clarity and hardness of the "prose tradition." While Pound rhapsodizes about Gautier's "perfectly plain statements" and attempts to follow him on this score, it is the Gautier of the "rêve flottant" singled out by Baudelaire and Mallarmé who comes to the fore in these early cantos and works to rend the fabric of the early cantos as a whole. In what follows, then, I argue that the attempt to identify Pound with the "poet as sculptor" backfires and, just as a subjectively elegiac Pound appears in the gaps and crannies of his "long poem including history," a romantic Pound reappears beneath the Gautieresque persona Donald Davie has captured so perfectly in the title of his study.

In advancing this argument on behalf of Pound's Gautieresque program, most discussions of these lines tend not to look beyond the initial line of the concluding stanza of "L'Art." With the simple shift of emphasis from "le bloc résistant" to the "rêve flottant," or in Gautier's case "la rêverie méditerranéenne,"[77] we discover a poem that argues for a mysterious world wherein matter and spirit are entirely interchangeable, a subjective, visionary world that Pound himself acknowledges when he appends the word "Subjectively" to his translation of Gautier's vision of Daphne. Whereas the Ovidian myth of Daphne's metamorphosis so important to both Gautier and Pound suggests a compensatory attempt on the part of a thwarted sexual or artistic desire to eternalize the fleeting moment in the real world, "Dans le bloc résistant," Gautier's allusion to this myth in "Le Château du Souvenir" occurs during a hallucinatory "promenade au Musée,"[78] which reverses the metamorphic trajectory in Ovid by having the painted images of Gautier's dead friends and lovers come to life:

> L'image au sépulcre ravie
> Perd son aspect roide et glacé;
> La chaude pourpre de la vie
> Remonte aux veines du passé.
>
> [The image in the open coffin
> Loses its stiff and frozen cast;
> The hot flush of the living
> Rises in the veins of the past.][79]

Similarly, "Affinités Secrètes," the opening poem of *Émaux et Camées* and one strangely ignored by Poundians discussing Gautier's influence, reverses the direction of artistic desire and, as with a drug-induced or hallucinatory state, suggests that this hidebound world of appearances can be dissolved and that a mysterious, primordial vision can be attained:

> Marbre, perle, rose, colombe,
> Tout se dissout, tout se détruit;
> La perle fond, le marbre tombe,
> La fleur se fane et l'oiseau fuit.
>
> .   .   .   .

Par de lentes métamorphoses,
Les marbres blancs en blanches chairs,
Les fleurs roses en lèvres roses
Se refont dans des corps divers.

[Marble, pearl, rose, dove,
All dissolves, all's destroyed;
The pearl melts, the marble falls,
The flower fades, the bird flees.

. . . .

Through slow metamorphoses,
White marble into white flesh
And rose flowers into red lips
Are made anew in other bodies.][80]

In Gautier's poetry, as in Pound's, the formal constraints of verse, the "sculpture of rhyme," serve only to contain a proliferating world of correspondences, sympathies, and "affinités secrètes" which compose the "rêve flottant." Gautier's visionary world is a paradoxical world composed of concrete, yet somewhat blurred, particulars which reflect one another and intermingle in a complex play of analogy. Whereas Pound's ideogramic method presupposes a "masculine" association or dissociation of particulars, Gautier's paradisal visions require a passive receptivity much like the drug-induced states recorded by Gautier: "Mon ouïe s'était prodigieusement développée, j'entendais le bruit des couleurs. Des sons verts, rouges, bleus, jaunes, m'arrivaient par ondes parfaitement distinctes" [My hearing was prodigiously developed. I heard the sound of colors. Green, red, blue and yellow tones over-whelmed me in waves that were perfectly distinct].[81]

Georges Poulet has with a great deal of penetration described the dilemma that results from Gautier's "aperception simultanée de l'éternelle beauté' et de l'éternel travail de dissolution qui en accompagne la présence" [simultaneous perception of "eternal beauty" and the eternal state of disintegration which accompanies it].[82] Attempting to reverse the typical romantic trajectory from "l'immanent au transcendant, du réel vers l'idéal," Gautier, "partant de l'idée abstraite, va chercher dans la réalité l'occasion d'incarner son idéal, de lui donner chair et substance" [Gautier, departing from the abstract idea, will search for an occasion to incarnate his ideal in the real world, to give it flesh and blood].[83] But whenever Gautier witnesses this reincarnation of eternal beauty in a temporal being, he also experiences a sense of déjà vu whereby "L'espace d'un instant, le sentiment de vivre dans le présent fait place à celui d'être transporté dans un passé infiniment lointain qui apparaît comme la vraie patrie temporelle" [For the space of an instant, the sensation of living in the present yields to one of being transported to an infinitely distant past which now seems the real temporal realm].[84] Poulet has convincingly demonstrated how Gautier, following Nerval's interpretation of *Faust*, attempts to escape this "rythme spasmodique" by adopting the Neoplatonic doctrine of emanation with its grounding concept of uninterrupted presence and plenitude: "Le platonisme initial de Gautier a donc fini par se méta-morphoser en un panthéisme d'allure mystique, qui se relie à Plotin et à toutes les doctrines d'émanations" [Gautier's initial Platonism is ulti-mately transformed into a pantheism with its mystical allure, a panthe-ism that returns to Plotinus and the doctrine of emanations].[85] In Gau-tier's eyes, Goethe's realm of the Mothers, the abode of the goddesses and of such immortal forms as the beautiful Helen, "ne contenait pas un passé immobile, un passé mort, mais des forces toujours actives, un passé toujours vivant et mouvant" [does not contain an immobile, dead past, but forces that are forever active, a past that is forever living and in motion].[86] As Gautier puts it:

> Goethe, dans son second Faust, suppose que les choses qui se sont passées autrefois se passent encore dans quelque coin de l'univers. Le fait est, selon lui, le point de départ d'une foule de *cercles excentriques* qui vont agrandissant leurs orbes dans l'éternité et dans l'infini: dès qu'une action est tombée dans le temps, comme une pierre dans un lac sans bornes, l'ébranlement causé par elle ne s'éteint jamais, et *se propage en ondulations* plus ou moins sensibles jusqu'aux limites des espaces. Ainsi, dans son étrange poème, la guerre de Troie étend ses rayonnements jusqu'à l'époque chevaleresque; la belle Hélène monte dans le donjon en poivrière du moyen-âge.

> [Goethe, in his second Faust, imagines that the things of the past happen again in another corner of the universe. An act is, according to him, the point of departure for a series of *eccentric circles* which expand their radii to eternity and to infinity: once an action happens in time, like a rock dropped into a lake without limits, the agitation caused by it never dimin-ishes, but spreads in more or less perceptible undulations to the limits of space. Thus, in this strange poem, the Trojan War extends its rays to the age of chivalry; the beautiful Helen climbs a castle keep in the middle ages.][87]

Gautier's discussion, with its emphasis on Helen, on Neoplatonic ema-nations, and on medieval light philosophy,[88] corresponds almost point for point to Pound's own philosophical-poetic program and, in addition, provides further support for Wyndham Lewis's contention that Pound was a "time-philosopher," a closet Bergsonian.[89]

More importantly, Gautier's visions are haunted by what Poulet and others have described as Gautier's romantic "hantise de la mort" [obsession with death].[90] And if Pound is following in Gautier's footsteps, we should not be surprised that Pound's Gautieresque imposition of form serves to contain only temporarily the threat of this "Wilderness of renewals, confusion / Basis of renewals, subsistence, / Glazed green of the jungle" (20/92). Thus, if we stress the importance of Pound's similarly timeless moments, we might want to reexamine the importance of visions such as Niccolò d'Este's delirium after he executes Parasina and Ugo:

> Jungle:
> Glaze green and red feathers, jungle,
> Basis of renewal, renewals;
>
> .   .   .   .
>
> Zoe, Marozia, Zothar,
>   loud over the banners,
> Glazed grape, and the crimson,
> HO BIOS,
>   cosi Elena vedi,
> In the sunlight, gate cut by the shadow;
> And then the faceted air:
> Floating. Below, sea churning shingle.
> Floating, each on invisible raft,
> On the high current, invisible fluid,
> Borne over the plain, recumbent,
> The right arm cast back,
>   the right wrist for a pillow,
> The left hand like a calyx,
> Thumb held against finger, the third,
> The first fingers petal'd up, the hand as a lamp,
> A calyx.
>
>   (20/91–92)

The metamorphic transfiguration of air into water, the hand into the calyx of a flower and then a lamp, the blue-pale incense into a river, the lotus-eaters into flame, all of this argues for a powerful visionary experience wherein the real world is dissolved or fragmented and where the crystalline world, "the faceted air," suggests a welter of new forms which subsequently assume the solidity of a phenomenological reality. Although critics have seized upon his characterization of this

vision as being "jumbled or 'candied' in Nicolo's delirium" in order to
distance Pound from the overtly negative description of nature, this
"general paradiso" (SL, 210) is but another instance of the luminous,
crystalline world Pound himself seeks:

> "as the sculptor sees the form in the air . . .
> "as glass seen under water,
> "King Otreus, my father . . .
> and saw the waves taking form as crystal,
> notes as facets of air,
> and the mind there, before them, moving,
> so that notes needed not move.
>
> (25/119)

Pound's is a crystalline world of identities and luminous reflections:
"the glass under water, the form that seems a form seen in a mirror,
these realities perceptible to the sense, interacting, 'a lui si tirì'" (LE,
154).

And yet, as critics are suggesting when they describe this vision as
being merely a "delirium," we must remember that Este's vision of the
"glazed green of the jungle," occasioned by his grief after the execu-
tion of Ugo and Parisina, is introduced by the negatively charged cata-
log of unfaithful women and contains an underlying sentiment not
wholly dissimilar to the one expressed by Pound in Three Cantos: "So
much for him who puts his trust in woman./So the murk opens" (P,
236).[91] Este's/Pound's recollection of Dante's "cosi Elena vedi" (Inferno
5.64) only reinforces this radical transformation of Pound's spirit of
romance, since it now situates ideal beauty in the realm of carnal trans-
gressions. Thus, while critics are undoubtedly correct in stressing the
central role of metamorphosis in the Cantos as a whole, there are meta-
morphic passages in the Cantos which suggest that this "divine energy"
is as troubling as it is uplifting. In a passage that continues the lotoph-
agoi passage discussed earlier, for example, a poetry of Eros is coupled
to a sense of chaos and of the dissolution of self:

> The young seek comprehension;
> The middleaged to fulfill their desire.
> Sea weed dried now, and now floated,
>   mind drifts, weed, slow youth, drifts,
> Stretched on the rock, bleached and now floated;
> Wein, Weib, TAN AOIDAN
> Chiefest of these the second, the female
> Is an element, the female
> Is a chaos

An octopus
A biological process
                    and we seek to fulfill . . .
TAN AOIDAN, our desire, drift . . .

                                        (29/144)

Woman, says Pound, "is submarine, she is an octopus, she is/A biological process," and as such she is wholly opposed to the "factive personality" Pound now champions. Because he now begins to consider Wine, Women, and Song as soporifics which lead to the dissolution of Self, Pound's own poetic strength, *melopoeia*, can only be seen as becoming increasingly suspect, as being a lapse in the persona Pound had created for himself, as being, perhaps, a literal "return of the repressed." Whereas Pound was able to contain this fear of drifting in *Mauberley* by means of an ironic externalization of the self, his outbursts in the *Cantos* become progressively shrill when he is faced with the possibility of his own drifting.

Later in the *Cantos*, we again see and can begin to understand the threat posed by this very powerful, although somewhat unsettling, mirage or "form that seems a form seen in a mirror":

Miss Tudor moved them with galleons
from deep eye, versus armada
from the green deep
                        he saw it,
in the green deep of an eye:
        Crystal waves weaving together toward the gt/
                                healing

. . . .
Light & the flowing crystal
        never gin in cut glass had such clarity
That Drake saw the splendour and wreckage
        in that clarity
Gods moving in crystal
                        ichor, amor
                                (91/625)

Although generally considered a paradisal vision, and therefore a wholly positive one, this crystalline world, linked indelibly in Pound's mind to Cavalcanti's *Amor*, is governed by *virtù*, that principle of sympathy or attraction which "draweth likeness and hue from like nature" (36/178) and is so strong that, at its limit, it erases all distinction between subject and object. In the above passage, the overlay of numerous agents and objects of vision, the "ply over ply" of Poundian perception, obliterates any objective means of validating this vision, of determining who sees what in "the green deep." The idealized Lady here, as is often the case with Pound, becomes a narcissistic reflection, but a reflection which, in its attempt to represent a historical reality and an idealized love, is undercut by a threatening, fragmented perception similar to that in Pound's "Near Perigord": "And all the rest of her a shifting change, / A broken bundle of mirrors! . . ."[92]

As a result, Pound's lyric vision becomes increasingly problematic as *Cantos I–XXX* draws to a close. Although the struggle with language in the *enoigandres* passage highlights the effort needed to enter paradise, the *lotophagoi* passage discussed above foregrounds the threatening abuleia that attends the visionary moment. Pound's attempts to represent these visionary moments risk becoming an entirely too passive mode of transcendence and would tend to confirm Nietzsche's insight regarding what Pound later defined as melopoeia: "Etymologically, *melos* is a tranquilizer, not because it is tranquil itself but because its aftereffects make one tranquil."[93] Pound's melopoeic strain, once the access to another realm via an absolute rhythm that intersects the cosmos,[94] now runs counter to Pound's project of "dissociation" and becomes subject to question as the proliferating correspondences and linguistic free-play within language itself threaten to spill over into the natural world, "the green virid of the jungle," now seen as a dangerous, feminine principle which threatens to overwhelm and dissolve the Self. In order to escape this narcissistic world fostered by the assimilating power of sympathy, there must emerge from this play of reflection an antipathetical force which permits a regime of similarity to supplant a regime of identity.[95] Although Pound maintains that the form inheres in the thing ("the stone knows the form"), his "male principle" is nonetheless required in order for the form to manifest itself, and it thus becomes the cornerstone of Pound's effort to escape the visionary *imaginaire* created by his adaptation of the metamorphic tradition.

•　　•　　•

Although we can begin (perhaps) to understand Pound's increasing willingness in subsequent cantos to lend his voice to this "male principle," to delegate his authority as poet to those with greater political authority, his ideogramic rendering of ideology clearly fails as poetry. No matter how conscientious Pound's rendering of his *documenta inventa*, these "gists and piths" can be read in two different ways: as a sign pointing toward a present intentionality imbricated in a network of socialized communications, or as a signifier in a language system creating the conditions of its own dispersion. "Helenaus and heleptolis" ["destroyer of ships and destroyer of cities"], for example, is, as a citation, a textual whole; but because of its linguistic associations, it is scattered throughout the *Cantos* in the form of Helen and her metaphorical doubles. Because "le mot juste" is couched in a larger discursive structure without an explicit narrative control, it tends to resonate beyond its immediate context. Thus, although we might be tempted to uphold as an instance of Flaubertian realism this overly meticulous description of . . . . . . r and . . . . m in the Hell Cantos—

> And with them. . . . . . r,
>   a scrupulously clean table-napkin
> Tucked under his penis,
>   and . . . . m
> Who disliked colloquial language,
> Stiff-starched, but soiled, collars
>   circumscribing his legs,
> The pimply and hairy skin
>   pushing over the collar's edge,
>
>   (14/61)

—there is in the context of the *Cantos* as a whole a kind of reverse irony, an unintentional reworking of Flaubert's pointed counterpoint during the awards presentation in *Madame Bovary*, since the ironic rendering of Pius II's scatological testimony to Malatesta's character forces us to question both the propriety and the precision of Pound's own denunciation of modern England.

And it is precisely this polyphonic and uncontrolled use of quotation that undermines Pound's intent in the middle cantos. Despite Pound's new firmness of tone, his new didacticism buttressed by "authority" and "right reason," the reader of these cantos cannot help but be struck by the seeming chaos contained within the borders of Pound's China. Chinese historiography certainly permits Pound to telescope several thousand years of Chinese history and at the same time provide his reader with an archetype of the "just ruler," but we must in all honesty acknowledge the overwhelming number of *hochangs*, *taozers*, *bhud-foés*, *eunuchs*, and *mandarins* who clutter the poem. Whereas Pound vehemently argues that "No slouch ever founded a dynasty" (56/307), many of these "just rulers" often disappear in the space of a line as if to underscore Pound's bitter observation on the capricious nature of religious worship:

> halls were re-set to Kung-fu-tseu
> yet again, allus droppin' 'em and restorin' 'em
> after intervals.

$$(54/284)$$

What we see, but are loathe to admit, is how easy it is to lose the Mandate. Even Pound's blind faith ought to have been shaken by the failures following the implementation of an economic program very similar to the one he himself advocates:

> And Ngan saw land lying barren
>   because peasants had nowt to sow there
> whence said: Lend'em grain in the spring time
>   that they can pay back in autumn
> with a bit of an increase, this wd/ augment the reserve
> .   .   .   .
> and Ssé-ma; said, all right in theory
>   but the execution will be full of abuse
> they'll take it, but not bring it back
> TSONG of TANG put up granaries
>   somewhat like those you want to establish
> a measure of ten or twelve pounds cost no more than ten pence
>   and when the price was put up
>   they went on buying
>   and the whole province was ruined

$$(55/297–98)$$

Despite the purported existence of a comfortingly fixed moral/ natural order based on sound economic policy, Pound's presentation here makes it hard to deny that avarice is the operative natural law in this world and that Pound's "right reason" is a transcendent idea only remotely connected to the human, all too human, civilization set forth in these cantos as an exemplary model for a world on the brink of war. As these cantos progress, Pound's "right reason" is so distant from any natural order that it can better be called a law imposed from above; the Four Tuan or Four Foundations—"Justice, d'urbanité, de prudence" (85/558)—become abstract, nominalized entities that are pronounced by fiat. Pound's ideogramic method now begins to depend upon a rigid series of binary oppositions ("strife is between light and darkness" [52/259]), so much so that these oppositions somehow become an a priori philosophical support that petrifies the verse. There is assertion, but no process of discovery, and Pound's lyric voice is not implicated in this dialectic, or, if it is, the "I" can only emerge with the almost poignant collapse of these rigid oppositions. And with the subsequent collapse of the economic and historical foundations of both the poem and his *paradiso terrestre*, Pound's holistic, social language also breaks down, and truth becomes individual, mystical, and intermittent. Pound can only revert to his earlier poetics of Eros, his spirit of romance, for poetry has once again become, in Pound's contradictory formulation, "the assertion of a positive, i.e. of desire" (*LE*, 324).

L'ÉTERNELLE RITOURNELLE IN THE
LATE CANTOS

> Now behind this parapet imagine persons carrying
> along various artificial objects, including figures of
> men and animals in wood or stone or other materials,
> which project above the parapet. Naturally, some of
> these persons will be talking, others silent.
>   It is a strange picture, he said, and a strange sort of
> prisoners.
>
> —Plato, *The Republic*

THE *PISAN CANTOS* present Pound in propria persona, a "lover mur-
muring name upon name,"[1] as the historical circumstances in which
he finds himself break through into his consciousness in an endless
chain of immaterial presences and disembodied voices: "Only shad-
ows enter my tent / as men pass between me and the sunset" (80/529).
Undergoing this "nox animae magna from the tent under Taishan"
(74/451), Pound must, like the prisoners in Plato's cave, decipher and
name the shadows and sounds passing outside his tent, proceeding
by degrees from the darkness and shadows to the sunlit world and,
finally, the empyrean:

> or Anchises that laid hold of her flanks of air
>   drawing her to him
>   Cythera potens, Κύθηρα δεινά
> no cloud, but the crystal body
>   the tangent formed in the hand's cup
>   as live wind in the beech grove
>   as strong air amid cypress
>
> (76/470–71)

Where Plato's allegory differs from Pound's narrative, however, is
that, unlike Plato's "strange prisoners" forced to invent and then un-
learn, so to speak, their private idiolect, Pound by no means disabuses
himself of his "false" private language. Pound relies on his memories
of a live tradition as a means to withstand the assault of an uncontrol-
lable reality, to organize and lend significance to the chaos in which he

finds himself. The much-noted but seldom discussed reprises of his early poetry in these late cantos suggest an almost preconceived structure to the *Cantos* as a whole. The *Pisan Cantos* repeat many of the thematic elements from earlier cantos and thus give the later ones a retrospective coloring, as do the transpositions to a new key of the lynx hymn in "Heather" and the Elizabethan lyricism seen formerly in the "Envoi" to *Mauberley*. Moreover, as the above quotation reminds us, the Aphrodite of Canto 25 reappears after a long absence, providing a satisfying return to the spirit of romance at the heart of his early poetry. Finally, Pound reverts in this sequence to a mode of writing very similar to the one he had described in a 1910 letter to his mother: "My mind, such as I have, works by a sort of fusion, and sudden crystallization, and the effort to tie that kind of action to the dray work of prose is very exhausting. One should have vegetable sort of mind for prose. I mean the thought formation should go on consecutively and gradually, with order rather than epigrams."[2] Having experimented with a "vegetable mind" in The Chinese Dynasty Cantos, Pound now returns, as Hugh Kenner has noted, to fusion and crystallization: "Pound's 'armor against utter consternation' is not gotten 'by constant elimination' but by vigorous fusion. The *Pisan Cantos* comment on *Mauberley* in a way Pound furthered by incorporating plangent scraps of the earlier poem in Canto LXXIV."[3]

Kenner's fine observation should undoubtedly lead us to examine how the *Pisan Cantos* "comment on *Mauberley*." Among other explicit references to *Mauberley*, both Capaneus and Elpenor return in these cantos, fulfilling the Odyssean reversal forecast in both *Mauberley* and *Three Cantos*, and, after nearly a quarter of a century, Pound once again voices his "praise of [Pisanello's] intaglios" (74/451):

> as against the half-light of the window
> with the sea beyond making horizon
> le contre-jour the line of the cameo
> profile "to carve Achaia"
> a dream passing over the face in the half-light
> Venere, Cytherea "aut Rhodon"
> vento ligure, veni
> "beauty is difficult" sd/ Mr Beardsley
>
> (74/458)

If *Mauberley* was Pound's farewell to England, the *Pisan Cantos*, with their many echoes of that earlier poem, amount to a reconciliation: "Oh to be in England now that Winston's out" (80/528). Pound's affectionate and compelling portraits of his friends and acquaintances in London and Paris, his many memories of that happier time when he was at the center of the modernist revolution, provide a long overdue answer to Wyndham Lewis's overly nasty (although somewhat accurate) description of Pound as "a little crowd," who, "when he writes about living people of his acquaintance . . . shows himself possessed of a sort of conventional malice . . . [and] never seems to have *seen* the individual at all."[4]

Surprisingly, the Decadent tradition is strongly represented here in Pound's elegiac roll call of friends, literary heroes, restaurants, and works of art lost with the war. Apart from brief, almost cameo appearances by Pound's modernist associates, the center of gravity in these cantos is Pound's affiliation with the previous generation of poets:

> Swinburne my only miss
> and I didn't know he'd been to see Landor
>   *and* they told me this that an' tother
> and when old Mathews went he saw the three teacups
>   two for Watts Dunton who liked to let his tea cool,
> So old Elkin had only one glory
>   He did carry Algernon's suit case *once*
> when he, Elkin, first came to London.
>   But given what I know now I'd have
>   got thru it somehow . . .
>
>   (82/537)

The majority of portraits, and certainly the most compelling of them, depict those literary figures of the late nineteenth and early twentieth centuries (Yeats, Swinburne, Ford, Beardsley, Whistler, Francis Thompson, Symons, Binyon, and Blunt) who helped foster Pound's belief that he was part of a live tradition passed down from generation to generation.

The *Pisan Cantos* also lead to Pound's reconciliation with France. In 1924, Pound wrote to Lewis that he had been "rejuvenated by 15 years in going to Paris, and added another ten of life, by quitting same, somewhat arid, but necessary milieu."[5] Now, returning to the roots of English poetry in the centerpiece of Canto 81—Chaucer's "Your eyen two wol sleye me sodenly / I may the beauté of hem nat susteyne" (81/534)—Pound vividly reaffirms his insights of 1917: "France and England have always been at their best when knit closest. Our literature is always in full bloom after contact with France. Chaucer, the Elizabethans, both built on French stock" (*SP*, 200). Indeed, the *Pisan Cantos* constitute almost a second edition of his "Study in French Poets," and the interplay and cross-fertilization of English and French letters is foregrounded throughout, whether through "Symons remembering Verlaine at the Tabarin" (80/508) or through Pound's

reminiscences of his own involvement in the Parisian literary
scene:

> Judith's junk shop
>> with Théophile's arm chair
> one cd/ live in such an apartment
>> seeing the roofs of Paris
>
>>>> (80/518–19)[6]

Although Pound's French portraits tend to emphasize his own genera-
tion or those older post-Symbolists with whom he corresponded or
was acquainted (Cocteau, Vanderpyl, Barzun, Spire, de Souza, Tail-
hade, Gauthier-Villars, Mockel, Romains, Vildrac), the really poignant
passages are surprising celebrations of the previous generation of
Symbolist poets like Verlaine and Mallarmé:

> Serenely in the crystal jet
>> as the bright ball that the fountain tosses
> (Verlaine) as diamond clearness
>
> . . . .
>
> This liquid is certainly a
>> property of the mind
> nec accidens est   but an element
>>> in the mind's make-up
> est agens and functions   dust to a fountain pan otherwise
>
>>>> (74/463)

Hugh Kenner long ago masterfully described how "the one word
'Verlaine' assembles 'crystal' and 'jet' and sculptor under the sign of
his 'Clair de Lune' which closes with great ecstatic fountains among
statues ('les grands jets d'eau svelte parmi les marbres'),"[7] and we
would be very unfortunate indeed to lose this allusion, for "Clair de
Lune" has become a part of the *Cantos'* phantastikon, lending Pound's
Pisan landscapes the reflected glory of its "calme clair de lune triste et
beau."[8] But this very personal allusion to Verlaine is not primarily a
reference to "Clair de Lune," but rather to Verlaine's "Fountain
Court: à Arthur Symons." In an unpublished letter to Dorothy
Shakespear circa 1912, Pound quotes the last two stanzas of this poem,
saying "bar the tag 'vil souci' it is very fine, I think, Ça c'est la chose
qu'on appelle le style by the way":[9]

> FOUNTAIN COURT
> à Arthur Symons
> La "Cour de la fontaine" est, dans le Temple,
> Un coin exquis de ce point délicat

Du Londres vieux où le jeune avocat
Apprend l'étroite Loi, puis le Droit ample:

Des arbres moins anciens (mais vieux, sans faute)
Que les maisons d'aspect ancien si bien
Et la noire chapelle au plus ancien
Encore galbe—aujourd'hui . . . table d'hôte!

Des moineaux francs picorent joliment
—Car c'est l'hiver—la baie un peu moisie
Sur la branche précaire, et—poésie!
La jeune Anglaise à l'Anglais âgé ment . . .

Qu'importe! ils ont raison, et nous aussi,
Symons, d'aimer les vers et la musique
Et tout l'art, et l'argent mélancolique
D'être si vite envolé, vil souci!

"Et le *jet d'eau* ride l'humble bassin"
Comme chantait, quand il avait votre âge,
L'auteur de ces vers-ci, débris d'orage,
Ruine, épave, au vague et lent dessein.

["The court of the fountain" is, in the Temple,
An exquisite corner in this choice part
Of old London where the young lawyer
Learns a narrow Law, and then broad Rights:

The trees are less ancient (but old indeed)
Than the houses of ancient aspect
And the even older black chapel
Curving outward still—today . . . the host's table!

The free sparrows joyfully peck
—Because it's winter—at the musty berry
On the precarious branch, and—poetry!
The young English girl lies to the old Englishman . . .

What's it matter! they have their reasons, as we do,
Symons, to love verse and music
And all art, and the melancholy silver
So soon departed, base thought!

"And the *water's jet* wears the humble basin"
As sang, when he was your age,
The author of that line, debris of the storm,
Wreckage, flotsam, in the slow eddies of a vague design.][10]

Written to memorialize his stay with Symons in November of 1893,[11] "Fountain Court" sets forth an insistent contrast between age and youth, between Old London around the Temple and the young law student who "Apprend l'étroit Loi, puis le Droit ample." Also, between a young English girl and an older gentleman, between a young Arthur Symons and the now renowned Verlaine, and, finally, between the younger and elder Verlaine himself. Like "Clair de Lune," the poem contains the *jet d'eau*, but, more importantly, it also contains the "bassin" (basin, bowl, pan) so central to Pound's ecstatic vision in the *Pisan Cantos*: "dust to a fountain pan otherwise." Finally, "Fountain Court" would have a personal significance for Pound, now writing in the DTC at Pisa and comparing himself to the mad Cassandra, since he would recall that Symons and Verlaine were both plagued by mental instability, and because the last two lines of the poem contain an eerie foreshadowing of Pound's current role as shipwrecked Odysseus amidst "the wreckage of Europe" ("when the raft broke and the waters went over me" [80/527]): "débris d'orage, / Ruine, épave, au vague et lent dessein."

While the poem does not seem to me the "very fine" poem Pound thought it to be, it would have been important to Pound because it celebrates poetry, as well as the meeting of different nations and different generations, and thus suggests that there was indeed a "live tradition" that could be handed down, a tradition to which Pound was once privy. Although Kenner's analysis is in no way invalidated,[12] Pound's allusion to "Fountain Court" is thus not only a positive celebration of a presently existing crystalline world, but also a remembrance of the past and of what might have been. Like the elder Verlaine, Pound is looking back on his "green youth" and wondering, perhaps, if he had not made a grave mistake with his programmatic rejection of a symbolist tradition exemplified by Verlaine (or Anglified by the Rhymers Club).

In Pound's earlier life, despite his ostensible break with symbolism, he nonetheless remained connected to it through his personal contact with people like Symons, Yeats, and Albert Mockel (the editor of the Symbolist periodical *La Wallonie*), writers who were part of that generation of "rarer spirits" (*Inst*, 88) like Verlaine and Mallarmé. Despite his "native distrust of *la belle phrase;* of '*temps doré*,' '*ferveur*,' '*belle confiance*,' etc." (*Inst*, 89), Pound took great pride in the apparent similarities between Mockel's *La Wallonie* and the *Little Review* and was pleased that Mockel was "gracious enough to call [*La Wallonie*] 'Notre *Little Review* à nous'" (*Inst*, 88). Responding to a letter from Mockel saying "qu'il serait intéressant, au point de vue de l'histoire litteraire, de voir notre groupement d'alors, formé autour du noble Stéphane Mal-

larmé, jugé à un intervalle de vingtaine années par le représentant
d'un groupe étranger et nouveau" [it would be interesting, from the
standpoint of literary history, to see our group, which had formed
around the noble Stéphane Mallarmé, judged after an interval of
twenty years by the representative of a new, foreign group],[13] Pound
wrote to his father on the same day: "Oct. L. R. sent off today w/greet-
ings from Mockel edtr. of *La Wallonie* a Little Review that published
Mallarmé, Verlaine, Maeterlinck & co. from '85–92."[14] Pound was ob-
viously pleased with Mockel's praise of his "Study in French Poets,"
and with Mockel's suggestion that he, like Mallarmé, had established a
cénacle.

And interestingly, after having been expurgated in Pound's revi-
sion of the ur-Cantos, Mallarmé makes a surprising reappearance in
the *Pisan Cantos:*

> "Il est bon comme le pain"
> > sd/ Mockel of "Willy"
> (Gauthier Villars) but I cdn't explain to him (Willy)
> what the Dial wanted and Gluck's "Iphigénie"
> > was played in the Mockel's garden
> Les mœurs passent et la douleur reste.
> "En casque de cristal rose les baladines"
> > Mallarmé, Whistler, Charles Condor, Degas
> and the bar of the Follies
> > as Manet saw it, Degas,
>
> > > (80/518)

Pound's mention of Mallarmé here brings to mind that he once de-
scribed Mallarmé's "Sonnet en -yx" as "exquisite" (*Inst*, 90), and it re-
turns us to the ur-Cantos, where "Mallarmé/Played for a fan, '*Rêveuse
pour que je plonge*' " (*P*, 236). Mallarmé's cénacle is also being invoked
in this passage when Pound highlights the mysterious resonances con-
tained in the first line of Stuart Merrill's "Ballet":

> En casque de cristal rose les baladines,
> Dont les pas mesurés aux cordes des kinnors
> Tintent sous les tissus de tulle roidis d'ors,
> Exultent de leurs yeux pâles de xaladines.
>
> [In their rose-crystal casques the danseuses,
> Whose steps are measured by the chords of the lyre
> And resound beneath their silk and spun-gold attire,
> Exult through their pale Chaldean eyes.][15]

Discussing this poem in 1918, Pound describes it approvingly in terms that recall his own efforts to emulate Bion in *Mauberley:* "The particular sort of fine workmanship shown in this sonnet of Merrill's has of late been too much let go by the board. One may do worse than compare it with the Syrian syncopation of *Diona* and *Adon in* in Bion's Adonis" (*Inst*, 92). And the final line of the quatrain becomes a refrain in subsequent cantos, lending the poem a symbolist coloring and celebrating a poet whose death Pound lamented along with Gourmont's as a direct and horrible consequence of World War I.[16] Resurrecting a world that he had often condescendingly described as *à la 1880*, these sincere and poignant portraits indicate a solid and mature appreciation on Pound's part of the importance of French poetry for his own poetic. Indeed, if we return to Pound's justly celebrated Canto 74, we will see that his meditation on French poetry marks a significant thematic and tonal shift in the *Pisan Cantos* and signals the beginnings of a redemptory awareness on his part.

Pound opens the Pisan sequence with this unsettling deification of Mussolini: "Manes! Manes was tanned and stuffed, / Thus Ben and la Clara *a milano*" (74/439). Then, after finding his Odyssean persona wanting, Pound accepts his "martyrdom" and self-pityingly identifies himself with Christ: "lay there Barabbas and two thieves lay beside him" (74/441). This religious mystification is of course unconscionable, but, paradoxically, it is this very meditation on the Bible that enables Pound to reaffirm his allegiance to France and, thus, to restore poetic balance to the sequence:

> a man on whom the sun has gone down
> and the wind came as hamadryas under the sun-beat
>   Vai soli [sic]
>   are never alone
>   amid slaves learning slavery
>
>   (74/445)

At first glance, it would seem that Pound's quotation from Ecclesiastes 4.10—*vae soli* (woe to him who is alone)—is simply in keeping with the Biblical theme, a continuation of his earlier quotation from Ecclesiastes 4.9 ("tempus tacendi, tempus loquendi" [74/443]), and a bridge to the other allusions to Ecclesiastes scattered throughout these cantos: "all is vanity," "under the sun," as well as the possible relevance of the Preachers warning—"A fool multiplies words"—to Ouan Jin's plight: "Ouan Jin spoke and thereby created the named / thereby making clutter" (74/441).

But Pound's vae soli is a very over determined allusion that also pays homage to Laforgue's "Pierrot: scène courte mais typique," a poem that Pound translated early in his career:

Il me faut vos yeux! Dès que je perds leur étoile,
Le mal des calmes plats s'engouffre dans ma voile,
Le frisson du *Vae Soli!* gargouille en mes moelles . . .

Your eyes! Since I lost their incandescence
Flat calm engulphs my jibs,
The shudder of *Vae soli* gurgles beneath my ribs.

(*T*, 438)

Because Pound translated Laforgue's "Pierrot: scène courte mais typi-
que," we know that he was aware of the irony contained in these lines:
"oui, divins, ces yeux! mais rien n'existe/Derrière! Son âme est affaire
d'oculiste" [yes! eyes divine, but nothing much exists / Behind. Her
soul is something from the oculist's].[17] But in the above homage,
Pound negates Laforgue's vae soli in the following line—"are never
alone"—insisting that some reality does inhere in the divine eyes
watching over him. And with this realization, like a screen memory
once the veil is torn, the repressed past comes flooding back: "she did
her hair in small ringlets, à la 1880 it might have been,/red, and the
dress she wore Drecol or Lanvin/a great goddess, Aeneas knew her
forthwith/by paint immortal as no other age is immortal/la France
dixneuvième" (74/449).

Pound has here corrected his previously one-sided emphasis on the
bitterly ironic Laforgue and is finally able to hear the plaintive and
very human cry underlying Laforgue's poetic vision. With the setting
sun, the moon, the sound of the wind, all of which come to symbolize
death for Laforgue, Pound's homage incorporates in miniature many
of the images of Laforgue's mature poetic, a poetic which transcends
a juvenile irony and voices a belief in and love of life. Now, in view of
Pound's powerful evocations of the "green world," we would have to
look for a tonal similarity between Pound and the more mature La-
forgue of *Derniers Vers*, wherein we find this concluding affirmation of
life by a poet on the verge of death:

O Nature, donne-moi la force et le courage
De me croire en âge,
O Nature relève-moi le front!
Puisque, tôt ou tard, nous mourrons. . . .

[Oh Nature, give me courage and strength
To think myself of age at length;
Oh Nature, raise my confidence high
Since sooner or later we die. . . .][18]

I have already shown how the early Pound championed a greatly
simplified Laforgue whose defensive irony enabled him, in Pound's

mind at least, to triumph over "l'inconsciente femme" who is allowed neither speech nor thought. In the Pierrot poem just mentioned, for example, the woman is said to have nothing behind her gaze, and Pound goes one step further by omitting the woman's spoken lines from his translation. Similarly, in Pound's most Laforguian poem, Mauberley adopts the putative mentality of one of Laforgue's lovers when he "passe[s], inconscient, full gaze / The wide-banded irides / And botticellian sprays implied / In their diastasis" (*P*, 198). But here, in the *Pisan Cantos*, as Pound returns to "her eyes as in 'La Nascita'" (74/460), he eschews the false assurance and unearned superiority of Laforgue's ironic stance, and he expresses a refreshing openness and uncertainty in his interrogation of Being:

> Ed ascoltando al leggier mormorio [and listening to the gentle murmur]
>   there came new subtlety of eyes into my tent,
> whether of spirit or hypostasis,
>   but what the blindfold hides
> or at carneval
>   nor any pair showed anger
>   Saw but the eyes and stance between the eyes,
> colour, diastasis,
>   careless or unaware it had not the
>   whole tent's room
> nor was place for the full Εἰδὼς
> interpass, penetrate
>   casting but shade beyond the other lights
>   sky's clear
>   night's sea
>   green of the mountain pool
>   shone from the unmasked eyes in half-mask's space.
>   (81/534)

Pound's vision not only harkens back to the similar apparition of Aphrodite's "liquid" eyes in *Mauberley*,[19] but raises a question of philosophical import that will haunt our understanding of Pound as he embarks upon the last part of his career. Is Pound, despite his seeming adherence to an Aristotelian empiricism, an Idealist or even a Platonic Realist? The *eidos* that appears to Pound in his tent recalls not only John Burnet's discussion of Pythagoras, as Carroll Terrell suggests,[20] but also Plato and Plotinus after him. If he is referring to Pythagoras, we might be able to adhere to our ideas about Pound's monism, since nature provides a fundamental ground for the pre-Socratics that obviates the need to posit a dualistic separation between appearance and being. If to Plotinus, as is most likely given Pound's earlier mention of hypostasis, although a monism is still a tenable position if we invoke Plotinus's theory of participation and emanation, a "relaxed dualism"[21] will inevitably creep into our discussion because of his reliance on the idea of an absolute, ineffable, and unknowable One. Moreover, a strong, and very Platonic, dualism will without doubt arise when it comes to the problem of body and soul. Whatever our attribution, however, it severely qualifies, if not contradicts, our critical suppositions regarding the privileged status of Aristotle in Pound's pantheon, as well as the generally unchallenged notion of Pound's "this-world-liness."

Taking our cue from Pound's references to Plotinus in the late cantos, I think it is safe to assume that his question as to whether the "new subtlety of eyes" is "of spirit or hypostasis" stems directly from Plotinus's philosophical investigation of Love, a hypothesis which, if true, bears witness to the undiminished influence of Plotinus on Pound (who had no access to his writings while at Pisa) and begins to explain the Emersonian cast of the natural world depicted in the *Pisan Cantos*.[22] Plotinus begins *Ennead* 3.5 with a question very similar to Pound's regarding the apparition in his tent: "What is Love? A God [a divine hypostasis], a Celestial Spirit, a state of mind? Or is it, perhaps, sometimes to be thought of as a God or Spirit and sometimes merely as an experience?"[23] And just as the *eidos* appearing to Pound is that of Aphrodite, Plotinus is forced to postpone his discussion of Love for a consideration of Aphrodite "since in any case Eros is described as being either her son or in some association with her."[24] Finally, Pound's uncertainty regarding the nature of this particular eidos results because there are two distinct Aphrodites according to Plotinus: the heavenly Aphrodite, the daughter of Ouranos or Heaven, and an earthly goddess, the daughter of Zeus and Dione, "who presides over earthly unions." The Heavenly Aphrodite emanates from the *Nous* or Intellectual Principle, and thus represents "the Soul at its divinest . . . remaining ever Above . . . never having developed the downward tendency, a divine Hypostasis essentially aloof . . . justly called not Celestial Spirit but God,"[25] whereas the Celestial Spirit is a lesser hypostasis, "the representative generated by each Soul when it enters the Cosmos":[26] "In the same way we must conceive many Aphrodites in the All, Spirits entering it together with Love, all emanating from an Aphrodite of the All, a train of particular Aphrodites dependent upon the first, and each with a particular Love in attendance."[27]

Whatever the status of Pound's philosophical sophistication or, indeed, of Neoplatonism itself, Pound seems to be in fundamental agreement with philosophical assessments of Plotinus's metaphysical monism.[28] In Canto 91, Pound invokes his theory of emanation and participation to describe the GREAT CRYSTAL or *Nous* as a "Light *compenetrans* of the spirits" (91/625) into which the Princess Ra-Set climbs for protection. And, again, in Canto 100 Pound celebrates the temple of the mind:

hieron

nous to ariston autou

as light into water compenetrans

that is pathema

ouk aphistatai"

Thus Plotinus

per plura diafana

neither weighed out nor hindered;

aloof.

(100/735–36)

Despite the idealistic thrust of both passages, Pound seems to subscribe to a real connection between mind and nature fostered by the participation of Nous or Spirit within the world and revealed to the adept through θεωρία or *contemplatio*.[29] *Pathema*, as Eva Hesse argues, "describes a condition in which the dualisms of subject and object, knower and known are dissipated."[30]

And even at Pisa, "from the death cells in sight of Mt. Taishan" (74/441), Pound insists on the plenary aura of his metaphysics of "presence, contact and, best of all, unity."[31] In the manuscript of Canto 74 Pound places the ideograms Ta (5956: intelligent, apprehend) and Shang (5669: supreme, top, first) next to the line, "How soft the wind under Taishan" (74/463), transforming the Pisan landscape into a symbol of the Supreme Intellect or Nous. Then, in Canto 83, he takes Baudelaire and Yeats to task for failing to recognize this omnipotent and omnipresent being:

Le Paradis n'est pas artificiel

and Uncle William dawdling around Notre Dame

in search of whatever

paused to admire the symbol

with Notre Dame standing inside it

(83/542)

Pound is here conflating and criticizing the decadence of Baudelaire's *paradis artificiels*, the Christian idea of Redemption ("I don't know how humanity stands it/with a painted paradise at the end of it" [74/450]), and Yeats's metaphysical yearnings which render him oblivious to the beauty of the real object in front of him. Although Yeats's "symbol-hunting" seems a reasonable mise-en-scène of Plotinus's notion that the "body is inside the soul," as Pound himself later admits in Canto 113, this vignette mocks Yeats by linking him to Baudelaire and Plotinus, the two writers whom Yeats was eager to read during a 1926 vaction.[32] And indeed, Plotinus's discourse on Love adds a new twist to Pound's overtly critical examination of Baudelaire's dualistic vision of Paradise: "Le Paradis n'est pas artificiel/states of mind are inexplicable to us" (76/474). Pound's refrain echoes the opening of *Ennead* 3.5—"What is Love? A God, a Celestial Spirit, a state of mind?"—thus pointing to this interesting discussion of Natural Love:

> Those that go after evil are natures that have merged the Love-Principles within them in the evil desires springing in their hearts and allowed the right reason, which belongs to our kind, to fall under the spell of false ideas from another source. . . . Those forms of Love that do not serve the purposes of Nature are merely accidents attending on perversion: in no sense are they Real-Beings or even manifestations of any Reality. . . .[33]

Baudelaire's almost Manichean sensibility aside, Pound reacts to Baudelaire's *Fleurs du mal* with a combination of prudishness and moralism that echoes the sentiments of Plotinus.[34] Comparing Baudelaire to Villon, Pound lambasts the former for his self-conscious exploration of "unnatural" mental states, that is, "the spell of false ideas from another source," whereas he praises Villon because his actions are entirely unself-reflexive: "In Villon filth is filth, crime is crime; neither crime nor filth is gilded. They are not considered as strange delights and forbidden luxuries, accessible only to adventurous spirits. Passion he knows, and satiety he knows, and never does he forget their relation. . . . Villon's actions are the result of his passions and his weaknesses. Nothing is 'sicklied o'er with the pale cast of thought'" (*SR*, 173–76).

But, as Pound would have known, Evil poses a real problem for Plotinus because its threatening presence forever lurks within or beneath nature. Describing the possible manifestations of Eros and Aphrodite in this world, i.e., as Celestial Spirit or Real-Being, Plotinus tells us how this third Hypostasis, or Real-Being, descends into matter, thereby cutting itself off from the Intellectual Principle, and, thus, "is not perfect, not self-sufficient, but unfinished. . . . It includes within itself an aspiration ill-defined, unreasoned, unlimited—it can never be sated as long as it contains within itself that element of the Indeterminate."[35] This Indeterminate, or Evil, haunts the plenary vision of both Plotinus and Pound and threatens the equilibrium of the *Enneads* and the *Cantos*. Neoplatonism, as the name suggests, remains on the other side of the Platonic divide, retaining the distinction between the Intellectual and Sensory worlds, and the even sharper divisions between body and soul or time and eternity.

That Pound himself recognizes this occulted dualism is indicated by his subsequent endorsement of at least one Baudelairian Contrary ("Le paradis n'est pas artificiel,/l'enfer non plus" [76/474]) and by his continued conjunction of Confucius and Heraclitus, of the *process* and *panta rei*,[36] instead of Plotinus. And despite the visionary thrust of the *Pisan Cantos*, Pound in his sober moments will admit that he is stranded in the sublunary world:

> lay on the cliff's edge
> 　　　　. . . nor is this yet *atasal*
> 　　　nor are here souls, nec personae
> 　　　neither here in hypostasis, this land is of Dione
> and under her planet
> 　　　to Helia the long meadow with poplars.
> to Κύπρις
> 　　　the mountain and shut garden of pear trees in flower
> here rested.

> (76/472)

Recalling Plotinus's discourse on Love, we begin to suspect that Pound is here describing the earthly Aphrodite, "the daughter of Zeus and Dione," in the garden of Zeus. And although this garden is, for Plotinus, "a place of beauty and a glory of wealth" where "Life is eternally manifest,"[37] the Love that resides there is "of mixed quality":

> Its Mother is Poverty, since striving is for the needy; and this Poverty is Matter, for Matter is the wholly poor: the very ambition towards the Good is a sign of existing indetermination; there is a lack of shape and of Reason in that which must aspire towards the Good. . . . To the thing aspiring the Good is an Ideal-Principle distinct and unchanging, and aspiration prepares that which would receive the Good to offer itself as Matter to the incoming power.[38]

Throughout *Ennead* 3.5, Plotinus adopts both the rhetoric of a "scarcity economics" and an asceticism that appealed to Pound at Pisa, but would have been anathema to the poet of the thirties and early forties, who, in his own eyes, had succumbed to the "Charybdis of action" (74/445). More important, Pound's seeming agreement with Plotinus regarding the objective existence of the Ideal-Principle or Archetype, as opposed to Aristotle's *hekasta* or particulars, suggests a move away from an epic "tale of the tribe" and a return to an earlier poetic program. Indeed, Plotinus's discussion in *Ennead* 3.5 sheds considerable light on Pound's cryptic reference to the imagists' "secret doctrine": "There are souls to whom earthly beauty is a leading to the memory of that in the higher realm and these love the earthly as an image; those that have not attained to this memory do not understand what is happening within them, and take the image for the reality."[39]

What has happened to Pound's prior empiricism? A hidden dualism has infiltrated his thought. Starting in the *Pisan Cantos*, he returns to an earlier visionary Neoplatonism, to such heroes of the ur-cantos as John Heydon, Helen of Tyre, and Apollonius. Should we regard the Pisan and late cantos as a further development of the political agenda of Pound's middle period then? Or are they an admission of defeat, an acknowledgment that the philosophical ground of the *Cantos* has been cut away?

· · ·

        not in memory,
                        in eternity
                                and "as a wind's breath
    that changing its direction changeth its name"

                                        (106/766)

The celebrated reprise of Cavalcanti's "dove sta memoria" (76/466) in the *Pisan Cantos* seems to indicate a continued adherence to a volitionist ideology whereby ideas go into action with an almost unreflexive celerity as a result of individual virtù. For Pound, who devoted much time and effort to his edition of "Donna mi prega," Cavalcanti was the Aristotelian poet par excellence. Pound's early fascination with the poem stems from its supposedly heretical content derived from "experience" outside the bounds of church dogma, and Cavalcanti's propensity for "*natural dimostramento*" (*LE*, 159) enables Pound to equate Cavalcanti's *Amor* with Dante's and still maintain a manifestly untranscendental epistemology. But as the above epigraph suggests, Pound's understanding of Cavalcanti has altered in the course of the *Cantos*, and he now admits of a cleavage between the real and the ideal, between time and eternity.[40]

Although this metaphysical conflict was clearly evident in Cavalcanti, Pound had tended in his reading of "Donna mi prega" to ignore the darker aspects of the poem and to align it with the pristine radiance of medieval light philosophy. But, as J. E. Shaw has argued, Cavalcanti's *Amor* contains a potentially threatening dualism that undercuts his vision of the Beloved and differentiates it from Dante's spiritualization of Beatrice:

Cavalcanti's Love is not consciously religious or moral. . . . It becomes a
passion of body and soul for a real woman, in which the Supreme Good
. . . is forgotten. This passion is destructive and often disastrous, and the
mind of the poet broods with tender melancholy over the impossibility,
demonstrated again and again by experience, of holding permanently
the temporary realization of his ideal. . . . The conflict between sense and
idealism which for Cavalcanti constituted the complete actuality of Love,
so that there could be no end to that conflict without the extinction of the
passion, was settled by Dante with the complete abandonment of all
earthliness in his attitude to Beatrice.[41]

This unresolved conflict between the sensory world and the ideal
world in Cavalcanti may help us understand Pound's move toward a
more Dantescan vision in the later *Cantos*. Although the many Dantes-
can elements are certainly in keeping with the paradisal motif of the
poem, we might find in them a deeper significance, a "lived reality," if
we take Pound at his word when he says that he was not writing to a
schema. Of these elements, many are concerned with Dante's political
vision (e.g., "'Not political', Dante says, a / 'Campagnevole animale' /
Even if some do coagulate into cities" [95/657]). These support
Pound's early contention that "Dante strives constantly for a nobler
state on earth" (*SR*, 171). But with this ever-increasing predominance
in the *Cantos* of a visionary Dante, we begin to move away from a world
shaped by individual virtù toward a world governed from above. As
Pound also noted, Dante "sought to hang his song from the absolute,
the center and source of light; art since Dante has for the most part
built from the ground" (*SR*, 166). We begin to see, in other words,
that this vision of paradise is intermittent and governed from above
by Fortuna (96/670): "above the Moon there is order, / beneath the
Moon, forsitan" (97/691). Whereas the middle cantos posit a harmoni-
ous society wherein ordering principles are immanent, Pound in the
later cantos cedes the real world to chance and begins to seek first
principles that are not necessarily embodied in the real. While Pound
still insists that "In nature are signatures/needing no verbal tradition"
(87/587), there is a strong contrary movement toward "not a lot of
signs, but the one sign" (85/560).

    Although Pound continues to affirm the political program for
which he risked his life, he knows that his Roma can only be resur-
rected anigrammatically through Dantescan AMOR and that he too,
like Dante, must be content to "[live] in his mind" (*SR*, 177). Pound has
become what he said of Dante: "He is in the real sense an idealist" (*SR*,
177). If, as Peter Nicholls remarks, the Pound of the thirties read
"Donna mi prega" as a vorticist would, "not in terms of the syntax of

connected thought, but as a mobile ensemble of intersecting images,"[42] the later Pound reverses his emphasis on the "proportion" of the canzone and reintroduces a more Dantescan emphasis on the poem's "relation to an external and extrapolatable idea."[43] As in Plato's allegory of the cave, we have the sense that Pound's language of the *chêng ming*, of the *verbum perfectum*, is now but a sign pointing to a higher, ecstatic, and esoteric knowledge that exists in the "purple patches" of Pound's "Neoplatonicks, etc." And as a result of this neo-idealism, the speed, energy, and sudden crystallization of thought implicit in the idea of a vortex is superseded by a stillness and slowness reaching toward the condition of silence that concludes the *Cantos*. Instead of the sudden crystallization, we have a litany celebrating slowness: "Beauty is difficult" (80/525); "Slowness is beauty" (87/586); "So slow is the rose to open" (106/766).

Like Plato's strange prisoner who has seen the truth but, because he is a good legislator, must return to the darkness, Pound too faithfully returns to his research with an even firmer resolve. But where the natural/social order of the Chinese Cantos formed a plenum in which a person's needs could be adequately represented, valued, and satisfied, we begin to see the scarcity economics Pound continually inveighed against make its appearance in his understanding of language and literature and in his more or less Byzantine researches into the history of money and the law (e.g., the *Codex Justinianus* and *The Eparch's Book*). Although Pound still maintains his belief in a historic blackout, there also emerges the sense that loss is an integral part of the process and not merely the product of a few evil and usurious men:

> Le Paradis n'est pas artificiel
> >   but is jagged,
> For a flash,
> >   for an hour.
> Then agony,
> >   then an hour,
> >   then agony,
> Hilary stumbles, but the Divine Mind is abundant
> >   unceasing
> >   *improvisatore* [improviser]
>
> . . . .
>
> also desensitization
> >   25 hundred years desensitization
> >   2 thousand years, desensitization

After Apollonius, desensitization
    & a little light from the borders:
Erigena,
Avicenna, Richardus.

                             (92/634–36)

Pound's acknowledgment of "25 hundred years desensitization" takes us back to his early China, to the time of Confucius himself (551–479 B.C.), curiously implying that this process of desensitization arose with the advent of classical Greece or with the codification of Confucian precepts. Documents are no longer celebrated as things in themselves, but as metonyms related, though only tenuously, to a hidden truth. There is certainly "a little light from the borders," but, to develop the implications contained in this image, the source of that light is hidden in a way heretofore unsuspected in the course of his researches ("and with one day's reading a man may have the key in his hands" [74/441]). If we take Pound's image seriously, it transforms discourse into what is for Pound a largely unacknowledged and undesirable palimpsest comprised of marginalia, which, in essence, is precisely what the *Cantos* have become, a palimpsest, in other words, that can never attain, adequately reflect, represent, or embody its source or origin. And because this "desensitization" or sense of loss is now seen to be inherent in a temporal world, Pound's quest, not so much for an "originary" word but for "first facts," is necessarily comprised of an intermittent and almost passive vision.

Needless to say, it is precisely this intermittent and passive awareness that comes to the fore in the fragmented rendering of paradise in the late cantos, particularly in *Drafts and Fragments*. Just as the initially whimsical Laforguian moon imagery of the *Pisan Cantos* gains in emotional resonance, culminating in the magically dark rites celebrating the moon and the Imagination in Canto 106, so too is Pound's regard for Laforgue's Buddhist passivity gradually qualified. Although Pound is still attacking the Buddhists (or Lotophagoi) as late as Canto 99 for their lack of "chao⁴ kuan³ / care for control," this criticism is followed, whether unconsciously or not, by one of the more tranquil and appealing passages in *Thrones*:

But to live as flowers reflected,
                as moonlight,
free from all possessiveness in affections

                           (99/717)[44]

And though this halcyon state may well be, "as Chu says, egoistical"

(99/717), it is sought out by Pound with increasing frequency in the
late cantos as he pleads with his Undine to surface:

> (Yes, my Ondine, it is so god-damned dry on these rocks)
> "The waves rise, and the waves fall
> But you are like the moon-light:
>   Always there!"
>
>   (93/637–38)

Until, finally,

> Gold mermaid up from black water—
>   Night against sea-cliffs
>   the low reef of coral—
> And the sand grey against undertow
>   as Geryon—lured there—but in splendour,
> Veritas, by anthesis, from the sea depth
>   *come burchiello in su la riva*
> The eyes holding trouble—
>   no light
>   ex profundis—
> naught from feigning.
> Soul melts into air,
>   anima into aura,
>   Serenitas.
>
>   (111/797)[45]

   Although Massimo Bacigalupo rightly argues that "we are delighted
by the decisive 'sincerity' of the poet, who, after much simplistic parti-
tioning, confesses that he does not know what the word coming to him
from the depths ('ex profundis') will import,"[46] we must also realize
that such sincere uncertainty is symptomatic of a reversal of Pound's
earlier poetics of assertion and signals his new willingness to entertain
previously threatening and unexplored states of mind. The depths (ex
profundis), especially in conjunction with the mermaid-siren-undine
cluster, can be seen as an analogue for—and, thus, an acceptance of—
that aspect of Laforgue's poetic vision, the submarine world of the
Unconscious or Nirvana, that Pound had found so threatening (see
Canto 29's "She is submarine") and had censored in his translation of
Laforgue's "Salomé." As Pound says in his final homage to Laforgue:
"And I have learned more from Jules / (Jules Laforgue) since then /
deeps in him [my italics]" (116/810). And if we take seriously La-
forgue's iconoclastic characterization of Mallarmé as a Buddhist sage
who is an exemplary model for his own world of the Unconscious,[47]
Pound's acceptance of Laforgue also entails a return to the symbolist

aesthetic that he had rejected earlier in his career. Whereas Mallarmé purges chance, *le hasard*, to arrive at the Absolute as Negation (the Blank page, Silence), Pound arrives at the same condition of Silence through the concatenation of contingent *realia*, with the ideogramic method, by now the "Ixionic method," ceding its place to wind-speech:

> Do not move
>> Let the wind speak
>>> that is paradise.

>>>> (117/816)

Although it would be an injustice to Pound's strongly held political beliefs to suggest that Pound in the late cantos has finally found safe haven in a Mallarméan poésie pure, there are nonetheless similarities that cannot be ignored. Both Mallarmé and Pound had undertaken the task of writing a "Book of the World," be it "L'explication orphique de la Terre"[48] or "the tale of the tribe," and both poets invoke a doctrine of correspondences ("le démon de l'analogie") irrevocably sundered from a primordial logos. Finally, both poets believe that there is a Real World behind the world of appearances. If Pound has a strong idealistic bent as I have argued, we must ask ourselves how far removed Pound's various idealisms are from Mallarmé's brand of Hegelianism. After all, both Plotinus and Hegel are proponents of a spiritual monism, be it Nous or Absolute Spirit. And if Mallarmé can say that "la destruction fut [sa] Béatrice," so Pound argues that we must periodically "break the icons" in our search for another gate to the divine world.[49]

Despite his early diatribes against symbolism, Pound himself has a propensity for, and in his lyrical moments is possessed by, "le démon de l'analogie." In Canto 106, for example, Pound creates what Bacigalupo terms a "late mythologem" celebrating the hidden presence of the Moon.[50] Admittedly, Canto 106 also contains much material foreign to a poésie pure. If Mallarmé ascends rapidly from the world of objects to the noumenal world of ideas (*verba*), Pound links together heterogeneous images, words, objects, and documents, all the while insisting on their status as real things (*res*) in a real world. He introduces numbing legal matter such as Kuan Chung's nine decrees, Antoninus's "coin-skill," and Aristotle's *Xreia;* he packs the canto with very specific and concrete references to places and things ("Aquileia, caffaris, caltha palistris, / ulex, that is gorse, herys arachnites" [106/769]); and he opens with a strong deictic emphasis evoking not "la disparition élocutoire,"[51] but the real presence of the poet seeing, remembering, or pointing at "Venice shawls from Demeter's gown":

"And was her daughter like *that* [italics mine]; / Black as Demeter's gown" (106/766). The poet is groping for true definitions, and the snippets of texts Pound quotes are intended to point us to a real world wherein such events did indeed happen and did have a specific intent and significance:

> At Zephyrium, July that was, at Zephyrium
> The high admiral built there;
>   Aedificavit
>
> TO APHRODITE EUPLOIA
>   "an Aeolian gave it, ex voto
>   Arsinoe Kupris.
>
>   (106/769)[52]

And yet, like Mallarmé, Pound is seeking the eternal Word that remains obscure to us in our forever changing sublunary world:

> ὁ θεός [the god]
> runs thru his zodiac,
>   misnaming no Caledon,
> not in memory,
>   in eternity
>   and "as a wind's breath
>   that changing its direction changeth its name"
>   (106/766)

Because he is trapped in this lower realm, Pound, like Mallarmé, can only suggest by negation (*abolir*): "not Circe / but Circe was like that. . . ./'not know which god'/nor could enter her eyes by probing/the light blazed behind her / nor was this from sunset. . . ./ —violet, sea green, and no name./Circe's were not, having fire behind them" (106/768–69). Finally, Pound's ideograms become so unhinged by the play of reflections that they are no longer linked to a specific referent but resonate within the field of the poem, creating a tissue of symbols not unlike those of Mallarmé. Here, many sources of illumination blend together to form one unworldly light, and the canto's many goddesses—Kore, Demeter, Artemis, Aphrodite, Athena—are fused into one unnamed lunar goddess who inspires the poet's imagination.

Massimo Bacigalupo underscores the Mother-Daughter relationship in this canto in order to isolate "the one goddess of vegetation" central to the Eleusinian Mysteries (Demeter/Persephone, Persephone/Circe).[53] But it might be better to stress an upward movement (*aufhebung*) whereby Circe and Persephone are identified with, and then subsumed by, Artemis and, later, the unnamed Selene. Pound's repeated prayers to Artemis in Cantos 106 and 110 ("And in thy mind beauty, O Artemis") suggest that he is invoking her in her lunar aspect and that the communion described in Canto 106, though it takes place at dawn,[54] occurs during an interregnum period, much like Mallarmé's *minuit*, which harbors traces of Verlaine's (and Pound's) "calme clair de lune, triste et beau." Undergoing a visionary experience at St. Elizabeth's, Pound returns to his early Noh translations to find expression for his ecstatic vision of the moon "still delaying above, though we've no skill to grasp it" (*CNTJ*, 98). Here, indeed, "is a beauty to set the mind above itself" (*CNTJ*, 98):

> At Miwo the moon's axe is renewed
> HREZEIN
> Selena, foam on the wave-swirl
> Out of gold light flooding the peristyle
> Trees open in Paros,
> White feet as Carrara's whiteness
>
> in Xoroi.
> God's eye art 'ou.
> The columns gleam as if cloisonné,
> The sky is leaded with elm boughs.
>
> (106/769)

Given Pound's invocations to the moon-god celebrated in the *Hagoromo* and to Selena, it is entirely possible that Pound is not (only) referring to the Selenaea,[55] but (also) to Selene or Luna, who drives the moon's chariot (i.e., the flame's barge). If so, though unnamed, Selene is the reigning diety of this canto, and, instead of seeking proper definitions, Pound is following Mallarmé in "painting not the thing, but the effect that it produces."[56] Selene-Artemis-Aphrodite become God's eye riding the "light into water compenetrans" (100/736). The golden moonlight floods the grove of trees and magically transforms it into a marble temple—"the palace of the moon-god is being renewed with the jeweled axe" (*CNTJ*, 102)—and then into the Xoroi whom Pound envisions dancing the Tennin's dance "symbolical of the daily changes of the moon" (*CNTJ*, 98). As in one of Mallarmé's night sonnets, the real world is banished in the play of reflections so that the poem itself becomes a veritable Temple of Art with its "columns gleam[ing] as if cloisonné." More than an arcane prayer to the moon, Canto 106 becomes a ritual celebration of what Pierrot has called the Decadent Imagination.[57]

Pound's allusion to the *Hagoromo* in Canto 106 is a particularly rich one, because it foregrounds the intersection of two very different applications of the material given Pound by Fenellosa's widow. For

Yeats, the Fenellosa papers enabled him to invent a modern symbolist drama adequate to "the mystical life." Describing the Noh in 1916, Yeats wrote: "When I remember that curious game the Japanese called . . . 'listening to incense,' I know that some among them would have understood the prose of Walter Pater . . . the poetry of Mallarmé and Verlaine."[58] For Pound, on the other hand, they gave rise to the ideogramic method and, as a consequence, dictated the unfolding of Pound's "poem including history" up to and including this visionary moment. But now, Pound reverses course and, after a long absence, returns to the mysterious world depicted in Gautier's "Symphonie en blanc majeur" (and, as we have seen, in Pound's own "Alchemist"):

Sur les blancheurs de son épaule,
Paros au grain éblouissant,
Comme dans une nuit du pôle,
Un givre invisible descend.

. . . .

A-t-on pris la goutte lactée
Tachant l'azur du ciel d'hiver,
Le lis à la pulpe argentée,
La blanche écume de la mer;

Le marbre blanc, chair froide et pâle,
Où vivent les divinités;

. . . .

Le vif-argent aux fleurs fantasques
Dont les vitraux sont ramagés;
Les blanches dentelles des vasques,
Pleurs de l'ondine en l'air figés? . . .

[Upon her bare white shoulders,
So dazzling, a Parian white,
An invisible rime descends,
As blinding as a polar night.

. . . .

Hast 'ou siezed the milky drops
Bespattering the azure winter sky,
The lily's silver pulp,
Or the white foam of the sea;

The white marble, pale-cool flesh,
Wherein live the ancient gods;

. . . .

The quicksilver in those strange flowers
Found in the cathedral's stained glass;

> The white lace at the fountain's base,
> Undine's tears frozen in midair? . . .] [59]

Here we find not only the Parian goddess(es), the "foam on the wave-swirl" ("La blanche écume de la mer"), and the "lead glass windows" of Canto 106, but also the divine "Ondine" who surfaces in Canto 93 and 111. Moreover, given the close connection between Cantos 106 and 110, we ought to include Pound's return to the Daphne depicted in Gautier's "Château du Souvenir":

> Laurel bark sheathing the fugitive,
>   a day's wraith unrooted?
>   Neath this altar now Endymion lies
>
> (110/793)

Is it too farfetched to see Pound firmly situating himself in the tradition of Mallarmé's "Toast Funèbre" and laying Gautier to rest here? Nonetheless, he inscribes in this honor roll a sense of loss which makes possible the poet's continued renewal of the word:

> God's eye art 'ou, do not surrender perception.
> And in thy mind beauty, O Artemis
>   Daphne afoot in vain speed.
> When the Syrian onyx is broken.
>   Out of dark, thou, Father Helios, leadest,
> but the mind as Ixion, unstill, ever turning.
>
> (113/804)

With this final bow to Gautier, Pound returns us not to the Gautier of "Carmen" but to the ideal Mallarméan poet of "La Nue":

> Elle plane dans la lumière
> Plus haut que l'Alpe ou l'Apennin;
> Reflet de la beauté première,
> Sœur de "l'éternel féminin."
>
> A son corps, en vain retenue,
> Sur l'aile de la passion,
> Mon âme vole à cette nue
> Et l'embrasse comme Ixion.
>
> La raison dit: "Vague fumée,
> Où l'on croit voir ce qu'on rêva,
> Ombre au gré du vent déformée,
> Bulle qui crève et qui s'en va!"
>
> Le sentiment répond: "Qu'importe!
> Qu'est-ce après tout que la beauté,

Spectre charmant qu'un souffle emporte
Et qui n'est rien, ayant été!

"A l'Idéal ouvre ton âme;
Mets dans ton coeur beaucoup de ciel,
Aime une nue, aime une femme,
Mais aime!—C'est l'essentiel!"

[She soars in all her radiance
Higher than the Alps or Apennines;
Reflection of primordial beauty,
Sister of "The Eternal Feminine."

Towards her on wings of passion,
Unmindful of any danger,
My soul ascends and, like Ixion,
Seeking beauty, grasps but air.

Reason says: "Vain mirage,
Though seeming real, really a dream,
Shadow changing with the breeze,
Bubble that bursts and disappears!"

Feeling answers: "What's it matter!
What's beauty but a charming ghost
Buffeted about by changing weather,
And, having once been, is forever lost!

"Open your soul to the Ideal;
Feed your heart a bunch of heaven,
Love a cloud, love a woman,
But love!—That's essential!"][60]

. . .

I have insisted so strongly on Pound's proximity to Mallarmé's version of symbolism in order to reestablish Pound's connection to a literary tradition that has been largely ignored by recent histories of modernism. Fittingly, Pound's poetic development itself begins to echo the consolatory refrain of the *Cantos:* "'How is it far, if you think of it?'" (77/479). The farther we move from the Decadent origins of Pound's poetic language, the nearer we come to its return.

For the purposes of my discussion here, I would like to invoke Michel Foucault's monumental study, *Les Mots et les choses*, which, through its examination of linguistics, economics, and natural history, delineates a history of Western thought that intersects Pound's "poem including history" in a curiously tangential fashion. Foucault sets forth a complex teleology whereby a Renaissance doctrine-of-signatures, "that uniform layer, in which the *seen* and the *read*, the visible and the expressible, were endlessly interwoven, vanishes" and is superseded by a classical theory of representation, which, in turn, dissolves and is replaced by a modern analysis of signification that has its poetic counterpart in a Mallarméan "poésie pure."[61] Strangely enough, *Les Mots et les choses* is a veritable compendium of Poundian themes and heroes (i.e., von Humboldt, Linnaeus, Law, etc.), and it might well be said that the drama of the *Cantos* is staged not in Browning's "showman's booth" (*P*, 232) but before a proscenium that has only of late been excavated and restored by Foucault's archaeological endeavors. At worst, Pound's belief that the world is composed of signatures and his promulgation of a Physiocratic economic doctrine derived from a classical representation of value are symptoms of an atavistic epistemological consciousness, of a premodern sensibility behind what has often been seen as a postmodern poem. But it may be more accurate to say that Pound is following Mallarmé in his quest for what Foucault describes as "the living being of language":

> And yet, throughout the nineteenth century, and right up to our own day—from Hölderlin to Mallarmé and on to Antonin Artaud—literature achieved autonomous existence . . . by finding its way back from the representative or signifying function of language to this raw being that had been forgotten since the sixteenth century. . . . From the nineteenth century, literature began to bring language back to light once more in its own being: though not as it had still appeared at the end of the Renaissance. For now we no longer have that primary, that absolutely initial, word upon which the infinite movement of discourse was founded and by which it was limited; henceforth, language was to grow with no point of departure, no end, and no promise. It is the traversal of this futile yet fundamental space that the text of literature traces from day to day.[62]

If we accept Foucault's characterization of a certain line of modern thought "in which the return is posited only in the extreme recession of the origin—in that region where the gods have turned away,"[63] we might be able to situate Pound's often anachronistic thought. Pound's gods are, as he himself tells us, "discontinuous gods" (21/99). More important, however, although the return of the gods provides us with some of the most sustained lyricism in the *Cantos*, these divine moments are not proofs of the successful realization of Pound's program; rather, they are compensatory moments underscoring Pound's failure to achieve an adequation between word and world:

> I sat on the Dogana's steps
> For the gondolas cost too much, that year,
> And there were not "those girls", there was one face,
> And the Buccentoro twenty yards off, howling "Stretti",
> And the lit cross-beams, that year, in the Morosini,
> And peacocks in Kore's house, or there may have been.
>   Gods float in the azure air.
> Bright gods and Tuscan, back before dew was shed.
> Light: and the first light, before ever dew was fallen.
> Panisks, and from the oak, dryas,
> And from the apple, maelid,
> Through all the wood, and the leaves are full of voices,
> A-whisper, and the clouds bowe over the lake,
> And there are gods upon them,
> And in the water, the almond-white swimmers,
> The silvery water glazes the upturned nipple,
>   As Poggio has remarked.

                                              (3/11)

This first appearance in the *Cantos* of Pound in propria persona is suggestive because it underlines the close proximity of desire (sexual and monetary) to visionary experience. Pound's gods fill the void created by frustration and lack, supplement it with their presence, but, because they do not adequately embody the reality of Pound's situation, because the dryas and maelids do not correspond to the "one face" who, in the *Three Cantos* version, is "young, too young," they must always return to the textual universe from whence they originated ("As Poggio has remarked."). There is a strange frustration in this citation, as though to suggest that even Pound's visionary moments are not his own. In short, Pound very much inhabited a "book of the world": "Titter of sound about me, always" (5/17).

If Pound is to be chastised, it should not be for his desire to "resurrect the gods," a desire common to other, more accepted modern heroes such as Hölderlin and Mallarmé, Nietzsche and Heidegger, but because he lacked the archaeological methods with which to interpret his findings. Pound incorporates his "facts" into the *Cantos* in an undifferentiated manner—that is, without any (archaeo)logical articulation, so that the *Cantos* become not a utopic paradiso terrestre, but what Foucault terms a heterotopia best exemplified by Borges's Chinese encyclopedia.[64] And yet, although Pound ultimately succumbs to this parodic heterotopia, his resistance to it is perhaps a more meaningful gesture. Pound's entire analysis of "2 thousand years, desensitization" could almost be deemed a scarcity economics transposed to the realm of a literary tradition. Pound sees language as a limited resource, one that is, according to Foucault, "the object of a struggle, a political struggle."[65] Although Pound may indeed have failed to navigate successfully the Scylla and Charybdis of res and verba, his attempt to rectify language for future generations, to restore the statue to Terracina, nonetheless underscores his desire for a better world. Despite his "errors and wrecks" (116/810), who can gainsay his vision?

> The Gods have not returned. "They have never left us."
> They have not returned.
> Cloud's processional and the air moves with their living.
> (113/801)

ROBERT DUNCAN'S REVISIONARY RATIOS: REWRITING *THE SPIRIT OF ROMANCE*

> my soul aroused to go forth on the godly sea, Pound
> then heroic,
> setting keel to breakers, our keel,
> the roar of surfs upon alien shores our boundaries—
> —Robert Duncan, "FOR ME TOO, I, LONG AGO
>   SHIPPING OUT WITH THE CANTOS"

> I knew nothing of Baudelaire, but I knew
> that the heart must be stripped bare.
> —Robert Duncan, *The H. D. Book*

FOR BETTER or for worse, Pound has left his indelible mark on American poetry. But if we are looking for a worthy successor to the Poundian countertradition described in the preceding chapters, we need not range outside that family of poets who claim Pound as their poetic forebear. Pound's symbolist inheritance finds its fitting culmination in Robert Duncan's extension of, or, more accurately, his return to, what he sees as the true Poundian tradition. Introduced to Pound's poetry just as he was entering his own vocation as poet, Duncan, with his concern for *techne*, faithfully adhered throughout his career to Pound's injunction that the poet "must know what is happening."[1] Duncan's preoccupation with melopoeia stems from Pound's emphasis on the "tone-leading of vowels";[2] his understanding of "Rime" derives from Pound's "doctrine of signatures"; and the *grande collage* contained in his sequence of *Passages* is an extension of the ideogramic method and open form of the *Cantos*.[3] Finally, with his syncretic mythology, his political and economic idealism, and his historical vision, Duncan recapitulates a great number of Poundian themes and thus continues the ambitious undertaking of the *Cantos*, a poem that is, in Duncan's view, a "vehicle for heterodox belief, a ground in which the divine world may appear."[4]

However, though firmly grounded in the Poundian tradition, Duncan differs from Pound's successors by virtue of the fact that, as he puts it, he reads "Modernism as Romanticism": "my ties to Pound, Stein, Surrealism and so forth all seem to me entirely consequent to their unbroken continuity from the Romantic period."[5] Moreover, as a self-professed "derivative poet," Duncan's "germinal masters" include not only Pound and Williams, but also, among others, H. D., Lawrence, Eliot, Stevens, Stein, Whitman, Dante, Milton, Blake, Shelley, Nerval, Rimbaud, and, most significantly, Charles Baudelaire and Stéphane Mallarmé. I want to focus on Duncan's return to those French Symbolists whom Pound rejected so vehemently, for, in conjunction with his reading of the *Cantos*, Duncan's understanding of our literary tradition reflects my study's attempt to chart the effects of repression and the critical lapses evident in Pound's very over-determined reading of French poetry.

Like Pound, Duncan insists on the ethical implications of language use and also makes it clear that he seconds aspects of, or at least the intention behind, Pound's economic thought: "What Pound wanted was not the pursuit of happiness but the pursuit of the good. This taking thought toward the distribution of goods was an extension of early democratic thought in America" (2, 11, n.p.). But here, in what seems to be a perfectly neutral account of Pound's economic thought, an almost imperceptible shift in emphasis rapidly becomes in Duncan's hands a thoroughgoing revision of the metaphysical and epistemological foundations of Pound's poetic vision. Although Duncan merely seems to be highlighting Pound's belief that a quantitative shift in the distribution of goods would lead to a qualitative one, an empirically demonstrable realization of the Good, he is also insisting that we recognize the linguistic freeplay permitting this equation between good(s) and the Good. Almost immediately, therefore, we are confronted with the underlying difference between Duncan's statement that "each name is a reification of things"[6] and Pound's "*nomina sunt consequentia rerum*" (*GB*, 84). While Duncan admits of an empirically grounded language permitting a reciprocal relation between man and the external world, he quickly reintroduces an Orphic notion of language wherein words obey a larger force and soon take precedence over mere things:

> Poems come up from a ground so
> to illustrate the ground, approximate
> a lingering of eternal image, a need
> known only in its being found ready.
>
> The force that words obey in song
> the rose and artichoke obey
> in their unfolding towards their form.[7]

To continue the economic metaphor, Duncan's Orphic language goes beyond the merely real or empirical and "refer[s] to/imagined goods where they/radiate" (*RB*, 26–27). And in such poems as "The Law I

Love is Major Mover" or "The Structure of Rime," Language is en-
shrined as Duncan's Muse, and his Freudian conception of language
as a palimpsest, his willingness to encounter the poem in its own world
of generative syntax—of unsuspected associations and contamina-
tions at both the level of sound and meaning—bespeak a remove from
Pound's dream of a stability inherent in language itself. In short,
Duncan continues Mallarmé's projected Book in the guise of an Amer-
ican version of *Les Mots Anglais*. As Duncan would put it in a late
interview,

> In the archaeologist's sense, the O.E.D. had opened up the layers of lan-
> guage, and the O.E.D. is another one of the complicating factors at every
> step of writing because that gives me the layers of every single English
> word through its layers of time. . . . It's going to look very odd, because
> it's a temporary thing in poetry how much we go by a belief in the magic
> of the root. The root is the one we're picturing in the "fiat lux." That
> there is a root binds us again very much to the Kabbalah.[8]

Duncan's mature conception of what poetry is or should be evolves out
of the notion of the *livre* embodied in the works of "those mystical Jews
who live in the Torah," as well as in the works of Mallarmé and Joyce.[9]
For Duncan, the Book is both nonexistent and nonreferential since
"the imagination is the final ground of reality":[10] "The 'fiat lux' ex-
cludes the possibility of referentiality . . . because in creating some-
thing, you don't refer to it. You can't refer to it. And what you then
create doesn't resemble something else."[11]

The Symbolists' notion of *correspondances* not only becomes a legiti-
mate literary analogue for the Swedenborgianism to which Duncan
was introduced at an early age by his foster parents, but it also enables
him to coordinate his poetic, theosophical, and psychoanalytic in-
terests:

> "The trembling of the veil of the Temple," Yeats had called the gener-
> ation of Mallarmé. Between the high-mindedness and the low thought-
> forms a Void—but it was also a Maelstrom—trembled, shimmered, began
> to cast forth its old fascination. What is on my mind is that Yeats too, like
> Freud, poetics as well as psychology, was drawn to find hidden content,
> working to bring us into a new consciousness in magic, away from the
> abstract and absolute, towards the coordination of above and below. (2, 8,
> 79–80)

In both theosophical and modern psychoanalytic thought, dualism is
all-pervasive and extends to such metaphysical and cosmological is-
sues as the problem of good and evil or light and dark: "In Alchemy,
so too in psychoanalysis, the work depended upon some equivalence
or ambivalence between the gold (the Good, the life, the essential) and

the shit (the waste, the contamination—but it was also that which was returned to the life or richness of the soil)" (2, 8, 81). In addition, the androgyny underlying the theosophical conception of the godhead, of the *Shekinah* or the *Adam Kadmon*, as well as the theory of bisexuality grounding early Freudian theory, permits a more fluid circulation of energies and desires, a variety of identifications that circumvent or at least minimize the aggressiveness implicit in Pound's and Williams's "hey-ding-dong" troubadour world.

It is for this reason that Duncan finds cause to celebrate and pay homage to H. D. in his monumental history of literary modernism, *The H. D. Book*. Not only do Duncan's and H. D.'s theosophical interests coincide, providing them with a symbolic language with which to represent immanence, but H. D.'s Freudian outlook strikes a sympathetic chord in Duncan for whom, in strong contrast to Pound, Freud is a major intellectual figure in the twentieth century. H. D.'s and Duncan's vision of language as being "either duplicit or complicit" (2, 3, 137) builds upon Freud's theories regarding a primordial "antithetical language" that functions in much the same manner as the dream work. From this perspective, words and images become hieroglyphs and depend more upon context for interpretation than upon any univocal meaning. Moreover, in all three writers this notion of "duplicity or complicity" extends to the field of human sexual behavior. Just as bisexuality is for Freud a central component of human sexuality, Kaspar, in H. D.'s *Flowering of the Rod*, is granted access to vision through Mary Magdalene because, says Duncan, "in the most real the two were always at one" (2, 9, 54). And Duncan himself follows H. D. in this attempt to recognize the crossing of genders:

> And of this other romance—Mallarmé's
> creative malaise—I have not truly undergone
>   that withdrawal from what Night has given me,
> that solitary bringing forth out of words,
>   offsprung and outcast poem,
> into the judgment of a woman's part in me,
>   seeking its hearing and sentence, yet
>
> I am not unfamiliar with the seepage of the light.
>
>   (*GW*, 154)

The strength of Duncan's poetic vision stems in large part from his willingness to voice that "woman's part in [him]," to embrace this "otherness" and thereby to find a creative freedom in and through this oft-repressed aspect of the male psyche. Duncan's Freudian and theosophical orientations, with their recognition and acceptance of dualism, differentiate him in marked fashion from Pound's monistic vision and permit him to open his poetry to realms of experience unavailable to the latter.

Thus, Duncan's continued preoccupation with Mallarmé is not surprising. Although he apprenticed under Rimbaud as did so many other postmoderns, he begins to grapple with *le Maître* as early as *Roots and Branches* (1964):

RISK

that there might, may, be

a last chance.

The last chance I had   had not

this die's immediacy

—an old rite I had forgotten

was a rite, cast, had feard

and put aside

le hazard.

It comes as an aside in a poem:

"the cast of the dice".

(RB, 56)

Nominally a poem treating Duncan's rather mundane concern as to whether he should risk his "day's allotment" to purchase a vase, "Risk" quickly evolves into a reflection on the lure of art and beauty. Just as "The sky on certain days has such a blue / that means no comfort, that intensifies" (*RB*, 57), so is Absolute Beauty an Ideal toward which we must continually strive only to fall back unsatisfied: "It's not Beauty it must reach, but / *towards* Beauty it must reach / unsatisfied" (*RB*, 58). And though in this poem Duncan shunned *IT*, "playd safe and did not / buy the vase," failed to "*draw [his] self out of the chance*," he nonetheless remains haunted by the human possibility of defining and filling the void through art, and he concludes the poem by reaffirming the existence of the Absolute, azure-filled realm of Mallarmé's *beauté:*

Outward the caravans go,

cut loose. The image *does*,

will *not* do. Lose sense toward what we do not know?

. . . .

Risk

for the sake of the lure, that there might be

this die's immediacy,

an old rite I had shunnd.

(RB, 59)

Curiously, though, Mallarmé's influence on Duncan undergoes a radical transformation in the course of his career, a transformation that sheds considerable light on Duncan's similar reappraisal of his Poundian inheritance. In *Ground Work* (1984), Duncan returns again to Mallarmé, but it soon becomes clear that his confidence in the Mallarméan Ideal has waned. Whereas he could still uphold that Ideal in "Risk" (1964), his meditations on Mallarmé's "Un Coup de dés" and "Don du poème" in "Passages: Jamais" and "An Interlude of Winter Light" subtly deconstruct Mallarmé's vision and serve to anchor both Duncan's poetic self and his art in *this* world. In "Passages: Jamais," for example, both Mallarmé and Heraclitus enter the field of the poem, forcing us to choose between the two incompatible positions implicit in Mallarmé's paradoxical "Un coup de dés jamais n'abolira le hasard": (1) the sceptical position in which the ever-changing phenomenal world precludes the existence of stable essences; or (2) Plato's dualism wherein these very appearances necessitate that we posit a transcendent realm of true essences or Ideas:[12]

JAMAIS

must extend   beyond the throw of the dice   "a" just now, yet
        no throw of the dice may   chance **IT**.
            Let us take the excellence of the style to be
                        lucidity—
        Clearly, there is no last chance
whether a certain word is to be taken with what precedes or with what follows
        hard to punctuate
        as in Herakleitos: *"Reason being such always*
                                men fail to understand"
All ways   men fail to understand.

                                                (*GW*, 147)

The various typographical oddities—the different fonts, the spacing, and the line breaks—are calculated, like Mallarmé's, to blur any univocal reading. Duncan begins with an imperative, "**JAMAIS**/must extend beyond the throw of the dice," which may be read in two ways: (1) "one should never tempt fate"; or (2) taking *jamais* as a synonym for the Mallarméan act of negation or *verneinung* that fuels the imagination, "the Imagination must extend beyond the quotidian world by denying it, thereby discovering the realm of Eternal Beauty." Similarly, where the early Duncan was still able to write in the optative— "that there might, may, be / a last chance" (*RB*, 59)—that possibility now seems closed off: "Clearly, there is no last chance." But even this formulation is ambiguous in that it might mean "there is no chance to finalize and clarify things" or "there is always another chance," and it is further complicated by the suggested enjambment linking "last chance" to the following lines: "whether a certain word is to be taken with what precedes or with what follows/hard to punctuate." Is Duncan suggesting that Heraclitus's gnomic fragment forever precludes the attribution of a univocal meaning? Or, as Duncan suggests in "Risk," do we have an unlimited series of chances to fix meaning: "the last chance I had had not/this die's immediacy" (*RB*, 59). And finally, Heraclitus's fragment provides no help since it reiterates rather than resolves this paradox: either reason is consistent and true ("reason being such always") or reason *al(l)ways* fails to encompass reality.

The second movement of the poem attempts to reconcile the two positions by invoking an almost Pythagorean sense of harmony, with God writing "the Nature of Sound" and with the Emersonian Poet reading "the Intention of a Universe," discriminating between "the 'sameness' of the note[s]" in an attempt to coordinate "the above and below": "Verse, linkt to the Idea of that Governance, / moves 'beyond.'" But the Poet is firmly grounded in the *Now* and, seemingly tone-deaf, more often than not misreads, dismisses, or misses God's sign or "key." Moreover, whatever harmony suggested here is shattered in the final movement of the poem:

> In the flicker   shutter/or shudder   ancient, absent-minded,
>   the granite massif   is/was?   present in Mind
>   disrupting the pervasive   overtones of Universe
> —so taking place
>   in the particular   now
> following,   is haunted,   a unique moment   taking over,
>   the Demon of Incident   "hugeness"   reorganizes
>   the insistent beating of the moth's wings at the screen
>   where panic tears apart
>
>   silence   .   the eternal   .   inertia
>
> thunderous outweigh
>   "the stability of the central triad"
>   in which the impression of a "key" wavers.
>
>   (*GW*, 148)

The "beating of the moth's wings" and the ensuing panic dissolve Mallarmé's "central triad" of silence, eternity, and inertia. Duncan is wholly content to let "the senseless arbitrate" and thereby to discover in chaos a *this-worldly* ground for the self. Instead of Mallarmé's *MAÎTRE*, Duncan celebrates the *Demon of Incident* or, in "An Interlude," the *Demon of the Psychopathology of Daily Life* (*GW*, 151). What James F. Mersmann has suggested with regard to Duncan's philosophical position is equally true of Duncan's encounter with Mallarmé and Pound: "Duncan appears to be a Platonist by natural inclination, an Aristotelian by choice."[13]

Duncan's growing dissatisfaction with Mallarmé's vision of stasis and coherence is even more evident in "An Interlude of Winter Light," the poem that follows "Passages: Jamais." Predominantly discursive (and thus almost impossible to excerpt from), "An Interlude" begins quite innocently and poignantly and in a typically Duncanesque fashion as he considers his seemingly eternal, though admittedly temporal, bond to his beloved. But the poem veers off course and the mood changes as Duncan attempts to respond to his recollection of a chance question asked by "the old crone" sitting next to him at the ballet: "What does 'Idumaean' mean?" His continued resistance to the question suggests that the word *Idumaean* conceals a significant and highly cathected internal conflict within Duncan himself, and it is only after several false starts that he lights upon his "oracular theme": "le Don du Poème / as it came to Mallarmé." Thus, turning to his Pleiade edition, he proceeds to give his own version of Mallarmé's poem:

> In the dance,   as if broken-wingd,
>   a failure,   he   approaches the Father—
>
> the phantom begotten of Idumaean Night.
>
> Thru the frosted panes,   thru the inner glass
>   burnt with aromatics and with gold,
> at last   dawn spurts forth upon the angelic lamp.
>   Palms!
> Forms of this world emerge within the
>   threshold of the light, and,
> if there were rapture, wrestling, the
>   advancing figure, the dread conception,
> it has all gone back to the other side,
>
>   it has entirely left
> this relic in the early morning light
>   to its father   who remains,
> trying an enemy smile.   the Solitude,
>   blue and sterile,   emptied of itself,
>   *shudders*.
>
>   (*GW*, 152–53)[14]

Although Duncan fully understands and sympathizes with Mallarmé's quest for the Absolute, he insists that Mallarmé's decision not to describe the poet's battle transforms the poem into nothing more than a "relic in the early morning light." Duncan's criticism of Mallarmé and his own understanding of the proper poetic stance is given voice in the conclusion of "An Interlude," when Thoth, *Master of us writing the Heart of the Truth in the Mouth of* 'IT'*s Risk, comes into the picture*":

> that you lead us on   to mis-take,   to mis-
> understand.   Misled we *must* be
>   or we would not have brought into the question
> the infant in the crèche hidden in Mount Ida,
>   we would have forgotten   it was in the heart
> the bread was broken; we would have known better
>   than to follow thru the legend of Idomeneo
> and the sacrifice again of the heart's treasure,
>   the promised surrender of the
> first born to the dawn's light;
>   and we would never have come along this way
> so burdend to Idumée.   It would all
>   have been untroubled by that informing
> duel of Night   and the betraying blast
>   of the Day's light.   There would not have been
> pleat upon pleat.   We would never have come   along this way
>   to this deserted Minoan shore.
>
> (GW, 153)

Duncan now considers pure poetry an ill-advised attempt to avoid "bring[ing] life to the risk" (*RB*, 58). And instead of seeking "the Solitude, blue and sterile," of Mallarmé's Absolute, Duncan insists that we continue to dwell on the bloody "initiation" and the "sacrifice again of the heart's treasure," the painful death and rebirth of the self. Although Mallarmé awakens in Duncan "links of feeling that send [him] again to the hidden spirit in history,"[15] Duncan fears that Mallarmé's "much more elusive idea of The Book" is too rooted in "the abstract and absolute," thus creating an insurmountable chasm between the real and ideal, the "above and below" (2, 8, 79–80).

• • •

But this criticism of Mallarmé is virtually identical to Duncan's most significant criticism and subsequent redirection of Pound's poetic vision. Again and again, Duncan notes and rejects a tendency on

Pound's part to situate his visionary world of Eros in a transcendent, empyrean realm. Once Pound comes to define love as "EX OUSIAS . . . HYPOSTASIN/III, 5, 3 PERI EROTAS" (100/735), as an emanation downward from transcendent essences, he has, according to Duncan, disowned his Spirit of Romance. Aphrodite is no longer a bodily presence in the late cantos but is transfigured into "THE GREAT CRYSTAL," which, Duncan argues, "in its capitalization [clearly insists that] . . . 'Right reason' takes the place of the earlier 'intellectual and emotional complex in an instant of time'" (2, 3, 133):

> The Aphrodite of the *Cantos* does not rise as Hesiod would have her from a *bloody wave* [my italics]; she is not the goddess of sexual love and life renewal Pound addressed in *The Spirit of Romance* but the Aphrodite of the higher intellect in which Beauty has become a pure essence. (2, 3, 133)

And if Pound comes in the late cantos to an empyrean realm and discovers there, albeit intermittently, a very Mallarméan *beauté pure*, Duncan too takes an unexpected detour. Having set sail early in his career for the safe haven of Mallarmé's radiant ideal world, Duncan now discovers that he had been mis-taken, that he had embarked instead upon a Baudelairean voyage culminating in *Ground Work II: In the Dark:*

> I know thru and thru the brutal
>   facts in which this unity
>   —grand illusion of what is lovely—
> takes hold. What I know
>   makes fierce indeed the drive
>   of my striving here. Hatreds
> as well as loves flowd thru as the
>   sap of me.   And we too,
>   my life companion and I,
> entertaind our projects and fancies,
>   playd house and kept company
> upon the edge of what we never knew then
>   you made clear was there
>   in the human condition—your *Ennui*
>
>   *plus laid, plus méchant, plus immonde,*
>
> that we would never have come to, yet
>   in the depths of Poetry
> I have so long ever gone to and ever
>   returned myself from,   beyond

the furies' nest, the squalor of these
            back streets, ravaged fields,
and the grinding, the drains,
            the sullen aftermaths of wars and
man's industrious sexuality,   there is a nursery
            deepest of all you knew
and pourd into our common stream
            this residue of an Eternal Admission,
whose nurse, formidable Muse of Man's Stupidities
            —we are surrounded by her evidence—
counts out into hours   the endlessness
            of a relentless distaste.

(GWII, 17–18)

The many invocations to Baudelaire in this his last volume reaffirm
Duncan's early allegiance to the romantic/symbolist tradition Baude-
laire exemplified. From very early on, Baudelaire served as a critical
benchmark by which to measure Duncan's own (and Pound's) distance
from his authentic self, his *coeur mis à nu*, and as an extremely valuable
model for his own attempts to strip bare his heart: "Finding my rime
in the opening propositions of Baudelaire's essay: 'De la vaporisation
et de la centralisation du Moi'" (2, 9, 37). Although Duncan uncovers
an uncanny resemblance between Baudelaire and Pound—"But what
ate at Pound's immortal Mind? for the Cantos, for *Les Fleurs du Mal/*
so eat at Mind's conscience / what malady? what undoing-of-all-Good
workt behind speech?" (*GWII*, 68)—his very willingness to entertain
the question, to expose himself to this malady, immunizes him, as it
were, against their "dis-ease or out-rage."

Paradoxically, the psychoanalytic method that Duncan uses to criti-
cize Pound also enables him to rescue the *Cantos*. Adopting Freud's
distinction between the manifest and latent content of the dream
work, Duncan argues that "it is this area between the manifest and the
conclusions of his enquiry that Pound cannot face as a conscious artist"
(2, 1, 9): "that the germinal consciousness, affecting mind about it, was
dark as well as light, Pound can never accept. . . . Wherever he faced
muddle, the digestive and excretory functions of the universe . . . he
could no longer think . . . he could only—closing his mind in distaste—
react" (2, 9, 72). Reading the *Cantos* as a dream work, Duncan discerns
signs of a repressed latent content and is consequently able to argue
that Pound's blind reaction to "metaphysical muddle" testifies to "the
authenticity of the Cantos" (2, 1, 9) and to the existence of a deeper
self which lies behind and legitimizes the poem:

> To render it true, then. Not only the truth of outrage in Swift or Bau-
> delaire, in Pound or Céline, that suddenly forces us to recognize the virus

(these passages, out-rages, are lesions of feeling and thought) that others would keep hidden or dressed up; but the truth of how consciousness moves, where form has been developed to bear testimony to undercurrent and eddy, shifts, breaks and echoes of content. . . . Here the virus is life, the hatred is emotion, the breaks in consciousness—that in conventional thought seem inroads of natural chaos or damaged passages that need surgery or correction—are surfs or sun-spots of the deep element. (2, 9, 75)

"Where intelligence is awareness," maintains Duncan, "Pound is a marred intelligence. But since intelligence is something larger and operates whether we are conscious in intelligence or not, the Cantos have their full poetic powers" (2, 1, 9).

Although *The H. D. Book* is not an entirely disinterested study of literary modernism and serves, by Duncan's own admission, to validate his own poetry of Eros, his arguments gain in force precisely because he is able to situate Pound in a specific literary tradition that we as critics have been more than willing to bury. For Duncan, that essential and authentic Pound through whom the *Cantos* attain "their full poetic powers" is the Pound of *The Spirit of Romance*, the poet who celebrated the heterodox paganism and the cult of Eros in a "Medieval romance-tradition" (2, 3, 133) that had been outlawed and suppressed, but which nonetheless led to the rebirth of lyric poetry in the West. More important, that tradition had been handed down to Pound by his own poetic forebears: "Back of H. D., as back of Pound or Yeats, was the cult of romance that Morris and Rossetti had derived from Dante" (2, 1, 21). Thus, revising accepted modernist history, Duncan views the Imagist Credo of 1912 not as the founding gesture of literary modernism, but as a step backward:

Essentially anti-modernist, in the Credo of 1912 with its insistence upon the ultimate reality of the image in itself and upon the magic of a cadence that corresponded with that image—what Pound called an "absolute rhythm"—the Imagists seek a return to Hellenic purity, even to the archaic Greek, in reaction to the theosophy and hermeticism of the Symbolist movement typified by Yeats. (1, 4, 82)

According to Duncan, the Imagist Credo permitted "Pound, deeply pre-Raphaelite in his affinities, [to] protest as a modernist in 1913 against Lawrence's 'middling-sensual erotic verses' as 'a sort of pre-raphaelitish slush, disgusting or very nearly so'" (2, 5, 345). "Behind his 'jesting'," Duncan argues, "is Pound's native Puritanical mind in its distaste for the sensual"; but, he adds, "deeper going, there is the intellectual disclaimer" (2, 5, 345).

Duncan considers Pound to have been from the outset "a man of divided mind" (2, 5, 339): "Pound and Williams, whose art belonged to the *trobar clus*, in their dis-ease were often ashamed of their Spirit. In Paterson that split . . . appears as a divorce within the language itself, a hidden divorce between man and woman. In the Cantos, where Pound is concerned with economics or politics, 'men's affairs', he will put on the man-in-the-street persona" (2, 9, 80). "Briefly, in the Cantos," Duncan laments, "Plotinus appears to rescue Pound from the hell-mire of politicians and dead issues, but Pound is eager to interrupt the inspiration of his poem and to direct its course" (2, 10, 64). In Duncan's view, Pound's failure as a poet was that of not accepting his true role as a "derivative poet" who unselfishly gives himself over to his language and his poetic tradition:

> It is the originality of Pound that mars his intelligence. The goods of the intellect are communal; there is a virtu or power that flows from the language itself, a fountain of man's meanings, and the poet seeking the help of this source awakens first to the guidance of those who have gone before in the art, then the guidance of the meanings and dreams that all who have ever stored the honey of the invisible in the hive have prepared. (2, 10, 64)

Having succumbed completely to what were merely *idées fixes*, argues Duncan, Pound in the twenties and thirties began to fear his poetic imagination: "Where in the essays of the London period Pound is exploring ideas of imagination and poetry, in the essays of Rapallo he speaks not as a visionary but as a pedagogue, a culture commissar, an economic realist, a political authority, and, in each of these roles, he feels that imagination and vision is unsound" (2, 4, 35). Only after the crisis at Pisa was Pound able to rediscover the psychological and emotional ground of his early poetry. With the fall of Mussolini, he is once and for all deprived of the authoritative center governing the poetry and criticism of his middle period, and, according to Duncan, "for the first time in the Cantos, in these Pisan Cantos, some attitude of authority, some self is surrendered, so that a pose seems to have fallen apart, exposing the genuine, confused, passionate mind. 'A lizard upheld me,' he testifies. He is in the condition of first things" (2, 2, 109).

With his proposed isolation of a "genuine, confused, passionate mind," Duncan is able to recover, both for himself and for a contemporary poetics, a Poundian legacy that had long been (and still is) under attack. Despite his poetic, philosophical, and political differences with Pound, Duncan is not blind to Pound's struggle to reveal the existence of a "vital universe," and Duncan's entire project, in both his poetry and his criticism, is one of re-scoring the syncopations and intermittences of Pound's "cosmic rhythm," of inflecting Pound's poetic so that the many aporias that appear briefly only to be immediately disavowed are made central to his own poetry. For example, whereas Pound sees history as a conflict between a creative vision embodying order, the "factive personality," and the disruptive forces of ignorance, Duncan counters Pound's dis-ease of (dis)order with his own more anarchic vision of chaos as a ground for order in both the cosmos and the individual.[16] As Duncan remarks of Pound, "wherever Hell appears in earlier *Cantos* it is exterior to Pound" (2, 9, 73); Duncan, on the contrary, is as willing to locate Hell in the individual, the "Eris in Eros" (*BB*, 6), as in repressive social institutions:

> Because of what we love   we are   increasingly at War.
>   That Sphere of all Attractions   draws us from what we are—
>
>   . . . .
>   Love ever contending with Hate.
>   Hate ever contending with Love.
> *"never, I think, shall infinite Time be emptied of these two"*
>   *"Never"*, being the name of what is infinite.
> In bright confusion.   White,   the interpresence of all colors,
>   shining back on us—
> Black, taking all back into itself.
>   They never cease their continuous exchange.
>
> <div align="right">(<i>GW</i>, 142–43)</div>

Duncan's Law is a rather manic Xris-cross of harmony and disharmony. In Duncan's cosmogony, the Good, the social face of Eros, rests on the principle of individual volition—"There being no common good, no commune,/no communion, outside the freedom of/individual volition" (*BB*, 73)—and Evil results from the legalized or institutionalized repression of Eros:

> *Evil* "referrd to the root of *up, over*"
> simulacra of law that wld over-rule
>   the Law man's inner nature seeks,
>
> <div align="right">(<i>BB</i>, 72)</div>

But because "new needs are new commands," Duncan's anarchic vision encompasses potentially disruptive forms of Eros:

> There are no
> final orders. But the Law
> constantly destroys the law.
>
> <div align="right">(<i>RB</i>, 26)</div>

Thus, although Duncan will admit to the existence of Pound's "right reason"—"Love prospers in right reason" (*OF*, 34)—he will also celebrate Eros as "outlaw," as a representation of desire which is potentially threatening to the rational imagination:

> The ear
> catches rime like pangs of disease from the air. Was it
> sign of a venereal infection raging in the blood? For poetry
> is a contagion   .   And Lust a lord
> who'll find the way to make words ake and take on
> heat and glow.
>
> (*BB*, 32)

Duncan's positing of a potentially disruptive desire and a fundamental ambivalence as a bedrock for human behavior marks a return to a more romantic conception of the individual and internalizes, in some very real sense, Pound's *agon*. Unlike Pound, who "wants to say that suffering is a mental error," Duncan can accept the fact that "the brooding mind correspondent with suffering and corruption . . . [and] the radiant mind correspondent with joy and purity" (2, 9, 73) are integral and interrelated parts of "the vital universe." Duncan recognizes that suffering and pain are necessary constituents of love simply by virtue of the fact that the Lover risks losing him or herself in the Beloved:

> I too, drawing the story again from Ovid's pen,
> know the bewildering knowledge in the beast's gaze
> that searcht with trust his lover's eyes
> and found his own wound repeated there.
> For love binds heart to human heart
> and would sound the depth
> from which the mortal life cries out.
>
> (*RB*, 166)

Although we are imprisoned in a subjectively ordered world of pain and decay, love, if we are willing to tolerate the suffering, enables us to embrace an Other, or, at worst, to find a truer reflection of our Self, and permits a brief and forbidden glimpse of Eros, of another Realm or another Law:

> If he be Truth
> I would dwell in the illusion of him
>
> His hands unlocking from chambers of my male body
>
> such an idea in man's image
>
> rising tides that sweep me towards him
>
> (*BB*, 63)

In the context of a love poetry, Pound's use of the idealized Lady as a mantra enabling the poet to attain atasal or union is indeed curious if we look a little more closely at the logic of the *trobar clus*. Although it idealizes the Beloved, the trobar clus, by virtue of its very unreadability, also contains an implicit denial of the possibility of attaining that love; moreover, the idealization of the Lady is determined by this very impossibility.[17] In essence, the process itself is self-defeating. Duncan's love poetry, on the other hand, represents the opposite extreme of the trobar clus, for unreadability or discursive failure becomes a condition of agonizing loss, but one which conditions a subsequent yearning for "first things":

> Such is the sickness of many a good thing
> that now into my life from long ago this
> refusing to say I love you has bound
> the weeping, the yielding, the
> yearning to be taken again,
> into a knot, a waiting, a string
>
> so taut it taunts the song,
> it resists the touch. It grows dark
> to draw down the lover's hand
> from its lightness to what's
> underground.

                                                                    (*BB*, 6)

For Duncan, "Death is prerequisite to the growth of grass" (*OF*, 43), and the benedictions of the Lover, the "intimations of the secret Mover," "are not permitted without corruption" (*OF*, 42). Whereas suffering is for Pound "a mental error" (2, 9, 73), Duncan views it as central to the human condition, fostering an earthly "inbinding" and, ultimately, giving him access to and a potential realization of the Truth and Life of Divine Being:

> Divine being shows itself
> not in the rising above,
> but embodied, out of
> deliberate committed lines of stone or flesh
> flashings of suffering shared.

                                                                    (*OF*, 84)

And it is precisely this unflinching realism that makes Duncan's unswerving faith in the Imagination, even in the face of death, so exemplary and poignant:

> Yes, I was afraid
> of not seeing you again,   of being
> taken away, not

> of dying, the specter I have long
> > known as my Death is the
> Lord of a Passage that unites us;
> > but of
> > never having come to you that other
> specter of my actually living is.
> > Adamant.

(GWII, 90)

In both his poetry and his criticism, and largely as a result of his encounter with Pound and the French Symbolists, Duncan has left us a legacy to be treasured. By living, reading, and writing (post)-modernism as romanticism, he provided us with unimpeachable testimony of a live poetic tradition. "In the gloom" of Duncan's *Ground Work*, as in Pound's Cantos, "the gold gathers the light against it" (11/51). In Duncan's re-reading and re-vision of the *Cantos*, the many aporias, "out-rages," and "lesions of feeling and thought" truly do become "surfs or sun-spots of the deep element" that help illuminate Pound and his poem, help make his "splendour" all the brighter, help us to see, then,

> from its flame
> the margins of the page flare forth.

(RB, 176)

NOTES

INTRODUCTION
EZRA POUND AND THE SYMBOLIST INHERITANCE

1. *Ezra Pound and Dorothy Shakespear: Their Letters 1909–1914*, ed. Omar Pound and A. Walton Litz (New York: New Directions, 1984), 193.
2. Ibid., 297.
3. In "Two Notes," *Egoist* 2, no. 6 (June 1915), May Sinclair writes:

> [Imagism] is not Symbolism. It has nothing to do with image-making. It abhors Imagery. Imagery is one of the old worn-out decorations the Imagists have scrapped.
> The Image is not a substitute; it does not stand for anything but itself. Presentation not Representation is the watchword of the school. The Image, I take it, is Form. But it is not pure form. It is form *and* substance. (88)

4. Frank Kermode argues, "In so far as the *Cantos* contrive to be an assemblage of ideograms in a significant relation to each other . . . they are one vast image. They are, in fact, the only kind of long poem the Symbolist aesthetic will admit" (*The Romantic Image* [London: Routledge & Kegan Paul, 1957], 136). Schneidau dismisses this argument in his "Pound, Olson and Objective Verse," *Paideuma* 5, no. 1 (Spring-Summer 1976): 24: "The Symbolist always desires to have the last word in his quarrel with language, and thus loses the argument. Pound is not a Symbolist." See also Donald Davie, *Ezra Pound* (New York: Viking, 1976), 40–41; and Herbert N. Schneidau, *The Image and the Real* (Baton Rouge: Louisiana State University Press, 1969), Chapters 1 and 2, especially p. 29.
5. Hugh Kenner, *The Pound Era* (Berkeley and Los Angeles: University of California Press, 1971), 133.
6. Glenn S. Burne, *Remy de Gourmont* (Carbondale: Southern Illinois University Press, 1963), 171: "In French criticism between 1900–1911, the *image* was replacing the ineffable *idée* as the crucial term in the definition of Symbolism." Also, René Taupin, *L'Influence du symbolisme français sur la poésie américaine* (Paris: Librairie Ancienne Honoré Champion, 1929), 114: "Comme l'image qui en est l'élément, le poème comme un dessin, non comme une arabesque, non comme les poèmes de Mallarmé; toutes ces courbes se répondent par une symétrie non préétablie, mais toujours réalisée quand l'émotion est sincèrement ressentie: 'Emotion is an organiser of forms' [Pound, *Blast*]" [Like the image which is the element of the poem, the poem as a drawing, not as the arabesques of Mallarmé's poems; these curves are not preestablished symmetries but are always the result of emotion that is sincerely felt].

7. William Carlos Williams, *Selected Essays* (New York: New Directions, 1969), 107.

8. William Carlos Williams, *Paterson* (New York: New Directions, 1963), 9.

9. "Lettres de France, II, Esquisse de la poésie française actuelle," *Rhythm* 2, no. 3 (Aug. 1912). Reprinted in *The Road from Paris: French Influence on English Poetry, 1900–1920*, ed. Cyrena N. Pondrom (London: Cambridge University Press, 1974), 155.

10. I am certainly not suggesting that Pound's engagement with French poetry is the *only* way to account for Pound's developing modernism. There have appeared in recent years a number of important revisionist studies of Pound's place in the very complex literary and philosophical milieu of the early twentieth century. George Bornstein's *Postromantic Consciousness of Ezra Pound* (Victoria: University of Victoria, 1977) anticipates my discussion of a latent romanticism in Pound. James Longenbach's admirable *Stone Cottage: Pound, Yeats, and Modernism* (Oxford: Oxford University Press, 1988) brought Pound's symbolism to life once more, only from an occult perspective which, I would argue, better explains Pound's poetic sensibility than his poetic practice. Sanford Schwartz's *Matrix of Modernism: Pound, Eliot, and Early Twentieth-Century Thought* (Princeton: Princeton University Press, 1985) and Michael Levenson's *Genealogy of Modernism: A study of English literary doctrine, 1908–1912* (Cambridge: Cambridge University Press, 1984) demonstrate Pound's connection to Hulme and Bergson. What becomes immediately clear in all of these studies is the complexity of, and our inability to circumscribe, the phenomenon we call modernism.

11. "The Approach to Paris," *New Age*, n.s., 13, nos. 19–25 (Sept. 4–Oct. 16, 1913); "Irony, Laforgue, and Some Satire," *Poetry* 11, no. 2 (Nov. 1917) and "The Hard and Soft in French Poetry," *Poetry* 11, no. 5 (Feb. 1918), both collected in *The Literary Essays of Ezra Pound* (New York: New Directions, 1968), 280–89; "A Study in French Poets," *Little Review* 4, no. 10 (Feb. 1918): 3–61, revised and reprinted in *Instigations*, 3–105; Pound's "Paris Letters," *Dial* 69 (1920); the French issues of the *Little Review*, vols. 8–9 (1921–1924); and the unpublished "French Poets: A Postscript" (1934) now in the Pound collection at the Beinecke Library, Yale University.

12. Kenneth Cornell, *The Post-Symbolist Period* (New Haven: Yale University Press, 1958), 42. Cornell provides an excellent and very detailed account of this period.

13. Ibid., 49.

14. Enid Starkie, *From Gautier to Eliot* (London: Hutchinson & Co., 1960), 138.

15. Pondrom, *Road from Paris*. Pondrom has assembled some indispensable and largely unavailable essays in this volume, and her introduction provides an invaluable, detailed account of the French influence on imagist poetry and theory.

16. F. S. Flint, "The History of Imagism," *Egoist* 2, no. 5 (May 1, 1915): 70–71. He discusses the Symbolists in the course of his "Recent Verse," *New Age*, n.s., 3 (July 11, 1908): 212–13; reprinted in Pondrom, *Road from Paris*, 50–53.

17. T. E. Hulme, "A Lecture on Modern Poetry," in *Further Speculations*, ed. Sam Hynes (Minneapolis: University of Minnesota Press, 1955), 67–76.

18. Flint, "The History of Imagism," 71.

19. Pondrom, *Road from Paris*, 12.

20. F. S. Flint, "Contemporary French Poetry," *Poetry Review* 1, no. 8 (Aug. 1912): 355–414. Reprinted in Pondrom, *Road from Paris*, 86–145.

21. Pondrom provides an excellent account of this battle for precedence in her introduction to *The Road from Paris*.

22. Ezra to Isabel Pound, Feb. 21, 1912, Paige Carbon #238, American Literature Collection, Beinecke Library, Yale University.

23. Flint, "History of Imagism," 71.

24. John Gould Fletcher, *Life Is My Song* (New York: Farrar & Rinehart, 1937): 73. Quoted in Pondrom, *Road from Paris*, 31.

25. Richard Aldington, *Life for Life's Sake* (New York: The Viking Press, 1941), 111. Quoted in Pondrom, *Road from Paris*, 33.

26. Jules Romains to Ezra Pound, May 1918, American Literature Collection, Beinecke Library, Yale University.

27. Flint, "Contemporary French Poetry," reprinted in Pondrom, *Road from Paris*, 86. Hulme argues that the atomistic perception contained in this "logical form of verse" is both poetically and epistemologically outmoded and that a symbolist vagueness better corresponds to a Bergsonian intuition of flux in his review of Tancrède de Visan's *L'Attitude du Lyrisme Contemporain* (*New Age*, n.s., 9 [Aug. 24, 1911]): 400–401; reprinted in Pondrom, *Road from Paris*, 58:

> Bergson represents a reaction against the atomic and rational psychology of Taine and Spencer. . . . The Symbolist reaction against the Parnasse is exactly the same reaction in a different region of thought. For what was the Parnassian attitude? It was an endeavour always to keep to accurate description. It was an endeavour to create poetry of "clear" ideas. They employed always clear and precise descriptions of external things and strove by combinations of such "atoms of the beautiful" to manufacture a living beauty. To the Symbolists this seems an impossible feat. For life is a continuous and unanalysable curve which cannot be seized clearly, but can only be felt as a kind of intuition. It can only be got at by a kind of central vision as opposed to analytic description, this central vision expressing itself by means of symbols. M. Visan would then define Symbolism as an attempt by means of successive and accumulated images to express and exteriorise such a central lyric intuition.

28. Flint, "Contemporary French Poetry," reprinted in Pondrom, ed. *Road from Paris*, 86.

29. Hulme, "A Lecture on Modern Poetry," *Further Speculations*, 70.

30. Ibid.

31. Flint, "Contemporary French Poetry," reprinted in Pondrom, *Road from Paris*, 86 and 91.

32. Although Pound argues that "De Régnier seems to verge out of Parnassianism into an undefined sort of poetry" (*LE*, 288), he also acknowledges that

"De Régnier is counted a successor to the Parnassians" (*Inst*, 40–41). Further-more, Pound omits a discussion of Samain and Heredia in *Instigations* because they are implicit in Gautier (*Inst*, 4).

33. Pierre Martino, *Parnasse et symbolisme*, 11th ed. (Paris: Librairie Armand Colin, 1964), 3–4.

34. Henry James, "Théophile Gautier," in *French Poets and Novelists* (New York: Grosset & Dunlap, 1964), 32. In *The Spirit of Romance* (1910), Pound discusses Baudelaire in a manner that should remind us of James's similar discussion in *French Poets and Novelists*, an essay following the one on Gautier and subsequently quoted by Pound in his 1918 essay on Henry James (*LE*, 295–338).

35. Ibid., 33.

36. Martino argues that the Romantic School was itself divided into the *l'école intime* and the *l'école pittoresque*, the latter, with its sensual materialism, ultimately leading via Sainte-Beuve and Hugo toward the aesthetic advanced in Gautier's *Mademoiselle de Maupin* and de Banville's and de Lisle's interest in Hellenism and in antiquity in general. See Martino, "Le Lendemain de 1830," *Parnasse et symbolisme*, 3–30.

37. John Porter Houston, *French Symbolism and the Modernist Movement: A Study of Poetic Structures* (Baton Rouge: Louisiana State University Press, 1980), 99.

38. Theophile Gautier, *Émaux et Camées*, ed. Claudine Gothot-Mirsch (Paris: Gallimard, 1981), 42–44. All translations of Gautier are mine.

39. Stéphane Mallarmé, *Oeuvres complètes* (Paris: Gallimard, 1945), 68.

40. David Kelley, "Gautier et Baudelaire—*Émaux et Camées* et les *Petits Poèmes en prose*," in *Baudelaire, Mallarmé and Valéry: New Essays in Honor of Lloyd Austin*, ed. Malcolm Bowie, Alison Fairlee, and Alison Finch (London: Cambridge University Press, 1982), 68. Here as elsewhere I follow Kelley's fine reading of Gautier.

41. Gautier, "Symphonie en blanc majeur," *Émaux et Camées*, 44.

42. Marcel Raymond, *From Baudelaire to Surrealism* (London: Methuen & Co Ltd, University Paperback, 1970), 1.

43. Francis Burch, *Tristan Corbière: l'originalité des Amours jaunes et leur influence sur T. S. Eliot* (Paris: Editions A.-G. Nizet, 1970), 169–70.

44. Pound does raise this question of the relationship between Gautier and Baudelaire in an offhand manner when discussing the inimitability of the for-mer and the relative translatability of the latter (*P&D*, 75). But, as we might expect, Pound's "bracketing" of Baudelaire leads to a great inconsistency in his canon formation. Although Pound acknowledges the proximity of Baudelaire to Corbière when discussing "the cult of ugliness" (*LE*, 45), he seems to reverse his position when he argues in another essay that Corbière "preceded and thereby escaped that spirit or that school which was to sentimentalize over ugliness with a more silly sentimentality than the early romanticists had shown toward 'the beauties of nature'" (*SP*, 372). We can hardly avoid linking this "sentimental school" with the "infinitely slighter volume" (*LE*, 308) of Baude-laire and the romantics. In addition, Pound obsessively refers to the anti-

romantic stance in Corbière's description of Hugo as the "Garde national épique" and of Lamartine as the "Inventeur de la *larme écrite*."

And yet, Corbière's borrowings indicate that he was obviously indebted to Baudelaire. Among other poems, Corbière's "Sonnet Posthume" contains a direct and unironic reference to Baudelaire's "Spleen," and the description of the Itinerant Singer in "La Rapsode Foraine," the poem singled out by Pound as the "best introduction to [Corbière]," is quintessentially Baudelairean. Indeed, this poem prompts C. F. MacIntyre to say that the Singer "is even more powerfully effective than Baudelaire's old women: he presents specimens, but Tristan gives us the archetype" (*Les Amours jaunes* [Berkeley and Los Angeles: University of California Press, 1954], 220). Moreover, Pound himself argues that Corbière "is more real than the 'realists' because he still recognises that force of romance which is a quite real and apparently ineradicable part of our life" (*SP*, 372).

Pound's characterization of Corbière's aesthetic also raises the interesting problem of accounting for Pound's attraction to the Parnassian Gautier. It is difficult, if not impossible, to link him to the Corbière who continually flouts poetic convention and the neoclassicism of the Parnassians—as he does in "Sonnet I," for example—or who pokes fun at Gautier in "Duel Aux Camélias." Pound's assertion that "criticism may be written by a string of names" (*SP*, 318) thus enables him to ignore some of the more important internal contradictions that would otherwise complicate his ideogram of good writing. It seems inconceivable that a serious critic can at one and the same time praise Gautier, castigate Baudelaire, and discover a group of satirical poets deriving from Corbière who are uncontaminated by a prior romanticism.

45. See, for example, Taupin, *L'Influence du symbolisme français*, 142, and Richard Sieburth, *Instigations: Ezra Pound and Remy de Gourmont* (Boston: Harvard University Press, 1978), 31–36.

46. Gautier, "Nostalgies d'obélisques," *Émaux et Camées*, 60–65.

47. Kelley, "Gautier et Baudelaire," *Baudelaire, Mallarmé and Valléry*, 71. The passage continues:

> Dans une telle société, vivre dans l'immédiat revient à vivre dans la laideur ou dans la fadeur, et tenter de faire de l'art vivant par son actualité, c'est courir le risque de tomber dans une banalité incompatible avec la noblesse quasi-religieuse de la poésie. Fuir par contre la seule réalité sociale possible pour chercher l'idéalité de l'art dans les traditions du passé, c'est se figer dans une aridité fatale non seulement à la vie, mais aussi à l'art.

> [In such a society, to live in the present means to live with ugliness and insipidity, and to attempt to make a living art in all its actuality is to risk falling into a banality incompatible with the quasi-religious nobility of poetry. But to flee the only available social reality and search for an artistic ideal in the traditions of the past is also to become fixed in an aridity fatal not only to life, but also to art.]

48. Similarly, as late as 1918 we will find Pound straddling the fence between the only "two tenable positions: the Mountain and the Multitude" (*Inst*, 77), between Lewis and Romains, between Nietzsche's Overman and a radical collectivism, between epic and lyric. I discuss this fence-straddling in Chapter 4.

49. Charles Baudelaire, *Oeuvres complètes* (Paris: Aux Editions du Seuil, 1977), 464.

50. Frank Kermode, as we saw, considered the *Cantos* "the only kind of long poem the Symbolist aesthetic will admit" (136). Similarly, Timothy Materer, in his *Vortex: Pound, Eliot, and Lewis* (Ithaca: Cornell University Press, 1979), associates Pound's technique in Canto 2 with that of Valéry and Mallarmé (210–11); and Akiko Miyake, in her "Ezra Pound and French Symbolists," *Kobe College Studies* (Sept. 1981), has made the strongest claims by far for the influence of Mallarmé on Ezra Pound, arguing that "Mallarmé's achievement was accepted by Pound, though criticized and corrected" (34). Similarly, Harold Bloom and Ian F. A. Bell see Pound as an Emersonian transcendentalist participating in the native strain of "American Orphism" (Harold Bloom, *Figures of Capable Imagination* [New York: Seabury Press, 1976], 75; Ian F. A. Bell, "Pound, Emerson and 'Subject-Rhyme',", *Paideuma* 8, no. 2 [Fall 1979]: 237–42). And even Pound himself provides us with a somewhat grudging admission that imagism did indeed owe something to the French Symbolists: "Mais 'voui': l'idée de l'image doit 'quelque chose' aux symbolistes français via T. E. Hulme, via Yeats ⟨ Symons ⟨ Mallarmé. Comme le pain doit quelque chose au vanneur de blé, etc" [But of course, the idea of the image owes "something" to the French Symbolists via T. E. Hulme, via Yeats ⟨ Symons ⟨ Mallarmé. Just as bread owes something to the man who processes the wheat, etc.] (*SL*, 218).

Such arguments on behalf of Pound's symbolism would certainly be extremely rewarding because they would provide a transcendental ground for the *Cantos* and would, at the same time, permit us to account for Pound's sympathy with the French post-Symbolists who derive from the Symbolists but who, like Pound, sought to reintroduce a social element into their poetry. Unfortunately, such arguments tend to make problematic any unified vision of Pound's poetry as a result of their disregard for the historical and referential aspects of the *Cantos*. Bloom, for example, seems to discount all of Pound's poetry except the *Pisan Cantos* (*Figures*, 123) and tends to minimize Pound's distance from romanticism:

> The Poundian dictum, that verse was to be as well written as prose, initially meant Browningesque verse and Paterian prose, as Pound's early verse and prose show. That literary Modernism ever journeyed too far from its Paterian origins we may doubt increasingly, and we may wonder also whether modern criticism as yet has caught up with Pater. (*Figures*, 43)

Attempts to link Pound with American Transcendentalism generally associate Pound with Whitman (Bloom), with American Puritanism (Schneidau), or with Emerson via Fenellosa or Agassiz (Bell). While there is a residual Emersonianism in Pound's poetry, particularly in the *Pisan Cantos*, Pound's cosmopolitan outlook, whether *recherché* or not, is, as Williams argues in *Kora in Hell*, much more European than "American Orphic."

51. T. S. Eliot, "Introduction," *Literary Essays of Ezra Pound*, xiv.

52. *Selected Prose of T. S. Eliot*, ed. Frank Kermode (New York: Harcourt Brace Jovanovich, 1975), 234.

53. Ibid., 231.

54. Henry James, *French Poets and Novelists*, 61–62. Quoted in Pound's *Literary Essays*, 308.

55. For an excellent analysis of Eliot's response to Baudelaire, see Patricia Clements's *Baudelaire & the English Tradition* (Princeton: Princeton University Press, 1985), 332–88.

56. Henry James acknowledges but sidesteps in a somewhat devious fashion the proximity of Gautier to Baudelaire: "The later editions of 'Les Fleurs du Mal' . . . contain a long preface by Théophile Gautier. . . . Of course Baudelaire is not to be held accountable for what Gautier says of him, but we cannot help judging a man in some degree by the company he keeps. To admire Gautier is certainly excellent taste, but to be admired by Gautier we cannot but regard as rather compromising" (*French Poets and Novelists*, 59).

57. James, *French Poets and Novelists*, 60.

58. Ibid., 59–60.

59. Ibid., 61. Most ironically, Eliot echoes almost verbatim James's wholly negative evaluation of Baudelaire when criticizing Pound's conception of Hell.

60. And not, as Robert Casillo argues in his *Genealogy of Demons* (Evanston: Northwestern University Press, 1988), "Le Vampire."

61. See Claude Pichois's commentary on the poem in his edition of Baudelaire's *Oeuvres complètes* (Paris: Gallimard, 1975), 893–94.

62. Ibid., 34; translation by Sir John Squire in *Flowers of Evil*, ed. Marthiel Mathews and Jackson Mathews (New York: New Directions, 1963), 43.

63. Leo Bersani, *Baudelaire and Freud* (Berkeley and Los Angeles: University of California Press, 1977), 46.

64. Mario Praz, *The Romantic Agony*, 2d. ed. (Oxford: Oxford University Press, 1970), 28. See also his chapter 1, "The Beauty of the Medusa," 25–52.

65. Charles Baudelaire, "Hymne à la Beauté," *Oeuvres complètes* (Paris: Gallimard, 1975), 24–25.

66. "Fusées, XVI" *Oeuvres complètes*, ed. Y. -G. Le Dantec (Paris: Gallimard, 1951), 1187–88.

67. Praz, *Romantic Agony*, 43.

68. Gautier, *Émaux et Camées*, 56.

69. Ezra Pound to Dorothy Shakespear, n.d., (Pound III, Box 1, Folder 2 [1910–14?]), Lilly Library, Indiana University. I return to this letter when I discuss Verlaine and Mallarmé's presence in the *Pisan Cantos* in Chapter 5.

70. *The Complete Works of Algernon Charles Swinburne*, vol. 3, the Bonchurch Edition, ed. Sir Edmund Gosse and Thomas James Wise (New York: Russell & Russell, 1968), 44–51. For two excellent discussions of Swinburne and Bau-

delaire, see Patricia Clements's *Baudelaire & the English Tradition* and David G. Riede's *Swinburne: A Study of Romantic Mythmaking* (Charlottesville: University Press of Virginia, 1978).

71. For a discussion of Pound's collage aesthetic, see Marjorie Perloff's "Portrait of the artist as collage-text: Pound's *Gaudier-Brzeska* and the 'italic' texts of John Cage," in *The Dance of the Intellect: Studies in the Poetry of the Pound Tradition* (London: Cambridge University Press, 1985), 33–70.

72. Pound criticizes Gosse for presenting "Swinburne as an epileptic rather than as an intemperate drinker" and adds, "We do not however wish a Swinburne coated with veneer of British officialdom and decked out for a psalm-singing audience" (*LE*, 290–91). In this respect he echoes Aldington's criticism of Plarr's *Life of Dowson:* "Mr. Plarr has admirably vindicated his friend, and the smiling statue of Dowson is now set up in the market-place agreeably smeared with the whitewash of a blameless life" (*Egoist* 2, no. 3 [March 1, 1915]: 42). Strangely, though, Pound criticizes Gosse for suppressing unseemly biographical detail like Moore's anecdote about Swinburne's drunken rantings in his room, which is in fact included by Gosse in an appendix.

73. Hulme, "A Lecture on Modern Poetry," 73. Cf. Flint's call for the "juxtaposition of images" quoted above.

74. Pound levels three specific charges at Swinburne: (1) "He habitually makes a fine stanzaic form, writes one or two fine strophes in it, and then continues to pour into the mould strophes of diminishing quality"; (2) "There is a lack of intellect in his work"; (3) "He neglected the value of words as words, and was intent on their value as sound. His habit of choice grew mechanical, and he himself perceived it and parodied his own systematization" (*LE*, 292).

75. James, says Pound, was "the hater of tyranny; book after early book against oppression. . . . The outbursts in *The Tragic Muse*, the whole of *The Turn of the Screw*, human liberty, personal liberty, the rights of the individual against all sorts of intangible bondage! The passion of it, the continual passion of it in this man who, fools said, didn't 'feel'" (*LE*, 296).

76. *Complete Works of Algernon Charles Swinburne*, vol. 1, 139.

77. In "Two Notes," May Sinclair levels an identical charge against Keats: "Keats . . . is in one sense a perfect Imagist since his Image *is* the thing he sees. In another he is hardly an Imagist at all. He gets his thrill, not directly through his Images, his casements and his foam and his seas and fairylands, but tortuously and surreptitiously through adjectives which Imagists would die rather than use" (89).

78. Hulme, "Lecture on Modern Poetry," 73.

79. Ibid., 74.

80. Ibid., 73.

81. Gautier, *Émaux et Camées*, 73.

82. Ezra to Dorothy Pound, Aug. 4, 1924, Pound III, Lilly Library, Indiana University.

83. See Noel Stock, *The Life of Ezra Pound* (San Francisco: North Point Press, 1982), 184; Humphrey Carpenter, *A Serious Character: The Life of Ezra Pound* (Boston: Houghton Mifflin, 1988), 287.

84. "Memorial Verses On the Death of Théophile Gautier," *The Complete Works of Algernon Charles Swinburne*, vol. 3, 55.

85. I discuss this issue at greater length in Chapter 5. Pound's entire oeuvre is rife with variations on the types of conflicts I describe in the following pages, and I think that the conflict in the late cantos is one between a transcendentalizing Neoplatonism and a Swedenborgianism that wants to preserve the sense of immanence that Pound fights for throughout the *Cantos*. I would like to thank Leon Surrette for the pleasant discussions-debates that helped to refine this formulation.

86. Michel Foucault, *The Order of Things* (New York: Vintage, 1973), 43.

CHAPTER ONE

POUND'S GRADUS AD PARNASSUM

1. Gautier, *Émaux et Camées*, 111. All translations of Gautier are my own.

2. Gothot-Mirsch, "Préface," *Émaux et Camées*, 13–14. As Harry Cockerham remarks of Gautier in his introduction to Théophile Gautier's *Poésies* (London: Athlone Press, 1973), 26: "His encyclopaedic memory, his taste for a realistic and technical vocabulary and his apparent delight in the rarer words and insistence on exact terminology all help to make him one of those who did most to rejuvenate the vocabulary of French poetry in the nineteenth century."

3. Charles Baudelaire, "Théophile Gautier," in *Oeuvres complètes* (Paris: Aux Éditions du Seuil, 1968), 464.

4. Kelley, "Gautier et Baudelaire" *Baudelaire, Mallarmé and Valéry*, 64.

5. Ibid., 65.

6. Marcel Voisin, *Le Soleil et la nuit: L'Imaginaire dans l'oeuvre de Théophile Gautier* (Brussels: Editions de l'Université de Bruxelles, 1981), 33. Pound merely hints at Gautier's transitional role when comparing Gautier and Baudelaire: "Baudelaire had, we presume, a 'message'. He had also a function in the French verse of his time. The poetic language had grown stiff, even Gautier is less miraculous if one consider the tradition of French eighteenth century writing. . . . and there was doubtless need of some new shaggy influx" (*P&D*, 75).

7. Baudelaire, "Théophile Gautier," *Oeuvres complètes* (1968), 464.

8. Taupin, *L'Influence du symbolisme français*, 142; Richard Sieburth, *Instigations*, 31–36. Sieburth rightly maintains that Pound's "Alchemist" adopts "a classic Symbolist strategy: the poem is not a statement about something beyond or outside itself but an autonomous lexical and aural event, based not on the referential but on the contextual function of words" (34–35). Because Sieburth has already discussed Gourmont's importance to Pound, I do not feel compelled to provide an extensive discussion here; instead, I would refer the reader to his *Instigations*.

9. P. E. Tennant, *Théophile Gautier* (London: Athlone Press, 1975), 104.

10. Gautier, "Symphonie en blanc majeur," *Émaux et Camées*, 43.

11. Tennant's characterization of Gautier's luminosity is equally appropriate for Pound's own "luminous details": "Gautier is an exceptionally luminous

poet. . . . Prismatic effects from the interplay of light and water are common in liquid imagery, while crystalline forms are another beautiful variant" (106).

12. This poem anticipates Pound's similar use of the image of the calyx in Canto 20. The close proximity between imagism and symbolism has been documented by René Taupin, and given the pervasiveness of the French influence it is not at all surprising to find Pound and H. D. pursuing similar lines. Just as Pound was intensely interested in Régnier, so too, argues Taupin, was H. D. (*L'Influence du symbolisme française*, 159):

> Parmi les Français modernes elle a lu Remy de Gourmont et Henri de Régnier qui sont bien les seuls poètes symbolistes français à aimer les lignes nettes et les couleurs claires dans la même atmosphère de pureté.

> [Among the modern French poets she read Remy de Gourmont and Henri de Régnier, the only French Symbolists who loved clean lines and bright colors in the same atmosphere of purity.]

A postcard from H. D. places her and Pound together in Paris in 1912 (Cyrena N. Pondrom, "Selected Letters from H. D. to F. S. Flint: A Commentary on the Imagist Period," *Contemporary Literature* 10, no. 4 [Fall 1969]: 559). In "H. D. and the Origins of Imagism," *Sagetrieb* 4, no. 1 (Spring 1985), Pondrom examines the connections between symbolism and imagism and sets forth a pursuasive argument for H. D.'s central role in the development of imagism.

13. Thomas H. Jackson develops this parallel between Pound's "Apparuit" and the poems of Rossetti in his *Early Poetry of Ezra Pound* (Cambridge: Harvard University Press, 1968), 154–55.

14. Gautier, *Émaux et Camées*, 73:

> Que tu me plais dans cette robe
> Qui te déshabille si bien,
> Faisant jaillir ta gorge en globe,
> Montrant tout nu ton bras païen!
>
> . . . .
>
> D'où te vient cette robe étrange
> Qui semble faite de ta chair,
> Trame vivante qui mélange
> Avec ta peau son rose clair?

> [O how you please me in that gown
> That reveals so much of you,
> It makes your firm breasts jut out,
> And bares your pagan arms!
>
> . . . .
>
> Where did you get that exotic dress
> That seems to be made of your flesh?
> Its life-like fabric of unblemished rose
> Blends so well with your skin.]

15. Cf. Baudelaire, *Oeuvres complètes* (1975), 159; translation by David Paul in *Flowers of Evil*, 1963), 27–28:

—Et la lampe s'étant résignée à mourir,
Comme le foyer seul illuminait la chambre,
Chaque fois qu'il poussait un flamboyant soupir,
Il inondait de sang cette peau couleur d'ambre!

[And the lamp having at last resigned itself to death,
There was nothing now but firelight in the room,
And every time a flame uttered a gasp for breath
It flushed her amber skin with the blood of its bloom.]

16. As W. G. Regier argues in his "Allusive Fabric of 'Apparuit'," *Paideuma* 9, no. 2 (Fall 1980): 321: "'Golden rose the house' is one of the earliest instances of 'logopoeia', Pound's terms for plurisignation and other forms of word-play, where 'rose' serves as a verb and, not remotely, as a noun whose appearance is made manifest in the second stanza, where 'roses bend'."

17. Gautier, "La Nue," *Émaux et Camées*, 135.

18. Gautier, "Caerulei Oculi," *Émaux et Camées*, 55.

19. In this respect, however, Pound differs somewhat from Gautier, who characteristically describes the woman in magical terms which suggest that the poet's desire leads to his own dissolution: "Mon âme, avec la violence / D'un irrésistible désir, / Au milieu du gouffre s'élance / Vers l'ombre impossible à saisir" [My soul, led by the violence / Of an irresistable desire, vainly / Leaps into the whirlpool's current / Toward the shadow that cannot be seized]. ("Caerulei Oculi," *Émaux et Camées*, 56). This important difference will be explored more fully in relation to *Mauberley*.

20. Tennant, *Théophile Gautier*, 37.

21. Ibid., 104.

22. "I think you will find all the verbal constructions of *Cathay* already tried in 'Provincia Deserta'" (*SL*, 101).

23. I borrow this term from a chapter heading in Marcel Voisin's *Le Soleil et la nuit*.

24. The Latin *modo pumice expolitum* is from Catullus 1.2 and translates as "polished with a pumice-stone."

25. *Oeuvres de Henri de Régnier* (Paris: Mercure de France, 1921), vol. 3, 240.

26. Ibid., vol. 1, 10. Pound praises a number of Régnier's poems: "L'Acceuil," from his *La Sandale ailée;* four poems from *Jeux rustiques et divins* ("Le Vase" and Odelettes I, IV, VI); and the introductory poem to *Médailles d'argile*. With Pound's mention of this range of poems, we must conclude that Pound has at least read outside of Leautaud and van Bever's *Poètes d'aujourd'hui*, 25th ed. (Paris: Mercure de France, 1917), despite the fact that Pound's discussion of Regnier's odelettes follows van Bever's estimation that the odelettes are poems "d'une souplesse de rhythme et une douceur incomparable" [of a rythmic suppleness and an incomparable gentleness] (116).

27. Taupin, *L'Influence du symbolisme française*, 142.

28. Régnier, *Oeuvres*, vol. 1, 11. The passage translates: "One by one, smiling you counted them, / And you said: He is clever; / And smiling you passed them."

29. Ibid., vol. 3, 246–48.

30. Pound's discussion of the Hellenic and Provençal aesthetic is an interesting one in the context of this poem. In his discussion of Cavalcanti, Pound defines the classic, Hellenic aesthetic as being "plastic to coitus. Plastic plus immediate satisfaction"; in Provence, on the other hand, "there is some proportion between the fine thing held in the mind, and the inferior thing ready for instant consumption. . . . The Tuscan demands harmony in something more than the plastic. He declines to limit his aesthetic to the impact of light on the eye" (*LE*, 151). Pound's "Apparuit," for example, is extremely plastic and yet does not yield to "immediate satisfaction"; moreover, despite the references to Hellenic godesses (Eos, Aphrodite), Pound, with his intricate verse form, also "declines to limit his aesthetic to the impact of light on the eye."

31. See, for example, Pound's borrowing from Rossetti in his "Fair Helena by Rackham" (*CEP*, 116).

32. "Sub Mare" was first published in *Poetry Review* 1, no. 2 (Feb. 1912). As I mention in the Introduction, Pound told his mother on February 21, 1912, that Flint had lent him some of Régnier's and Gourmont's works.

33. Régnier, "Refrain," *Oeuvres*, vol. 3, 254.

34. Régnier, *Oeuvres*, vol. 1, 406.

35. See Praz, *Romantic Agony*, 2d ed., 310–11.

36. Cf. Sieburth, *Instigations*, 34–35.

37. van Bever, 116. As Amy Lowell says of this poem: "Suffice it to say that it is the most perfect presentation of the creative faculty at work that I know of in any literature" (*Six French Poets*, 175).

38. Régnier, *Oeuvres*, vol. 3, 129. Translation by Amy Lowell, in *Six French Poets*, 389.

39. According to van Bever, in his *Poètes d'aujourd'hui*, 117: "*La Sandale ailée*, publiée en 1907, est à ce jour le dernier volume de vers de M. de Régnier. Le changement marqué dans les poèmes dont nous venons de parler,—l'abandon du decor pour l'expression directe des sentiments,—y est encore plus sensible" [*La Sandale ailée*, published in 1907, is the most recent volume of verse by Régnier. The marked change in the poems of which we speak—the abandonment of the decorative for the direct expression of his sentiments—is here even more apparent].

40. Martino, *Parnasse et symbolisme*, 187. Although too long to translate, I include Samain's introductory poem to his *Au Jardin de L'Infante*, 9th ed. (Paris: Mercure de France, 1904) for the convenience of the reader:

> Mon âme est une infante en robe de parade,
> Dont l'exil se reflète, éternel et royal,
> Aux grands miroirs déserts d'un vieil Escurial,
> Ainsi qu'une galère oubliée en la rade.
>
> Aux pieds de son fauteuil, allongés noblement,
> Deux lévriers d'Écosse aux yeux mélancoliques
> Chassent, quand il lui plaît, les bêtes symboliques
> Dans la forêt du Rêve et de l'Enchantement.
>
> Son page favori, qui s'appelle Naguère,
> Lui lit d'ensorcelants poèmes à mi-voix,

Cependant qu'immobile, une tulipe aux doigts,
Elle écoute mourir en elle leur mystère . . .

Le parc alentour d'elle étend ses frondaisons,
Ses marbres, ses bassins, ses rampes à balustres;
Et, grave, elle s'enivre à ces songes illustres
Que recèlent pour nous les nobles horizons.

Elle est là résignée, et douce, et sans surprise,
Sachant trop pour lutter comme tout est fatal,
Et se sentant, malgré quelque dédain natal,
Sensible à la pitié comme l'onde à la brise.

Elle est là résignée, et douce en ses sanglots,
Plus sombre seulement quand elle évoque en songe
Quelque Armada sombrée à l'éternel mensonge,
Et tant de beaux espoirs endormis sous les flots.

Des soirs trop lourds de pourpre où sa fierté soupire,
Les portraits de Van Dyck aux beaux doigts longs et purs,
Pâles en velours noir sur l'or vieilli des murs,
En leurs grands airs défunts la font rêver d'empire.

Les vieux mirages d'or ont dissipé son deuil,
Et dans les visions où son ennui s'échappe,
Soudain—gloire ou soleil—un rayon qui la frappe
Allume en elle tous les rubis de l'orgueil.

Mais d'un sourire triste elle apaise ces fièvres;
Et, redoutant la foule aux tumultes de fer,
Elle écoute la vie—au loin—comme la mer . . .
Et le secret se fait plus profond sur ses lèvres.

Rien n'émeut d'un frisson l'eau pâle de ses yeux,
Où s'est assis l'Esprit voilé des Villes mortes;
Et par les salles, où sans bruit tournent les portes,
Elle va, s'enchantant de mots mystérieux.

L'eau vaine des jets d'eau là-bas tombe en cascade,
Et, pâle à la croisée, une tulipe aux doigts,
Elle est là, reflétée aux miroir d'autrefois,
Ainsi qu'une galère oubliée en la rade.

Mon Ame est une infante en robe de parade.

(7–10)

41. Remy de Gourmont, *Le Livre des masques* (Paris: Mercure de France, 1896), 65. Although Pound's "Study in French Poets" (*Little Review*) and "Hard and Soft in French Poetry" (*Poetry*) both appeared in February of 1918, we can determine that the latter was a subsequent development in Pound's thinking about French poetry because he incorporates his discussion of "hardness" into his reprint of "A Study in French Poets" in *Instigations* (1920).
42. Samain, *Au Jardin de L'Infante*, 8.

43. K. K. Ruthven, *A Guide to Ezra Pound's Personae* (Berkeley and Los Angeles: University of California Press, 1969), 76.

44. Gautier, *Émaux et Camées*, 111.

45. Kelley, "Gautier et Baudelaire," *Baudelaire, Mallarmé and Valéry*, 73.

CHAPTER TWO
POUND'S GRADUS A PARNASSO:
MISANTHROPY, POUND, AND SOME FRENCH SATIRE

1. See, for example, Pound's discussion of Régnier, Samain, and Heredia in the Feb. 1918 *Little Review*.

2. Pound's interest in Arthur Rimbaud would also be relevant here. I omit such a discussion because Marjorie Perloff has discussed this topic very extensively in her important "Pound and Rimbaud: The Retreat from Symbolism," *Iowa Review* 6 (Winter 1975) and *The Poetics of Indeterminacy: Rimbaud to Cage* (Princeton: Princeton University Press, 1981). Although Perloff's discussion of Pound and Rimbaud is, as always, very suggestive, I believe that Pound's interest in Rimbaud corresponds to, and is better illustrated by, his fascination with Tailhade. Perloff looks to Pound's 1918 *Study in French Poets* for evidence of a Rimbaldian influence on the "collage-text" of the *Cantos*, saying that "Rimbaud's influence on Pound has gone largely unnoticed, no doubt because Pound paid no attention to Rimbaud's major works: *Saison en Enfer, Illuminations*, or even such late great poems as 'Mémoire' and 'Larme.' But one must remember that Pound's interest in a given poet was almost always stylistic rather than thematic" ("Pound and Rimbaud," 93). However, Perloff's argument is, I think, undermined by Pound's reference to "Aube" and "Villes" (*Illuminations*) and to "Vierge Folle" (*Un Saison en enfer*) in his 1913 "Approach to Paris" (*AP* 7, 727). That Pound chose to ignore these poems in his later *Study in French Poets* would seem to indicate that his interest in Rimbaud stems from something other than Rimbaud's "anti-paysages" ("Pound and Rimbaud," 111). As Perloff rightly argues, the poems mentioned in *A Study in French Poets* are not poems that would lead to the collage-text; rather, Rimbaud's "Au Cabaret-Vert," "Vénus Anadyomène," and "Les Chercheuses de poux" are, as Pound stresses, closer in spirit to the poems of Laurent Tailhade. Of "Vénus Anadyomène" Pound says, "Tailhade has painted his 'Vieilles actrices' at greater length, but smiling; Rimbaud does not endanger his intensity by a chuckle" (*Inst*, 30–31). And, again, of "Les Chercheuses de poux" Pound writes, "The poem is 'not really' like Tailhade's, but the comparison is worth while" (*Inst*, 34). These poems contain hard, clean images not unlike those in Tailhade's *Poèmes Aristophanesques*, a fact underscored by Pound's decision to follow his translations of Rimbaud with a translation of Tailhade's "Rus" (*T*, 434–37).

3. The dilemma which faces us is conveniently framed by two divergent evaluations of Pound's poetry in this period. In his *Genesis of Ezra Pound's Cantos* (Princeton: Princeton University Press, 1976), Ronald Bush argues that, "despite the small successes of 'Les Millwin' and his other realist verse . . . and despite his respect for the 'prose tradition,' Pound was then unable to turn realism into major poetry" (151). Schneidau takes a divergent approach in *The*

Image and the Real which perhaps overemphasizes the breakthrough in this volume: "The 'Contemporania' poems . . . imply a new freedom of attitude, a new unpretentiousness of subject, a new brilliance of himself as *persona*—all taking rise from Pound's desire to bid good-bye to his earlier style, and the postures in which it had involved him" (8).

4. In the former category, I would include as conversational or confessional poems: "Silet," "In Exitum Cuisdam," "Sub Mare," "Plunge," "Portrait d'une Femme," and the two picture poems, "The Picture" and "Dans un Omnibus de Londres." In the latter, I would include as metamorphic: "Apparuit," "Doria," "A Virginal," "The Return," "N.Y.," "A Girl," and "Effects of a Company." Such categories, of course, mean little or nothing by themselves; what is important, however, is how easily one can in fact categorize the tonal variants in this volume.

5. Remy de Gourmont, *Le Livre des masques*, 100. Guy Michaud echoes this evaluation in his *Message poétique du symbolisme* (Paris: Librairie Nizet, 1947), 473:

> Cet émule de Juvénal et de Pétrone mêle la satire au pamphlet, fustigeant, dans une langue dont la truculence n'hésite jamais devant le scatologique ou l'obscène, faux poètes, faux dévots, et toute cette fausse humanité qui n'a qu'un mufle ou un groin pour visage. . . . Ce Parnassien . . . grand trouveur de mots après Laforgue, passa auprès du Symbolisme sans le comprendre.

> [This emulator of Juvenal and Petronius mixes satire with pamphleteering, thrashing, in a colorful language which doesn't hesitate before the scatological or the obscene, false poets, hypocrits, and a false humanity wearing a muzzle or a snout for a face. . . . This Parnassian, a great discoverer of words after Laforgue, went beyond Symbolism without realizing it.]

6. C. T. Lewis, *Elementary Latin Dictionary* (Oxford: Oxford University Press, 1977).

7. Hugh Witemeyer, "Clothing the American Adam," in *Ezra Pound among the Poets*, ed. George Bornstein (Chicago: University of Chicago Press, 1985), 94.

8. *Oeuvres de Laurent Tailhade*, vol. 2 (Paris: Mercure De France, 1923), 15. All translations of Tailhade are my own.

9. Pound is of course expressing a resentment regarding "High Bohemia" common among the avant-garde and later summarized nicely by Wyndham Lewis in *Time and Western Man* (London: Chatto & Windus, 1927), 48:

> Mr. Diaghileff is a 'revolutionary' impresario; that is to say, what he provides is designed to pass as the 'latest' and most 'revolutionary' fare possible. In Western Europe there is no other stage-performance so original and experimental as his Ballet. Although invariably full of people, a very fashionable and wealthy audience, his performances are supposed, on account of their daring originality, not to pay. And every one who has the interests of experimental art at heart is supposed to experience a fervent sympathy for those performances.

10. Hugh Kenner, *The Poetry of Ezra Pound* (New York: New Directions, 1951), 118.

11. Jackson, *The Early Poetry of Ezra Pound*, 106.

12. Ibid.

13. In "H. D. and the Origins of Imagism," Cyrena N. Pondrom argues convincingly that the woman described in "Ortus" is H. D., which, if true, makes the poem all the more sinister. This article is a significant revision of standard accounts of H. D.'s "marginal" role in the history of poetic modernism.

14. In his *Guide to Ezra Pound's Personae*, K. K. Ruthven cites Pound's allu-
· sion to Shakespeare's *Midsummer Night's Dream*, V, i, 17–18: "gives to airy nothing/A local habitation and a name."

15. Schneidau, *The Image and the Real*, 6.

16. Taupin, *L'Influence du symbolisme français*, 145.

17. Tailhade, *Oeuvres*, vol. 2, 56.

18. Taupin, *L'Influence du symbolisme français*, 146.

19. Tailhade, "Hydrotherapie," *Oeuvres*, vol. 2, 30. Because this poem is, I think, far superior to any of Pound's similar satires, I quote it in full:

"Hydrotherapie"

Le vieux monsieur, pour prendre une douche ascendante,
A couronné son chef d'un casque d'hidalgo
Qui, malgré sa bedaine ample et son lumbago,
Lui donne un certain air de famille avec Dante.

Ainsi ses membres gourds et sa vertèbre à point
Traversent l'appareil des tuyaux et des lances,
Tandis que des masseurs, tout gonflés d'insolences,
Frottent au gant de crin son dos où l'acné point.

Oh! l'eau froide! la bonne et rare panacée
Qui, seule, raffermit la charpente lassée
Et le protoplasma des sénateurs pesants!

Voici que, dans la rue, au sortir de sa douche,
Le vieux monsieur qu'on sait un magistrat farouche
Tient des propos grivois aux filles de douze ans.

"Au Pays du Mufle" is the title of one of the sections of Tailhade's *Poèmes Aristophanesques* wherein he satirizes the bourgeoisie. Richard Aldington translates it as "In the Land of the Mugs" (*Egoist* 2, no. 10; reprinted in Pondrom, *Road from Paris*, 295). *Mufle* signifies "snout" but connotes a person who is poorly educated and very crass.

20. According to Taupin, for example, "Tailhade l'influence plus que Corbière alors. Il admirait en lui les mêmes vertus qu'il admirait chez Pétrone, Catulle et Villon, le nombre et la qualité des images, la verdeur du style" [Tailhade influenced him more than Corbière therefore. He admired him for the same virtues he saw in Petronius, Catullus, and Villon, for the number and quality of their images and the vigour of their style] (*L'Influence du symbolisme français*, 145).

21. Ibid., 145.

22. Verlaine, for example, makes this same claim in his *Les Poètes maudits* (Paris: Vanier, 1888), 8: "Villon et Piron se complairaient à voir un rival souvent heureux." Pound was certainly familiar with Verlaine's essay—he mentions it in his revised discussion of Corbière in *Instigations* (19), and in his 1913 essay Pound echoes Verlaine's claim that it would be "impossible de tout citer de ce *Pardon* dans le cadre restreint que nous nous sommes imposé" (11): "One garbles it so in quotation and it is much too long to give in full" (*SP*, 372).

23. Corbière, *Les Amours jaunes*, 27; trans. MacIntyre, 29. Pound quotes the first two sections of "Paris" in *Instigations*.

24. Ibid., 206; my translation.

25. Ibid. Pound notes that "the dots are in the original" (*SP*, 371). Significantly, *Mauberley*, a poem which was, I think, influenced to a certain extent by Corbière, makes extensive use of such "dots."

26. Cf. Corbière's "Très mâle . . . et quelquefois très *fille*" (*Les Amours jaunes*, 32).

27. Pound's "Our Contemporaries" (*P*, 122) contains a similar ironic reference to a poet that Pound "a lu mourir," that is, to Rupert Brooke, who, unfortunately for Pound, died fighting in World War I shortly after the publication of this poem.

28. Kenner, *Poetry of Ezra Pound*, 118.

29. Michel Dansel, *Langage et modernité chez Tristan Corbière* (Paris: Librairie A.-G. Nizet, 1974), 83.

30. Pound is not alone, of course, in emphasizing Corbière's Breton poems. As Francis Burch has remarked in his *Tristan Corbière: l'originalité des Amours jaunes et leur influence sur T. S. Eliot* (Paris: Editions A.-G. Nizet, 1970), 158: "Ni Baudelaire ni Laforgue n'ont évoqué la mer ou la campagne avec la puissance et la sensibilité d'un Corbière dans ses poèmes bretons" [Neither Baudelaire nor Laforgue have evoked the sea or the countryside with the power and the sensibility of Corbière in his Breton poems].

31. Corbière, *Les Amours jaunes*, 167; trans. MacIntyre, 177.

32. Ibid., 149; trans. MacIntyre, 151.

33. Ibid., 154–55; 171.

34. Dansel, *Langage et modernité*, 130.

35. Edwards and Vasse, trans. *Annotated Index to* ***The Cantos*** (Berkeley and Los Angeles: University of California Press, 1957), 64.

36. Pound writes: "Leger has approved the section of XVI that deals with his account of Verdun" (Ezra Pound to Dorothy Shakespear, Oct. 20, 1923, Pound III, Lilly Library, Indiana University).

37. Starkie, *From Gautier to Eliot*, 162.

38. Corbière, *Les Amours jaunes*, 140; my translation.

39. Ibid., 144; my translation.

40. Ibid., 177; trans. MacIntyre, 181.

41. See C. F. MacIntyre's commentary in his translation of *Les Amours jaunes*, 215.

42. Corbière, *Les Amours jaunes*, 123; trans. MacIntyre, 113.

43. "Épitaphe," *Les Amours jaunes*, 31.

44. In his *Tristan Corbière* (Boston: Twayne Publishers, 1979), Robert Mitchell describes the poem as follows: "The style of 'Paysage mauvais' is totally different from that of the poems in the first four sections of *Les Amours jaunes*. . . . It is basically a kind of 'tone poem' which attempts to present the mood of Brittany with its Celtic mythology, its fantasy, and its sinister qualities. . . . Its structure is also quite different, consisting of a series of nouns (with or without verbs), one following the other, which produces the effect of cumulative description rather than the suspense, antithesis, undercutting, etc." (130).

45. This one passage alone, with its echo of Shakespeare's *Tempest*, would substantiate Francis Burch's claim that "Corbière se rattache, enfin, en recourant à une prosodie quelque peu âpre, à un langage et à une imagerie qui fuient le «precieux», à la tradition qu'illustre Shakespeare" [In resorting to a somewhat harsh prosody, to a language and an imagery that avoids the "precious," Corbière in the end rejoins that tradition exemplified by Shakespeare] (Burch, *Tristan Corbière*, 171).

46. Pound uses a similar constellation of images in his discussion of the mathematics of the "image" in *Gaudier-Brzeska*, 92.

47. *The Aeneid of Virgil* 6.270, ed. R. D. Williams (London: Macmillan, 1972).

48. Corbière *Les Amours jaunes*, 131; trans. MacIntyre, 125.

49. Ibid., 217. MacIntyre gives us one of the few accounts in English of this poem (216–25). I would like to take this opportunity to express my indebtedness to his translation and commentary, for it was my initial entrée to Corbière's world, as my discussion of this and other of Corbière's poems would indicate.

50. Ibid., 132; trans. MacIntyre, 127.

51. Ibid., 133–34; 129–33.

52. Ibid., 135; 137.

53. Ibid., 218.

54. Pound does quote the entire hymn in his *Instigations*.

55. Corbière, *Les Amours jaunes*, 129–30; trans. MacIntyre, 119–21.

56. Cf. Mitchell, *Tristan Corbière*, 130.

57. Corbière, *Les Amours jaunes*, 128–29; trans. MacIntyre, 117–19.

58. Ibid., 132; 125.

59. The epigraph to "Épitaphe," *Les Amours jaunes*, 31.

60. Pound's "To a Friend Writing on Cabaret Dancers" is a powerful corrective to Hermann Hagedorn's "The Cabaret Dancer," which appeared in *Poetry* 7 (1915–16), 125:

> Breathe not the word Tomorrow in her ears.
>> Tomorrow is for men who send their ships
>> Over the sea to moor at alien slips;
> For dreamers, dawdlers, martyrs, pioneers,
> Not for this golden mote. To her appears
>> No hovering dark that prophesies eclipse.
> Grace of the swallow in the swaying hips,
> Heart of the swallow, knowing not the years! . . .

61. Pound's allusion to Catullus establishes a link with Gautier's "Carmen," *Émaux et Camées*, 111:

> Elle a dans sa laideur piquante
> Un grain de sel de cette mer
> D'où jaillit nue et provocante,
> L'âcre Vénus du gouffre amer.

> [Her piquant ugliness contains nonetheless
> A grain of the salt of that sea
> From which the naked Venus of the bitter abyss
> Bursts forth provocatively.]

62. Corbière, *Les Amours jaunes*, 108; my translation. My interest in this poem is not entirely arbitrary; there is internal evidence that supports my claim that Pound would have read this poem. "To a Friend Writing" contains a mention of "kohl and rouge" ("I search the features, the avaricious features / Pulled by the kohl and rouge out of resemblance— / Six pence the object for a change of passion" [*P*, 159]), which echoes lines from Corbière's "Déjeuner de soleil," a poem in *Raccrocs* preceding "Veder Napoli": "Kh'ol, carmin et poudre de riz; / Pour fair dire—la coquette— / Qu'on fait bien les ciels à Paris" (*Les Amours jaunes*, 107).

63. Dansel, *Langage et modernité*, 97.

64. Ibid., 162–63.

65. Corbière, *Les Amours jaunes*, 98; my translation.

66. Albert Sonnenfeld, *L'Oeuvre poétique de Tristan Corbière* (Paris: Presses Universitaires de France, 1960), 161. For an alternative reading, see Mitchell, *Tristan Corbière*, 53–60.

67. Corbière, *Les Amours jaunes*, 37. Pound quotes from both "A l'éternel madame" and "Féminin singulier" to illustrate Corbière's ironic treatment of love.

68. Ibid., 37; trans. MacIntyre, 47.

69. Ibid.

70. Mitchell, *Tristan Corbière*, 123.

71. Lewis, *Time and Western Man*, 85–86.

72. "Browning wrote to a theory of the universe, thereby cutting off a fair half of the moods for expression" (*LE*, 293).

73. Peter Makin, *Pound's Cantos* (London: George Allen & Unwin, 1985), 283.

CHAPTER THREE
THE CITADEL OF THE INTELLIGENT: POUND'S LAFORGUE

1. The letters to Iris Barry are included in *Selected Letters*, 92–93; "Irony, Laforgue, and Some Satire" appeared in *Poetry* 11, no. 2, and is reprinted in *Literary Essays*, 280–84.

2. Remy de Gourmont, *Le Livre des masques*, 205–9; Arthur Symons, *The Symbolist Movement in Literature* (London: William Heinemann, 1899), 105–14.

3. As Hugh Kenner argues in *The Pound Era*, "Eliot after some years' infat-

uation with a peripheral Symbolist poet, Jules Laforgue, worked more and more deeply into the central Symbolist poetic, translated Perse, sponsored the reputation of Valéry in England, and wrote his last principal work, the *Four Quartets*, under the sign of Mallarmé himself and with a title that remembers Verlaine ('De la musique avant toute chose')" (p. 133). Although Eliot's religious orthodoxy does not approach Mallarmé's atheistic version of Platonism, his concern for the logos permits a parallel to be drawn at the level of form.

4. Pound refers here to a 1918 letter from Spire thanking him for an introduction to Laforgue's works: "Je vous remercie de m'avoir révélé Laforgue que je connaissais seulement par les extraits publiés dans la première Anthologie en 1 volume par Van Bever et Leautaud. Celui là c'est un vrai génie." (Spire to Pound. Aug. 22, 1918. American Literature Collection, Beinecke Library, Yale University.)

5. Houston, *French Symbolism*, 82–83.

6. Jules Laforgue, *Poésies* (Paris: Librairie Armand Colin, 1959), 114–15; trans. Peter Dale, *Poems of Jules Laforgue* (London: Anvil Press Poetry Ltd., 1986), 133.

7. David Arkell, *Looking for Laforgue: An Informal Biography* (Manchester: Carcanet Press, 1979), 151.

8. Laforgue, *Poésies*, 91; trans. Dale, *Jules Laforgue*, 105.

9. Ibid., 97; 113.

10. See, for example, the discussion of the popularity during Laforgue's lifetime of Camille Flammarion's *La Pluralité des mondes habités* in Warren Ramsey's *Jules Laforgue and the Ironic Inheritance* (New York: Oxford University Press, 1953), 52–53.

11. Laforgue, *Poésies*, 97; trans. Dale, *Jules Laforgue*, 113.

12. Donald Davie suggests this parallel in *Ezra Pound: Poet as Sculptor* (New York: Oxford University Press, 1964), 91–96.

13. Laforgue, says Pound, has "dipped his wings in the dye of scientific terminology" (*LE*, 283).

14. Raymond Poggenburg, "Laforgue and Baudelaire," in *Jules Laforgue: Essays on a Poet's Life and Work*, ed. Warren Ramsey (Carbondale: Southern Illinois University Press, 1969), 32.

15. N. Christophe de Nagy, "The Place of Laforgue in Ezra Pound's Literary Criticism," in Ramsey, *Essays*, 111–29.

16. Kenner, *Pound Era*, 142.

17. Ramsey, *Ironic Inheritance*, 211.

18. Schneidau, *The Image and the Real*, 161.

19. W. G. Hale, "Pegasus Impounded" in *Ezra Pound: The Critical Heritage*, ed. Eric Homberger (London: Routledge & Kegan Paul, 1972), 157: "If Mr. Pound were a professor of Latin, there would be nothing left for him but suicide. I do not counsel this. But I beg him to lay aside the mask of erudition. And, if he must deal with Latin, I suggest that he paraphrase some accurate translation, and then employ some respectable student of the language to save him from blunders which might still be possible."

20. J. P. Sullivan, *Ezra Pound and Sextus Propertius: A Study in Creative Translation* (Austin: University of Texas Press, 1964), 5.

21. *Propertius*, trans. H. E. Butler (London: Loeb Classical Library, William Heinemann, 1924), 2.28.18—19: "So Io wore a strange guise and lowed her earlier years; but now a goddess, that once drank Nilus' waters in likeness of a cow." Unless otherwise indicated, all subsequent references are to this text. Other notable errors include Pound's misreading *rigere* ("stiffen") for *rigare* ("conduct water," "to wet or moisten"), and his mistranslation of "Nocturnaesque canes" as "Night Dogs."

22. Pound, "Propertius and Mr. Pound," in Homberger, *Critical Heritage*, 169.

23. Adrian Collins, "Grumbles about the 'Homage'," in Homberger, *Critical Heritage*, 161.

24. Pound, "Propertius and Mr. Pound," in Homberger, *Critical Heritage*, 169.

25. *Propertius* 2.28.31–34.

26. "But now 'tis time with other measures to range the slopes of Helicon" (*Propertius* 2.10.1).

27. "Such music makest thou as the Cynthian god modulates with fingers pressed upon his well-skilled lyre" (*Propertius* 2.34.79–80). See Sullivan's *Ezra Pound and Sextus Propertius* (102–4) for a detailed discussion of this passage.

28. As Ruthven notes in his *Guide to Ezra Pound's Personae*, 83–124, Pound parodies Yeats's "Withering of the Boughs" in the lines "and the desolated female attendants / Were desolated because she had told them their dreams" (*P*, 211). Ruthven also cites Pound's "Impressions . . . de Voltaire" as the source for "orfevrerie" (*P*, 211), "In Durance" for "For her hands have no kindness me-ward" (*P*, 209), "Spring" for "Bright tips reach up from Twin Towers" (*P*, 209), and "Homage to Quintus Septimus" for "Death has his tooth in the lot" (*P*, 219).

29. Kenner, *Pound Era*, 29.

30. Laforgue, "Complainte à Notre-Dame des Soirs," *Poésies*, 36; "Pierrots," *Poésies*, 175. Trans. Dale, *Jules Laforgue*, 197.

31. Lawrence Richardson, "Ezra Pound's Homage to Propertius," *Yale Poetry Review* 6 (1947): 23.

32. Pound, "Propertius and Mr. Pound," in Homberger, *Critical Heritage*, 170.

33. Kenner, *Pound Era*, 285.

34. Friedrich Nietzsche, *The Gay Science*. Trans. Walter Kaufmann (New York: Vintage Books, 1974), 137.

35. May Sinclair, "The Reputation of Ezra Pound," in Homberger, *Critical Heritage*, 184.

36. Bush, *Genesis*, 174.

37. Ruthven, *Guide*, 86.

38. "A. R. Orage on Pound, Propertius and 'decadence'," in Homberger, *Critical Heritage*, 158.

39. Sullivan, *Ezra Pound and Sextus Propertius*, 85.

40. *Propertius* 2.28.3–4: "For the season has come when the scorching air seethes with heat and earth begins to glow beneath the parching Dog-star."

41. Ruthven, *Guide*, 90.

42. Sullivan, *Ezra Pound and Sextus Propertius*, 32.

43. Bush, *Genesis*, 174.

44. Sullivan, *Ezra Pound and Sextus Propertius*, 89.

45. Ibid., 31.

46. *Propertius* 2.26 and 4.7. J. P. McCulloch, trans. *The Poems of Sextus Propertius* (Berkeley and Los Angeles: University of California Press, 1972), 115 and 228.

47. Sullivan, *Ezra Pound and Sextus Propertius*, 57. Pound is correct, of course, if he means by this that the love interest is, as in Ovid, meant as a challenge to Augustan *mores*. See Hans-Peter Stahl, *Propertius: "Love" and "War": Individual and State under Augustus* (Berkeley and Los Angeles: University of California Press, 1985.)

48. Ramsey, *Ironic Inheritance*, 162.

49. Ibid., 83.

50. Ibid., 84.

51. As William Jay Smith argues in his "Introduction" to the *Selected Writings of Jules Laforgue* (New York: Grove Press, 1956), 21:

> The Unconscious is what the poet saw as "the law of the world, which is the great melodic voice resulting from the symphony of the consciousness of races and individuals." Laforgue gives to Hartmann's metaphysical concept a psychological and imaginative extension. Poetry for him was no longer the romantic outpourings of the individual, as it had been in his early poems, but rather the expression of the many individuals that go to make up the one. The strength of the *Complaintes* lies in Laforgue's realization of the complex nature of the subconscious mind. Although he affected the air of a dilettante, he was a psychologist in poetry long before the advent of modern psychology. The discoveries of Freud and Jung, which lie behind so much of the writing of the twentieth century, owe a great deal to Hartmann. Laforgue's interest in the Unconscious and his interpretation of it prepared the way, in a very real sense, for Eliot and Joyce.

52. Jules Laforgue, *Feuilles volantes* (Paris: Editions Le Sycomore, 1981), 86; my translation. As Erika Ostravsky describes it in "Laforgue and Samuel Beckett," in Ramsey, ed. *Jules Laforgue: Essays*, 142: "Its topography and the conditions which exist there are almost identical: fixity, calm, and silence prevail. The light is vague or failing, the senses are restricted or dead, a physical and spiritual numbness has taken over. Reason is obliterated, the will is weakening, all the functions of the human creature are slowly stripped away."

53. In a draft of *Our Tetrachal Précieuse* now contained in the Beinecke Library, Pound includes these references to the Unconscious, making his censorship in the published version all the more curious.

54. William Jay Smith, trans. *The Moral Tales* (New York: New Directions, 1986), xxiv.

55. Ramsey, *Ironic Inheritance*, 226.

56. Jules Laforgue, *Moralités légendaires* (Paris: Mercure de France, 1964), 152; trans. Smith, *Moral Tales*, 107.

57. Ibid., 127.

58. Ramsey, *Ironic Inheritance*, 226.

59. Laforgue, *Moralités légendaires*, 154; trans. Smith, *Moral Tales*, 109.

60. Pound's "Conduct, on the other hand, the soul / 'Which the highest cultures have nourished'" (*P*, 194) is a rough translation of Laforgue's line, "Menez L'âme que les Lettres ont bien nourrie."

61. John Espey, *Ezra Pound's Mauberley* (Berkeley and Los Angeles: University of California Press, 1955), 66.

62. Ibid., 65–66.

63. William V. Spanos provides an excellent summary of this critical debate in "The Modulating Voices of *Hugh Selwyn Mauberley*," *Wisconsin Studies in Contemporary Literature* 6, no. 1 (Winter-Spring 1965): 73–96. I have merely extended Spanos's "basic categories" by including his own reading of the poem. Spanos suggests a more subtle reading whereby Pound identifies with Mauberley's attacks on the British cultural milieu but himself attacks Mauberley's personal perceptions.

The confusion caused by *Mauberley* is conveniently illustrated by comparing the grounding premises of the two book-length studies of the poem. Pound's own suggestion that Mauberley may be "merely a translation of the Homage to S. P., for such as couldn't understand the latter" (*SL*, 239) has led John Espey to argue that "both *Propertius* and *Mauberley* are works of self-justification, concerned with the fate of the artist in an age unsympathetic to his art" (*Ezra Pound's Mauberley*, 103–4). For Espey, the poem "moves from Pound (*Ode*-V) through Pound's and Mauberley's contacts (*Yeux Glauques*-XII) to the disappearance of Pound (*Envoi*) and the independent emergence of Mauberley (*Mauberley*-III), with Pound acting now, at least on the surface, only as tolerant observer, and concludes with Mauberley's single poem (*Medallion*)" (ibid., 16).

Jo Brantley Berryman, on the other hand, argues that "Pound, beginning with the 'E. P. Ode' and ending with 'Poem XII,' has created a consistently ironic portrait of the untrustworthy critic—Hugh Selwyn Mauberley.... Mauberley tells us about E. P. in the 'Ode,' but what he says reveals his own limitations—what he does *not* understand about the poet he presumes to explain.... By exhibiting such misinformed critical views, Pound hoped to expose critics who misread the writer and mislead the reader" (*Circe's Craft* [Ann Arbor: UMI Research Press, 1983], 1). Using Pound's discussion of logopoeia to buttress her argument, Berryman in a sense transforms the "Ode" into a Browningesque monologue that reveals the limitations of Mauberley (ibid., 26); thus, Berryman reverses the terms of Espey's argument when she says that Mauberley speaks in the first half of the poem and that Pound in fact speaks in the second.

64. Ramsey, *Ironic Inheritance*, 207.

65. See Pound's "Religio" (*SP*, 47): "By what characteristic may we know the divine forms? By beauty."

66. Hugh Witemeyer, *The Poetry of Ezra Pound: Forms and Renewal, 1909–1920* (Berkeley and Los Angeles: University of California Press, rpt. 1981), 179–80.

67. Berryman, *Circe's Craft*, 11.

68. Stock, *Life of Ezra Pound*, 242.

69. Maxwell Bodenheim, "The Isolation of Carved Metal," *Dial* 72 (Jan. 1922): 87–91; reprinted in Homberger, *Critical Heritage*, 206.

70. Pound's note reads as follows: "The sequence is so distinctly a farewell to London that the reader who chooses to regard this as an exclusively American edition may as well omit it and turn at once to page 205" (*Personae* [New York: New Directions, 1971], 185). The epigraph from Nemesianus's "Eclogue 4"—"vocat aestus in umbram" ("the heat calls us to the shade," trans. J. Wight Duff and Arnold M. Duff in *Minor Latin Poets* [London: Loeb Classical Library, William Heinemann, 1935], 4.38)—is a puzzling one that has been discussed little or not at all by critics. Nemesianus was a Carthaginian poet of the Silver Age working in the pastoral tradition perfected by Virgil. He can be seen either as a derivative poet who adds very little to the tradition or as a minor artist who nonetheless manages to do what he can within the constraints of that tradition. Strangely enough, "Eclogue 4" possesses the alternative title "Eros" and thus bears witness to one thematic aspect of *Mauberley*. Additionally, the Eclogue presents two shepherds, Lycidas and Mopsus, each lamenting their futile loves:

> Populea Lycidas nec non et Mopsus in umbra,
> pastores, calamis ac versu doctus uterque
> nec triviale sonans, proprios cantabat amores
> nam Mopso Meroe, Lycidae crinitus Iollas
> ignis erat; parilisque furor de dispare sexu
> cogebat trepidos totis discurrere silvis.

The shepherds, Lycidas and Mopsus too, both of them skilled on the reed-pipes and in verse, were singing each of his own love in the poplar shade, uttering no common strain. For Mopsus the flame was Meroe, for Lycidas 'twas Iollas of the flowing locks; and a like frenzy for a darling of different sex drove them wandering restlessly through all the groves. (*Nemesianus* 4. 1–6)

The parallel is of course striking, particularly since the homosexual theme is prevalent throughout Decadent literature, but we can only guess at its significance.

71. "A. R. Orage on Pound's Departure from London," *New Age* (Jan. 13, 1921); reprinted in Homberger, *Critical Heritage*, 199.

72. Ibid., 200.

73. Ibid.

74. Ibid., 201–2.

75. Ibid., 202.

76. In a letter to Harriet Monroe, Pound writes: "I dislike the paragraph about Hamlet, but it is an early and cherished bit and T. E. won't give it up" (*SL*, 50).

77. Spanos, "Modulating Voices," 96.

78. Laforgue, *Poésies*, 89–90; trans. Dale, *Jules Laforgue*, 103.

79. Ibid., 184; 209. Even a cursory examination of the more extended list of poems that Pound quotes in his *Instigations* indicates that he favors the defensively aggressive Laforguian persona over the "philosophical" Laforgue or the Laforgue whose irony rebounds onto and threatens to overwhelm his "ironic equilibrium." Although Pound assures us that his selection of poems from Laforgue's oeuvre is "representative" (*Inst*, 8), he concentrates most characteristically on those poems ("Complainte des consolations," "Complainte des printemps," "Complainte des pianos," "Pierrot III," and "Locutions des Pierrots") wherein Laforgue triumphs over "l'éternel féminin" by his blatant disregard for—or, better, his intentionally uncomprehending and malicious attitude toward—her feelings.

In *Jules Laforgue* (London: Athlone Press: 1977), Michael Collie offers a more carefully articulated discussion of the types of poems that make up Laforgue's *Les Complaintes* and his *L'Imitation*. Collie notes that the poems in *Les Complaintes* "fall into several categories": (1) "witty, iconoclastic verses where the interest lay in the brilliance of verbal formulation and the impudence of technique" ("Complainte de l'orgue de Barbarie" and, I would argue, "Complainte des pianos qu'on entend dans les quartiers aisés"); (2) "philosophical poems" written prior to *Les Complaintes* ("Complainte des voix sous le figuier bouddique"); and (3), the majority of poems "in which metrical and verbal freedom combined, not with raw 'philosophizing' but with sets of psychological responses to give a more unified type of effect. These are poems in which there is an emphasis upon the poet's response to experience as opposed to his ideas about the Universe" (39).

80. Collie, *Jules Laforgue*, 91.

81. Ibid., 95.

82. For a discussion of Laforgue's eye imagery, see Collie, *Jules Laforgue*, 96.

83. Laforgue, *Poésies*, 184; trans. Dale, *Jules Laforgue*, 209.

84. Collie, *Jules Laforgue*, 98.

85. Ian F. A. Bell, "A Mere Surface: Wyndham Lewis, Henry James and the 'Latitude' of Hugh Selwyn Mauberley," *Paideuma* 15, nos. 2–3 (Fall-Winter 1986): 55–56.

86. Ibid., 58.

87. Jo Brantley Berryman makes a similar observation in *Circe's Craft*, although she argues for the continuity between these two visions (175–77).

88. Laforgue, "Autre complainte de lord Pierrot," *Poésies*, 95; trans. Dale, *Jules Laforgue*, 111.

89. Kelley, "Gautier et Baudelaire," *Baudelaire, Mallarmé and Valéry*, 65.

90. Gautier, *Émaux et Camées*, 73 and 109.

91. Ibid., 45.

92. Ibid., 93. All translations of Gautier are my own.

93. Ibid., 55.

94. Ibid., 82.

95. Ibid., 121–29.

96. Silvestre de Sacy, Théophile Gautier, and Ed. Thierry, "Rapport sur les progrès de la poésie," in *Recueil de Rapports sur les progrès des lettres et des sciences en France* (Paris, 1868), 125.

97. Davie, *Poet as Sculptor*, 98.

98. Berryman, *Circe's Craft*, 144.

99. Ibid., 153.

100. S. Reinach, *Apollo*, trans. Florence Simmonds (New York: Charles Scribner's Sons, 1908), 58.

101. Berryman's ellipses are in this respect fascinating.

102. Reinach, *Apollo*, 59.

103. Gautier, *Émaux et Camées*, 135.

104. Ibid., 30. Reinach compares Apelles and Correggio in the following passage: "The most renowned painter of the fifth century, Polygnotus, was, we are told, less pre-eminent as a colourist than as a draughtsman, whereas those of the fourth century, Parrhasius, Zeuxis, and Apelles, were above all colourists. If their pictures had been preserved to us, we should perhaps have found them more akin to Correggio than to Mantegna, or Bellini" (*Apollo*, 59).

105. Friedrich Nietzsche, *The Will to Power*, trans. Walter Kaufmann and R. J. Hollingdale (New York: Vintage Books, 1968), 396.

106. Gautier, *Émaux et Camées*, 31.

107. Ibid., 55.

108. Ibid., 56.

109. Ibid., 57.

110. Davie, *Poet as Sculptor*, 100.

111. "The metal finish alarms people. They will no more endure Joyce's hardness than they will Pound's sterilized surgery" (*P&D*, 73).

112. Davie, *Poet as Sculptor*, 100.

113. Berryman, *Circe's Craft*, 150–51.

114. Gautier, *Émaux et Camées*, 126–27.

115. Pound, *Personae*, 185.

CHAPTER FOUR
THE WOBBLING PIVOT:
SURFACE AND DEPTH IN THE EARLY CANTOS

1. Kermode, *Romantic Image*, 136.

2. Rejecting the notion that the "symbolist" counterpointing of Pound's ideogramic method provides an efficacious solution to the problem of the long poem, critics have seized upon Pound and Gaudier's discussion of modernist sculpture as a series of "planes in relation" in order to analyze the *Cantos* in vorticist terms as a collage superposition. Such critics as Myles Slatin, Marjorie Perloff, and, most recently, Peter D'Epiro suggest that Pound's extensive labor and singular emphasis on the Malatesta Cantos attest to his realization that the technique of superposition alone was not an adequate structural principle for the *Cantos*. According to Slatin, for example, "It seems significant that only after he had finished the Malatesta group was Pound able to rethink the poem sufficiently to change drastically those parts of it left untouched since the appearance of the *Lustra* volumes" ("A History of Pound's *Cantos I–XVI*, 1915–1925," *American Literature* 35 [May 1963] 191–92). Like Slatin, Perloff locates the real shift in Pound's poetic in the Malatesta Cantos where, accord-

ing to Perloff, he finally adopts a "collage method" which "decompose[s] and fragment[s] historical time so as to create a new landscape without depth, what Jean-Pierre Richard calls, with reference to Rimbaud, an 'anti-paysage'" ("Pound and Rimbaud," 111).

3. The grafting of Ovidian metamorphosis onto Homeric epic has long been considered a principal structural device in the *Cantos*, and arguments of this sort are certainly supported by the recurrence of Homeric and Ovidian themes and motifs throughout the poem, particularly in the Pisan section where they become a haunting refrain signaling a major, if only temporary, reversal. However, recent criticism has extended this relatively simple notion of a "cultural overlaying" by exploring the implications of the epic/metamorphic tradition in light of more overtly formal issues like metaphor and metonymy, the difference between poetry and prose realism, or between myth and history. Such theoretical approaches are truly generative in that they permit us to discover the logical problems necessitating drastic stylistic and thematic shifts in Pound's "long poem including history." In his *Tale of the Tribe: Ezra Pound and the Modern Verse Epic* (Princeton: Princeton University Press, 1980), for example, Michael André Bernstein convincingly demonstrates the weakness of the Ovid/Homer parallel as an explanatory model. Ovid's static rendering of essences undermines Pound's "ideogrammic juxtaposition" of historical particulars: "Metamorphosis implies some universal *forma*, some constant element which finds expression in a multitude of changing guises. . . . With the ideogrammic juxtaposition, on the other hand, the emphasis resides in the new insight that emerges from the combination of two or more apparently unrelated elements" (43). The Homeric parallel, however, while it does correspond to Pound's attempt to write a "tribal encyclopedia," "is over-valued as the text's main integrating principle" because "large sections of the poem simply do not fit such a paradigm or belong within so fixed a scaffolding" (170). Instead, Bernstein turns to Chinese historiography with its moral framework of a "conservative revolution" as an explanatory model for Pound's attempt to mediate between the mythical and historical codes—to render, that is, an unchanging and mythically grounded historical/temporal progression.

4. Pound's *Three Cantos* appeared in *Poetry* 10, nos. 3–5 (June–Aug. 1917) and have been reprinted in the revised *Personae*, ed. Lea Baechler and A. Walton Litz (New York: New Directions, 1990).

5. Myles Slatin has outlined the significant dates marking Pound's progress on the *Cantos* in the following fashion: (1) Pound completes a draft of *Three Cantos* by December 1915, a date which underscores the proximity of *Three Cantos* to Pound's "Near Perigord," and he publishes them in the June-August 1917 issues of *Poetry*; (2) after a two-year hiatus, Pound publishes Canto 4 in October 1919 and writes his father in December of that same year that he has finished Cantos 4–7, which are published in the *Dial* in late 1921; (3) Canto 8 (now Canto 2) appears in the May 1922 *Dial*, and by July 1922 Pound writes as though he had completed the first eleven, or perhaps even thirteen, cantos; (4) Pound's initial Canto 9, the Malatesta Canto, grows into four cantos upon which Pound works from July to December 1922 and finally publishes in the

July 1923 *Criterion;* after completing his draft of the early cantos, Pound makes extensive revisions from February to May 1924, revisions which include the elimination of much material in *Three Cantos,* particularly the Browningesque voice which governs these cantos, and he finally decides to transfer Canto 8 to its present position as Canto 2.

For a more detailed treatment, see Myles Slatin, "A History of Pound's *Cantos I–XVI,*" 183–95, and Bush, *Genesis.*

6. Houston, *French Symbolism and the Modernist Movement,* 83.

7. Ramsey, *Ironic Inheritance,* 212.

8. Ibid., 208.

9. Ibid., 209.

10. Christine Froula, *To Write Paradise: Style and Error in Pound's Cantos* (New Haven: Yale University Press, 1984), 11.

11. Ibid., 26.

12. Ibid., 41.

13. N. Christophe de Nagy, "The Place of Laforgue in Ezra Pound's Literary Criticism," *Essays,* ed. Ramsey, 121.

14. Pound's comment on Pius—"stone in his bladder / *testibus idoneis*" (10/ 45)—approaches the misappropriation of etymological detail characteristic of *Propertius,* but it is less ironic than it is sarcastic, unless we choose to read it as "sufficient testicles," applying the phrase to Malatesta himself.

15. Guy Davenport, *Cities on Hills: A Study of Cantos I–XXX,* Studies in Modern Literature, no.25 (Ann Arbor: UMI Research Press, 1983), 220.

16. See Bush, *Genesis,* 261ff.

17. Pound's reservation about the Unanimistes is contained in this confusing formulation: "The thing that puzzles me in attempting to appreciate both Romains and Vildrac is just this question of 'hardness', and a wonder how poetry can get on without it—not by any means demanding that it be ubiquitous. For I do not in the least mean that I want their poems rewritten 'hard'; any more than I should want Jammes' early poems rewritten 'hard'" (*LE,* 289).

18. Michel Décaudin, ed., "Preface" to Jules Romains, *La Vie unanime* (Paris: Gallimard, 1983), 12. Unless otherwise noted, all translations are my own.

19. Ibid., 46. Pound quotes the passage in *Instigations,* 70.

20. André Cuisenier, *Jules Romains et l'unanimisme,* vol. 2 (Paris: Flammarion, 1948), 29.

21. Romain, *La Vie unanime,* 103.

22. Ibid., 14.

23. See, for example, "Gaudier-Brzeska Vortex" in *GB,* 20–24.

24. See Michel Décaudin, *La Crise des valeurs symbolistes* (Toulouse: Privat, 1960), 226–40.

25. Romains, *La Vie unanime,* 49.

26. As, for example, in Romains's "Pendant une guerre" (*La Vie unanime,* 127):

> Pourtant j'ai hâte. Allons, j'ai faim; non d'une idée.
> L'idée et l'idéal me dégoûtent. Je veux

Un être! Nous voulons un dieu! Il faut des dieux!
Non pas des dieux perdus au ciel, des cause blêmes;
Il faut des dieux charnels, vivants, qui soient nous-mêmes,
Dont nous puissions tâter la substance; des dieux
Qui souffrent par nos corps et qui voient par nos yeux,
Des animaux divins dont nous soyons les membres;
Qui tiennent tout, nos corps, notre espace, nos chambres,
Enclos dans leur réelle et palpable unité.

27. Cuisenier, *Jules Romains et l'unanimisme*, 31.

28. "Postscript to the *Natural Philosphy of Love* by Rémy de Gourmont" (*P&D*, 203–14). Pound refers to it as his "sperm-essay" in an undated letter to Dorothy Shakespear circa July 1921 now in the Pound Collection (Pound III) at the Lilly Library, Indiana University. As we shall see, this is a particularly modernist formulation, for, when Lewis tells us to "eschew all clichés" in "The Code of a Herdsman" (*Little Review* 4, no. 3 [July 1917]: 4), his examples of permissable "personal epithets" include "He has a great deal of *sperm*" and "I like a fellow with as much *sperm* as that."

29. Romains, *La Vie unanime*, 119.

30. Pondrom, *Road from Paris*, 26.

31. Romains, *La Vie unanime*, 55.

32. Romains's wartime career, however, runs strangely parallel to Pound's: both had strong fascist and collaborationist tendencies. See Denis Boak, *Jules Romains* (New York: Twayne, 1974), 103–4.

33. Ezra Pound, "Unanimisme," *Little Review* 4, no. 12 (April 1918): 32.

34. Discussing "Benevolence" in *The Gay Science*, Nietzsche asks: "Is it virtuous when a cell transforms itself into a function of a stronger cell? It has no alternative. And is it evil when the stronger cell assimilates the weaker? It also has no alternative; it follows necessity, for it strives for superabundant substitutes and wants to regenerate itself. Hence we should make a distinction in benevolence between the impulse to appropriate and the impulse to submit, and ask whether it is the stronger or the weaker that feels benevolent" (Nietzsche, *The Gay Science*, trans. Kaufmann, 175–76).

35. In his editorial for the *Little Review* 4, no. 1 (May 1917), Pound writes that he has "accepted the post of Foreign Editor of *The Little Review:* chiefly because [I] . . . wished a place where the current prose writings of James Joyce, Wyndham Lewis, T. S. Eliot, and myself might appear regularly, promptly, and together, rather than irregularly, sporadically, and after useless delays" (3). Pound's editorial was followed by Lewis's "Imaginary Letters, I: Six Letters of William Bland Burn to his Wife" (19–23), and Lewis then published the following pieces in subsequent issues: "Imaginary Letters, II," *Little Review* 4, no. 2 (June 1917): 22–26; "Imaginary Letters, III: The Code of the Herdsman," *Little Review* 4, no. 3 (July 1917): 3–7; "Inferior Religions," *Little Review* 4, no. 5 (Sept. 1917): 3–8; "Cantleman's Spring-Mate," *Little Review* 4, no. 6 (Oct. 1917): 8–14; "The Starry Sky," *Little Review* 4, no. 7 (Nov. 1917); "A Soldier of Humor, I," *Little Review* 4, no. 8 (Dec. 1917): 32–46; "A Soldier of Humor, II," *Little Review* 4, no. 9 (Jan. 1918): 35–51; "Imaginary Letters,

VIII," *Little Review* 4, no. 11 (March 1918): 23–30; "The Ideal Giant," *Little Review* 5, no. 1 (May 1918): 1–18. Pound also reviewed *Tarr*.

36. *Little Review* 4, no. 11 (March 1918): 25. The entire passage reads: "But when twenty men are conglomerated into a giant, it is not, in the case of genius, simply an addition sum. The fine fellow is the head of the Colossus. But we must admit that he never succeeds in quite actively canalizing the mass. There is always the slovenly character of all giants about the organism. His superb megaphone is not so successful as the attenuated voice of the whittled-down human reed."

37. *Little Review* 5, no. 1 (May 1918): 1–18. Subsequent page references will be incorporated into the body of the text.

38. "Imaginary Letters, I," *Little Review* 4, no. 1 (May 1917): 22–23. Although Lewis later claimed that he "was reasonably immune then to Superman," he does nevertheless admit that "'La Gaya Scienza,' or those admirable maxims . . . which he [Nietzsche] wrote after the breakdown in his health, were among [Lewis's] favorite reading in those years" (*Rude Assignment* [London: Hutchinson, 1950] 120). Notably, *The Gay Science* is the book in which Nietzsche first introduced Zarathustra and the Uebermensch, and much of this book is devoted to Nietzsche's condemnation of the "herd instinct" and to his arguments on behalf of "egoism": "Surely, the faith preached so stubbornly and with so much conviction, that egoism is reprehensible, has on the whole harmed egoism (while *benefiting*, as I shall repeat a hundred times, *the herd instincts!*)—above all, by depriving egoism of its good conscience and bidding us to find in it the true source of all unhappiness." (*The Gay Science*, 258). Nietzsche characterizes his contemporaries "as *tame animals* . . . [who] are a shameful sight and in need of the moral disguise . . . because he has become a sick, sickly, crippled animal that has good reasons for being 'tame'; for he is almost an abortion, scarce half made up, weak, awkward" (ibid., 295). Finally, in an extremely important passage occuring shortly after the introduction of Zarathustra, Nietzsche contrasts the "multitude" with the Uebermenschen or "born guessers of riddles who are, as it were, waiting on the mountains" (ibid., 279).

39. Lewis, "Imaginary Letters, I," 21.

40. Significantly, Remy de Gourmont echoes this characterization in his "Nietzsche sur la montagne," *Revue du Nouveau Siècle* (March 15, 1902).

41. Lewis, "Code of the Herdsman," 3.

42. Ibid., 7.

43. Ibid., 4–7.

44. Ibid., 5: "Never lie. You cannot be too fastidious about the truth. If you must lie, at least see that you lie so badly that it would not deceive a pea-hen.— The world is, however, full of pea-hens."

45. Nietzsche, *The Gay Science*, 279: "The greatest recent event—that 'God is dead,' that the belief in the Christian god has become unbelievable—is already beginning to cast its first shadows over Europe."

46. Quoted in Ronald Paterson, *The Nihilistic Egoist: Max Stirner* (London: Oxford University Press, 1971), 81.

47. Nietzsche, *The Gay Science*, 275.

48. Friedrich Nietzsche, ibid., 281; *Werke*, vol. 2 (Berlin: Walter de Gruyter, 1973), 258.

49. Ibid., 282.

50. *The Odyssey of Homer*, trans. Richmond Lattimore (New York: Harper Torchbooks, 1968), 27. See also Kaufmann's note in *The Gay Science*, 282.

51. Pound would have been exposed to Nietzsche earlier through his association with the *New Age*, but his interest in Nietzsche at no other time assumes the proportions that it does here.

52. Letter of August 10, 1922, to John Quinn. Quoted in Daniel Pearlman, *The Barb of Time* (New York: Oxford University Press, 1969), 302.

53. Although it is true that the Malatesta Cantos do suggest a flattening of perspective and a suspension of inwardness, particularly with the elimination of the unifying voice contained in the Verona scene, depth is reintroduced with the moral analysis implicit in Pound's "totalitarian" synthesis and becomes the strongest argument against the notion of a "collage" method. With the notion of the moral exemplum ("'History is a school book for princes'" [54/280]), Pound reintroduces the "symbolist principles" for which Perloff criticizes Cantos I–VII ("Pound and Rimbaud," 91–117), and, thus, we should be careful not to attribute too much significance to his prosaic solution to the difficulties of epic narrative in the Malatesta Cantos, especially when Pound immediately reverts to his earlier technique of juxtaposition, if in a less fragmented and more accessible manner, with his portraits of Baldy Bacon, Dos Santos, and Kung. Indeed, Pound's seeming reluctance to adopt his new prosaic mode is merely a more elaborate manifestation of the initial doubt that accompanied Pound's composition of *Three Cantos*.

54. See, for example, Jacob Burkhardt, *The Civilization of the Renaissance in Italy* (New York: Harper Colophon Books, 1958), 50: "Unscrupulousness, impiety, military skill, and high culture have been seldom so combined in one individual as in Sigismondo Malatesta (d. 1467). But the accumulated crimes of such a family must at last outweigh all talent, however great, and drag the tyrant into the abyss." Also, John Addington Symonds, *Renaissance in Italy: The Age of the Despots*, vol. 1 (London: John Murray, 1926), 134–35.

55. P. J. Jones, *The Malatesta of Rimini and the Papal State: A Political History* (London: Cambridge University Press, 1974), 176: "It is now understood that Sigismondo Malatesta, like other bad characters of the past, owes much of his evil reputation to hostile testimony, and especially, as often in the Middle Ages, the testimony of the church. The worst allegations against him were all transmitted to posterity by one authority: the Piccolimini Pope Pius II, whose interests as ruler, and possibly as Sienese, envenomed him against the Malatesta, and whose published anathemas and, still more, his widely read historical *Commentaries*, represented Sigismondo with medieval gusto and indiscriminacy as a monster guilty of every possible public and private outrage. Many of these charges can be dismissed at once as the conventional invective of *curia* and church. Others, among the most grave, convicting him of the murder of his first two wives . . . and of killing and dishonouring the corpse of a German noblewoman, were either inaccurate, improbable, or the offspring of malicious rumour."

56. Michael F. Harper, "Truth and Calliope: Ezra Pound's Malatesta," *PMLA* 91, no. 1 (Jan. 1981): 86–103.

57. Ibid., 96.

58. Carroll F. Terrell, *A Companion to the Cantos of Ezra Pound*, vol. 1 (Berkeley and Los Angeles: University of California Press, 1980), 52: "Ravisher, butcher, adulterer/murderer, parricide, and perjurer,/killer of priests, reckless, lecher,/ . . . fornicator and assassin,/traitor, rapist, committer of incest, arsonist, and keeper of concubines."

59. Peter D'Epiro, *A Touch of Rhetoric: Ezra Pound's Malatesta Cantos*, Studies in Modern Literature, no. 2 (Ann Arbor: UMI Research Press, 1981), 63.

60. Andrew Clearfield makes this point in "Pound, Paris, and Dada," *Paideuma* 7, no. 1–2 (Spring-Fall 1978): 133.

61. Peter D'Epiro's discussion of the early drafts of the Malatesta section is interesting in that it demonstrates Pound's continuing reluctance to edit out completely both the dramatic and the introspective aspects of his work. In the final draft Pound all but eliminates a fairly long section involving his and Eliot's trip to Verona in 1920 wherein they undertake "somber ruminations on the transcience of human relationships and the decline of great civilations" (D'Epiro, *Touch of Rhetoric*, 21). Although the refrains—"And we sit here. I have sat here/For forty four thousand years" (11/50) and "In the gloom, the gold gathers the light against it" (11/51)—continue to appear throughout the *Cantos*, divested of their context, they become, as D'Epiro suggests, an "*ex abrupto* voice . . . emanating from an eerie, surrealistic dimension of its own, provid[ing] the canto with a somber, sibylline resonance" (ibid., 48). The autobiographical scene is finally recontextualized in the *Pisan Cantos* (78/495) when Pound appears in propria persona.

62. Peter Nicholls, *Ezra Pound: Politics, Economics and Writing: A Study of the Cantos* (London: Macmillan, 1984), 60. Nicholls makes a fascinating argument similar to that which follows, but from a purely economic point of view.

63. Foucault, *Order of Things*, 199.

64. Modern economic theory, according to Foucault, undoes this classical representation of value and substitutes an analysis of the labor embodied in the object:

> Needs, and the exchange of products that can answer to them, are still the principle of the economy: they are its prime motive and circumscribe it; labour and the division that organizes it are merely its effects. But within exchange, in the order of equivalences, the measure that establishes equalities and differences is of a different nature from need. It is not linked solely to individual desires, modified by them, or variable like them. It is an absolute measure, if one takes that to mean that it is not dependent upon men's hearts, or upon their appetites; it is imposed upon them from outside: it is their time and their toil. (Ibid., 224)

65. Here and elsewhere I am greatly indebted to Michael Bernstein's influential *The Tale of the Tribe*, one of the first studies to explain the significant role that the Chinese Dynasty Cantos play both in the poem and in Pound's developing poetic.

66. Although Fenollosa denies that either a "true noun" or a "pure verb" exists in nature (*CWC*, 10), he nonetheless maintains that "the sentence form was forced upon primitive men by nature itself" (*CWC*, 12) and that, because "all natural processes . . . redistribute force" (*CWC*, 12), any linguistic component will contain a *"verbal idea of action"* (*CWC*, 9). For Fenollosa, then, the link between a linguistic sign and its referent is not guaranteed by an adequate and transparent representation as it is in the classical period, but by a transitivism that language and the world both share: "The form of the Chinese transitive sentence, and of the English (omitting particles), exactly corresponds to this universal form of action in nature. This brings language close to *things*, and in its strong reliance upon verbs it erects all speech into a kind of dramatic poetry" (*CWC*, 13).

67. Foucault, *Order of Things*, 289.

68. Ibid.

69. Fenollosa and Pound reject this tendency by insisting on the metaphorical naturalism of the Chinese ideogram. Confronted with the opacity of language, Fenollosa can only salvage the luminous relationship between word and world and still escape a syllogistic logic by positing a metaphorical relationship inherent in nature, that is, a relationship which does not result from the subjective intervention of man. Whereas the attribution of a predicate to a subject is, according to Fenollosa, an arbitrary act performed by a "pure subjectivity" and thus permits "no possible test of the truth of a sentence" (*CWC*, 11), the metaphorical nature of language is wholly objective:

> But the primitive metaphors do not spring from arbitrary *subjective* processes. They are possible only because they follow objective lines of relations in nature herself. The forces which produce the branch-angles of an oak lay potent in the acorn. . . . Had the world not been full of homologies, sympathies, and identities, thought would have been starved and language chained to the obvious. There would have been no bridge to cross from the minor truth of the seen to the major truth of the unseen. (*CWC*, 22–23)

70. Hugh Kenner, *The Poetry of Ezra Pound* (New York: New Directions, 1951), 204. According to Foucault, a simple order of resemblances would not allow the degree of displacement necessary to transform a similitude into a signature: "the totality of these marks, sliding over the great circle of similitudes, forms a second circle which would be an exact duplication of the first, point by point, were it not for that tiny degree of displacement which causes the sign of sympathy to reside in an analogy, that of analogy in emulation, that of emulation in convenience, which in turn requires the mark of sympathy for its recognition" (*Order of Things*, 29).

71. Kenner, *Pound Era*, 116.

72. In "Pound and Ovid" (Bornstein, ed. *Ezra Pound among the Poets*, 13–34), Lillian Feder argues that Pound "does not, like Ovid, reveal the human emotions projected on divinity but rather converts metamorphosis into a deification of natural phenomena" (22). Thus, Tyro's love is not an issue here for Pound, but "appear[s], like Proteus, with whom the canto ends, as part of the

continuous process of merging and transformation through which the natural and divine become indistinguishable" (22). While Feder's discussion is extremely suggestive, particularly her attempt to situate Pound's rendering of Ovidian metamorphosis within a Neoplatonic tradition, it seems that such a notion of metamorphosis has to be balanced against the many instances of metamorphosis in these early cantos resulting from sexual violation or from violation of rituals, the majority of which derive from Ovid (Actaeon, Philomela, etc.). While Feder's argument might well be true in the case of Tyro, a myth deriving not from Ovid but from Homer (*Odyssey* 11, 235), it is not clear, for example, how the Itys/Cabestan episode can be seen as a "deification of nature"; rather, it is a complicated ideogram conflating unrestrained sexuality, human jealousy, infanticide, murder, and cannibalism. And in the Ignez da Castro incident we have a literalization of metamorphic fixity so perverse that it forces us to recognize the need for a finite temporal horizon. Thus, once we move beyond Pound's hypnotic and compelling depictions of these nymphs, his "deification of natural phenomena," we might begin to ask ourselves, with Nietzsche, "When will we complete our de-deification of nature?" (*Gay Science*, 169).

Similarly, although Feder is, I think, largely right when she argues that, "In Ovid, myth is merged with nature, human and inanimate. . . . In the *Cantos* mythical beings transform nature to reflect their presence" (20), she relies somewhat heavily on the differences between Ovid's and Pound's handling of the Bacchus episode and ignores the fact that Pound's emphasis "on the appearance of Bacchus' animals" (19) stems just as much from the "Homeric Hymns" as do Pound's early depictions of Aphrodite. Thus, Pound's reversion to a more archaic religious poem might indeed force us to qualify Feder's otherwise suggestive assertion that, "whereas Ovid's gods are all too human in their desires, limits, indulgences, and anger, in the *Cantos*, chosen human beings are allowed the prerogatives of gods" (19). As Jean Pierre Vernant describes Dionysius in his *Myth and Thought among the Greeks* (London: Routledge & Kegan Paul, 1983), 325:

> The god who suddenly takes possession of a man in the midst of paroxysms of excitement makes him lose possession of himself, 'overrides' him, and even when he has taken charge of him, remains inaccessible and incomprehensible. . . . Both within man and in nature, he embodies what is radically other.

While such a god might appeal to the mystical side of Pound, it would not appeal to Pound, the "factive personality," for Dionysus is here the "Inspirer of frenzied women" ("Hymn to Dionysus, I," *Hesiod: The Homeric Hymns and Homerica*, trans. Hugh G. Evelyn-White" [London: William Heinemann, 1920], 289), and, as Vernant argues, not only is the Dionysiac ecstasy "first and foremost the province of women" (*Myth and Thought*, 324), but it "is a collective hysteria, the god suddenly seizing possession of the man, is an impersonal state passively undergone" (Ibid., 354).

73. Pound is alluding to Gautier's "Le Château du Souvenir," *Émaux et Camées*, 123:

Daphné, les hanches dans l'écorce,
Étend toujours ses doigts touffus;
Mais aux bras du dieu qui la force
Elle s'éteint, spectre confus.

Pound later returns to this theme in *Drafts and Fragments:* "Laurel bark sheath-
ing the fugitive/a day's wraith unrooted?" (110/793).

74. Gautier, *Émaux et Camées*, 150.

75. Cuisenier, *Jules Romains et l'unanimisme*, vol. 2, 127.

76. "*The H. D. Book*, Part 2, Chpt. 3," *IO* 6 (Summer 1969): 133.

77. I borrow this term from a chapter heading in Marcel Voisin's *Le Soleil
et La Nuit: L'Imaginaire dans l'oeuvre de Théophile Gautier* (Brussels: Editions de
l'Université de Bruxelles, 1981).

78. Gabriel Brunet, *Théophile Gautier poète*, 312.

79. Gautier, *Émaux et Camées*, 128.

80. Ibid., 26–27.

81. *La Presse* (July 10, 1843). Quoted in Tennant, *Théophile Gautier*, 63.

82. Georges Poulet, *Études sur le temps humain* (Edinburgh: Edinburgh Uni-
versity Press, 1949), 291.

83. Ibid.

84. Ibid., 293.

85. Ibid., 316.

86. Ibid., 303.

87. *Le Panthéon, peintures murales*, septembre 1848, et *L'Art moderne*, 70.
Quoted in Poulet, *Études sur le temps humain*, 309.

88. As Poulet points out, Gautier transforms Dante's concentric circles into
"*cercles excentriques*," but the image of the lake which "se propage en ondula-
tions" and the "rayonnements" should remind us of Pound's similar use of a
Dantescan light imagery which "non si disuna" (*Paradiso* 13.56).

89. Lewis, *Time and Western Man*, passim.

90. Poulet, *Études sur le temps humain*, 291.

91. As Guy Davenport tells us in *Cities on Hills*: "We are shown the Empress
Zoe, of Byzantium, who poisoned her husband, thereby reducing her civila-
tion to the moral advantages of the rawest nature; and the queen Marozia,
wife of Alberic I, who became mistress of Pope Sergius III; and the mythical
Zothar whom we saw in Canto XVII" (207).

92. I have argued this previously in "After Strange Gods: Robert Duncan
Reading Ezra Pound and H. D.," *Sagetrieb* 4, nos. 2–3 (Fall–Winter 1985):
237–38.

93. Nietzsche, *Gay Science*, 139.

94. For a discussion of "cosmic rhythm," see Kenneth Cornell's *The Post-
Symbolist Period*, 42.

95. See Michel Foucault's *Order of Things*, 23–24: "Sympathy is an instance
of the *Same* so strong and so insistent that it will not rest content to be merely
one of the forms of likeness; it has the dangerous power of *assimilating*, of
rendering things identical to one another, of mingling them, of causing their
individuality to disappear. . . . This is why sympathy is compensated for by its
twin, antipathy. Antipathy maintains the isolation of things and prevents their

assimilation." If the surprising resemblance between Pound and Foucault has not yet been made clear, compare Pound's "form seen in a mirror" and his "Titter of sound about me, always" (5/17) with Foucault: "The great untroubled mirror in whose depths things gazed at themselves and reflected their own images back to one another is, in reality, filled with the murmur of words" (*Order of Things*, 27).

CHAPTER FIVE
L'ÉTERNELLE RITOURNELLE IN THE LATE CANTOS

1. Bernstein, *Tale of the Tribe*, 178.

2. Ezra Pound to Isabel Pound, Feb. 23, 1910, Paige Carbon #153, Beinecke Library, Yale University.

3. Kenner, *Pound Era*, 178.

4. Lewis, *Time and Western Man*, 85–86.

5. Pound to Wyndham Lewis, Dec. 3, 1924, Paige Carbon #704, Beinecke Library, Yale University.

6. In a 1922 letter (Ezra Pound to Dorothy Shakespear, Aug. 29, 1922, Pound III, Lilly Library, Indiana University), Pound mentions "Pratz in Judith Gautier's old apart. with Theophile's arm chair and varied holy relics." In a December 1915 letter to his father (Paige Carbon #406, Beinecke Library, Yale University), we learn that Mlle. de Pratz was a friend of both Judith Gautier and Laurent Tailhade and was helping Pound translate some of his poetry into French.

7. Kenner, *Pound Era*, 482–83.

8. Verlaine, *Oeuvres poétiques complètes* (Paris: Gallimard, 1962), 107.

9. Ezra Pound to Dorothy Shakespear, n.d., (Pound III, Box 1, Folder 2 [1910–14?]), Lilly Library, Indiana University. Although the sequence of these undated letters might lead us to believe that this particular letter was written in 1911 or before, Dorothy tells Pound in a letter of May 3, 1912, "I like the Verlaine" (Pound and Litz, eds. *Ezra Pound and Dorothy Shakespear*, 94–95). This reference remains unidentified but could conceivably refer to this poem. Pound quotes the two stanzas in reverse order.

10. Verlaine, *Oeuvres*, 599.

11. See the "Chronologie" to Verlaine's *Oeuvres*, xliv.

12. Verlaine is, of course, misquoting his "À la Promenade" ("Et le vent doux ride l'humble bassin" [*Oeuvres*, 109]), and we can certainly rescue "Clair de Lune" (107) for the *Cantos* by noting that "À la Promenade" follows hard upon "Clair de Lune" in Verlaine's *Fêtes galantes*.

13. Mockel to Pound, July 18, 1918, American Literature Collection, Beinecke Library, Yale University.

14. Ezra Pound to Homer Pound, July 18, 1918, Paige Carbon #492, American Literature Collection, Beinecke Library, Yale University.

15. The Merrill refrain repeats 78/494 and will continue through the late cantos. As Pound so often does, Merrill is, I think, transliterating the Greek *chi* (χ) as x to create a neologism combining Chaldean and Saladin (Sultan or Salah el Din, and, by extension, the woman dancing for the Sultan). *Chaldean*

also fits the context of Pound's poem because it suggests another occult tradition discussed in Burnet's *Greek Philosophy: Thales to Plato*, a book of which Pound was very fond. Also, the Chaldean Oracles was considered a sacred book by later Neoplatonists.

16. Ezra to Homer Pound, Dec. 18, 1915, Paige Carbon #406, American Literature Collection, Beinecke Library, Yale University.

17. Laforgue, *Poésies*, 185; trans. Dale, *Jules Laforgue*, 209.

18. Ibid., 298; 421.

19. See my discussion in Chapter 3 where I refer to Reinach's *Apollo*, 58.

20. Carroll F. Terrell, *A Companion to the Cantos of Ezra Pound*, vol. 2 (Berkeley and Los Angeles: University of California Press, 1984), 453. In his *Greek Philosophy: Thales to Plato*, 2d ed. (London: Macmillan, 1964), John Burnet discusses Pythagorean *eide* (figures, musical scales, mathematical ratios) extensively in his chapter on Pythagoras (35ff). Also, the arcane *diastasis* (separation) in this passage certainly corresponds to Burnet's discussion of Anaximander's "natural [impulse] to speak of the opposites as being 'separated out' from a mass which is as yet undifferentiated than to make any one of the opposites the primary substance" (17), as opposed to Pythagoras's more sophisticated notion of the (Un)limited: "We hear nothing more of 'separating out' or even of rarefaction and condensation. Instead of that we have the theory that what gives form to the Unlimited ($\check{\alpha}\pi\epsilon\iota\rho o\nu$) is the Limit ($\pi\acute{\epsilon}\rho\alpha\varsigma$)" (34–35).

21. Paul Henry, S. J., "Introduction: The Place of Plotinus in the History of Thought," in Plotinus, *The Enneads*, 3d edition rev., trans. Stephen MacKenna (London: Faber & Faber Limited, 1962), lvi.

22. Pound's conception of both language and nature in the Pisan and later cantos is very reminiscent of Emerson's discussion in "On Nature," which helps to explain his unflinching support of Fenellosa, who was very much in line with Transcendentalism. Although Pound downplayed Emerson, we have seen throughout this study the residual effects of Pound's early training. One of the few instances of Pound's "anxiousness" is evident in this response to his mother's complaint about his helping some Hamilton freshmen with Emerson's "Self-Reliance" (Ezra to Isabel Pound, Feb. 1905, Paige Carbon #28, American Literature Collection, Beinecke Library, Yale University):

> Also madam you needn't begin to crow just because I happen to hear a little Emerson. He and all that bunch of moralists, what have they done? Why, all that is in their writings that's good is from the Bible and the rest is rot. They have diluted Holy Writ. They have twisted it awry. They have it is true weakened it sufficiently for the slack-minded and given vogue to the dilutation. The chief benefit of reading them is this. You can't trust a word they say and the exhilaration produced by this watchfulness for sophistries is the only benefit. The joy I get from the mediaevalians is this: you current eventers think you're *so* modern and so gol darn smarter than anybody else that [it] is a comfort to go back to some quiet old cuss of the dark, so-called silent centuries, and find written down the sum and substance of what's worthwhile in your present day frothiness.
>
> I'm not yelling anti-progress, but it's good to know what is really new. Only if you want to boast your progress stick to chemistry and biology,

etc., things that change per decade. But for love of right mercy and jus-
tice, don't try to show off modern literature and brain quality.

23. Plotinus, *Enneads*, 191. This translation first appeared in five volumes
beginning in 1917, with the third Ennead appearing in 1921. Although David
Gordon (*Paideuma* 3.3 [1974]: 420) cites the Budé edition translated by Émile
Bréhier (seven volumes appearing between 1924 and 1938) as a text used by
Pound, it is entirely likely that Pound would have read MacKenna's translation
given Yeats's overwhelmingly positive response to it, which would explain the
echos between MacKenna's translation and Pound's allusions.

24. Plotinus, *Enneads*, 192.

25. Ibid., 193.

26. Ibid., 196.

27. Ibid., 194–95.

28. W. R. Inge, an avowed disciple of Plotinus's philosophy, makes one of
the strongest cases for Plotinus's monism, and a case with which Pound would
have sympathized, I think, in his *Philosophy of Plotinus*, vol. 2, 2d. ed. (London:
Longmans, Green and Co., 1923), 148: "The 'exile of God from the world' is
part of the 'extreme dualism' which Caird supposes in Plotinus, but which, I
venture to think, no careful student of the Enneads will find there. There are
certainly two movements—a systole and diastole, in which the life of the Soul
consists. Spiritual progress is on one side an expansion, on the other an inten-
sification or concentration. But it is not true that one is the core of Plotinus's
philosophy, the other of his religion."

29. For a compelling account of Plotinian (and, I think, Poundian) con-
templation see Inge, *Philosophy of Plotinus*, 178ff.

30. Eva Hesse, "Notes and Queries," *Paideuma* 1, no. 2 (1972): 272–73. Ter-
rell glosses the Greek lines as follows in his *Companion*, 652: "nous to ariston
autou" (the mind in itself most sacred); pathema (affection) . . . ouk aphista-
tai" (not separate [from mind]); per plura diafana (through more diaphanes
or layers of translucency). The source for this passage remains unidentified
but is not *Ennead* III.5. *Per plura diafana* is from Grosseteste's *De Luce* as Car-
roll F. Terrell has shown in "A Commentary on Grosseteste with an English
Version of *De Luce*," *Paideuma* 2, no. 3 (1973): 449–70. Pound quotes Plotinus
again in Canto 102:

> KAI ALOGA,
> nature APHANASTON,
> the pine needles glow as red wire
> OU THELEI EAEAN EIS KOSMOU
> they want to burst out of the universe
>
> (102/730)

David Gordon (*Paideuma* 3, no. 3 [1974]: 420–21) traces KAI ALOGA (irra-
tional living things) and APHANASTON (without the power to form mental
images) to *Ennead* 3.8 and says:

Here Plotinus indicates contemplation as the life spring and at the same
time the goal of all action and production on every possible level of being.

There is no separation between the lowest and highest levels of activity. This does not conflict with the two phases, one ascending toward the Good, & the other descending toward the last phase of Soul which is the immanent principle of growth, Nature. . . . This also comments quite pointedly to Pound's criticism of Aristotle's view of contemplation as being quite impossibly narrow, non-organic and most definitiely non-humane. (See *Guide to Kulchur* p. 339) Again his remark describes just what Aristotle would have us do in order to contemplate, "to bust out of the universe."

31. Plotinus, *Enneads*, xlviii–xlix.

32. *The Letters of W. B. Yeats*, ed. Allan Wade (New York: Farrar, Straus & Giroux, 1980), 714–15.

33. Plotinus, *Enneads*, 198.

34. Pound's response to Baudelaire is not an uncommon one. In *French Poets and Novelists*, Henry James says that Baudelaire's "evil is represented as an affair of blood and carrion and physical sickness—there must be stinking corpses and starving prostitutes and empty laudanum bottles in order that the poet shall be effectively inspired" (61). Similarly, in *The Symbolist Movement in Literature*, Arthur Symons writes: "Even Baudelaire, in whom the spirit is always an uneasy guest at the orgie of life, had a certain theory of Realism which tortures many of his poems into strange, metallic shapes, and fills them with imitative odours, and disturbs them with a too deliberate rhetoric of the flesh" (6).

35. Plotinus, *Enneads*, 197.

36. Pound creates an ideogram conjoining Confucius and Heraclitus in 80/526 and 83/543.

37. Plotinus, *Enneads*, 199–200.

38. Ibid., 200–1.

39. Ibid., 191.

40. Pound acknowledges this dualism in his Cavalcanti essay when he says, "The '*dove sta memoria*' is Platonism. The '*non razionale ma che si sente*' is for experiment, it is against the tyranny of the syllogism, blinding and obscurantist" (*LE*, 159).

41. J. E. Shaw, *Guido Cavalcanti's Theory of Love: The Canzone d'Amore and Other Related Problems* (Toronto: University of Toronto Press, 1949), 123–24.

42. Nicholls, *Pound, Economics, and Writing*, 66.

43. Ibid., 66–67.

44. This despite his sympathetic rendering of Swedenborg's 3d sphere, "above which, the lotus, white nenuphar/Kuanon, the mythologies" (77/486).

45. Both the 1968 New Directions *Drafts and Fragments* and the Yale typescripts read "Gold mermaid." The Undine is a highly charged figure for Pound that takes him back to his early occult interests. As James Longenbach has shown, Pound encouraged Olivia Shakespear to translate the very esoteric *Le Comte de Gabalis*, which includes a discussion of "rivers and seas . . . full of Undines and Nymphs." Longenbach discusses Pound's fascination with this tale in his important *Stone Cottage*, 86–91. This and other passages should also remind us of Yeats's discussion of "Porphyry on 'the Cave of the Nymphs'" in

his "Philosophy of Shelley's Poetry" in *Essays and Introductions* (New York: Macmillan, 1961), 82.

46. Massimo Bacigalupo, *The Forméd Trace: The Later Poetry of Ezra Pound* (Chicago: University of Chicago Press, 1980), 483.

47. In *Mélanges posthumes*, 6th ed. (Paris: Mercure de France, 1919), 128, Laforgue writes the following "fragment sur Mallarmé":

> L'Inconscient; le principe, après l'effort, l'apothéose de la conscience artistique parnassienne se consolant dans des protestations bouddhiques, le principe en poésie du bégaiement, de l'en allé.
>
> Chez M. Mallarmé, contemporain des Parnassiens à facture raisonnée et du premier engouement de la poésie faisant de la psychologie descriptive et didactique (Sully-Prudhomme, Bourget), ce n'est pas le bégaiement de l'enfant qui a mal, mais le *Sage qui divague;*—ce n'est jamais une divagation d'images comme dans le rêve et l'extase inconsciente, c'est-à-dire de sentiments exprimés avec l'immédiat de l'enfant qui n'a à sa disposition que le répertoire de ses besoins, mais de la divagation *raisonneuse*. Sa technique est également *raisonnée*, consciente et l'on voit souvent qu'elle n'est pas de premier jet.

> [The Unconscious: the principle, after the effort, the apotheosis of the Parnassian artistic consciousness consoling itself with Buddhist protestations, the principle in poetry of stammering, of withdrawal.
>
> With M. Mallarmé—a contemporary of the Parnassians with their reasoned style and their first infatuation with a poetry that creates a descriptive and didactic psychology (Sully-Prudhomme, Bourget)—it's not the stammering of a sick child, but of the Sage who divagates. It is never the imagistic divagation that happens in a dream or in an unconscious rapture, that is, the kind of sentiments expressed with the immediacy of a child who only has at his command the repertoire of his needs, but it is a *reasoned* divagation. His technique is equally reasoned, conscious, and one often sees that it is not a first draft.]

Ramsey takes issue with Laforgue's account and notes the apparent contradiction between the two descriptions of Mallarmé's poetic (*Ironic Inheritance*, 93–94).

48. Mallarmé, *Oeuvres complètes*, 663.

49. Ezra Pound, *Correspondances*, ed. Henri Mondor (Paris: Gallimard, 1959), vol. 1, 246. Pound speaks of breaking the icons in a typescript draft from the forties. I thank Ronald Bush, who discusses this passage in his *Ezra Pound and the Ideologies of Modernism*, for pointing it out to me (forthcoming from Oxford University Press).

50. Bacigalupo, *Forméd Trace*, 425. Bacigalupo provides a most exhaustive reading of this canto, a reading to which I am indebted and which I follow with some slight shifts in emphasis.

51. Mallarmé, *Oeuvres complètes*, 366.

52. As Bacigalupo has shown in his "Who Built the Temple? Or, Thoughts on Pound, Res and Verba" (*Paideuma* 13, no.1 [1984]: 56), Pound found these

historical details in A. W. Mair's note on Callimachus' Epigram 14 in *Hymns,
Epigrams*, Loeb Classical Library (London: Heinemann, 1921), 141.

53. Bacigalupo, *Forméd Trace*, 436. Citing Pound's account of Circe's par-
entage—"Helios, Perse: Circe" (106/768)—Bacigalupo argues that Pound was
"surely aware that Perse and Persephone, the brides of Helios (the sun of day)
and Dis (the sun of night), are ultimately one lunar goddess" (*Forméd Trace*,
435–36). Thus, the Persephone-Circe contrast—"Circe, Persephone / so dif-
ferent is sea from glen/ the juniper is her holy bush" (106/767)—recapitulates
the Demeter-Persephone contrast that opens the canto: "The two are unlike
as Enna and Nysa, sea and glen, pine and juniper—the passage is a set of
dissociations—yet they are *like* each other. . . . In context both names serve (on
good mythological evidence) as approximate definitions of the one goddess of
vegetation" (*Forméd Trace*, 436).

54. Bacigalupo, *Forméd Trace*, 437.

55. In "Who Built the Temple" (56), Bacigalupo argues that the reference
to Selena comes from Callimachus's Epigram 14: "And old shell am I, O Lady
of *Zephyrium*, but now, *Cypris*, I am thine, a first offering from *Selenaea:* I the
nautilus that used to sail upon the sea" (Loeb Classical Library, 141–43). Here,
Bacigalupo elaborates upon his prior treatment of this passage in *Forméd Trace*
and makes explicit Selena's connection to Artemis as a lunar deity: "Pound
does quick work, selecting a few details for his pattern: he calls Selenaea Se-
lena for short and in order to align her with the moon-goddess Artemis previ-
ously invoked, and conflates her with Arsinoe, the 'queen risen into heaven,'
later repeating the name as Arsinoe Kupris: the Queen is both lover and vir-
gin, sun and moon, Ra and Set."

56. Mallarmé to Cazalis, Oct. 1864.

57. Pierrot, *The Decadent Imagination* (Chicago: University of Chicago Press,
1981).

58. Yeats, *Essays and Introductions*, 236.

59. Gautier, *Émaux et Caméees*, 43.

60. Ibid., 135–36.

61. Foucault, *Order of Things*, 43.

62. Ibid., 43–44.

63. Ibid., 334.

64. Ibid., xviii.

65. Michel Foucault, *Archaeology of Knowledge* (New York: Harper & Row,
1972), 120.

CONCLUSION
ROBERT DUNCAN'S REVISIONARY RATIOS:
REWRITING *THE SPIRIT OF ROMANCE*

1. Quoted by Duncan in "Letters on Poetry & Poetics," *Ironwood* 22 11, no.
2 (Fall 1983): 121.

2. Ibid., 100.

3. Although Michael Bernstein rightly distinguishes between Duncan's
grande collage and Pound's ideogram in his "Robert Duncan: Talent and the

Individual Tradition," *Sagetrieb* 4, no. 2–3 (Fall-Winter 1985), his argument in no way precludes the idea of *grande-collage-as-derivation* and, in fact, supports my own.

4. Robert Duncan, "Part 2, Chapter 5 of *The H. D. Book*," *Stony Brook* 3/4 (1969): 339. The published chapters of *The H. D. Book* are available in the following journals; as it has, most regrettably, not yet appeared in book form: Part I (*Beginnings*): chapter 1, *Coyote's Journal* 5/6 (1966): 8–31; chapter 2, *Coyote's Journal* 8 (1967): 27–35; chapter 3, *Tri-Quarterly* 12 (Spring 1968): 67–82; chapter 4, *Tri-Quarterly* 12 (Spring 1968): 82–98; chapter 5: "Occult Matters," *Stony Brook* 1/- (Fall 1968): 4–19; chapter 6: "Rites of Participation," *Caterpillar 1* (Oct. 1967): 6–29 and *Caterpillar 2* (Jan. 1968): 125–154. Part II (*Nights and Days*): "From the Day Book,—excerpts from an extended study of H. D.'s poetry," *Origin* 10, first series (1963): 1–47; chapter 1, *Sumac* 1, no.1 (1968): 101–46; chapter 2, *Caterpillar* 6 (Jan. 1969): 16–38; chapter 3, *IO* 6 (Summer 1969): 117–40; chapter 4, *Caterpillar* 7 (April 1969): 27–60; chapter 5.1, *Stony Brook* 3/4 (1969): 336–47; chapter 5.2, *Credences* 2 (July 1975): 50–52, see also *Sagetrieb* 4, no. 2–3 (1985): 39–85; chapter 6, *Southern Review* 21, no. 1 (1985): 26–48; chapters 7–8, *Credences* 2 (1975): 50–95; chapter 9, *Chicago Review* 30, no. 3 (1979): 37–88; chapter 10, *Ironwood 22* 11, no. 2 (1983): 48–64; chapter 11, *Montemora* 8 (1981): 79–113.

Subsequent references will be signaled in the body of the text by (part, chapter, page).

5. "Interview with Robert Duncan," *Towards a New American Poetics: Essays and Interviews*, ed. Ekbert Faas (Santa Barbara: Black Sparrow Press, 1978), 82.

6. Ibid., 83.

7. Robert Duncan, *The Opening of the Field* (New York: New Directions, 1960), 60. Subsequent references to this and other volumes will be signaled in the text by the following abbreviations—*BB: Bending the Bow* (New York: New Directions, 1968); *GW: Ground Work: Before the War* (New York: New Directions, 1984); *GWII: Ground Work II: In the Dark* (New York: New Directions, 1987); *OF: The Opening of the Field*; *RB: Roots and Branches* (New York: New Directions, 1964).

8. Roger Kamenetz, "Realms of Being: An Interview with Robert Duncan," *Southern Review* 21, no. 1 (Jan. 1985): 15.

9. Ibid., 13.

10. Ibid., 13.

11. Ibid., 14.

12. If Mallarmé's gamble is deemed a failure, it is because Thought (toute pensée emet un coup de dés) will never triumph over chance and the world of appearances. But if we read *le hasard* as a synonym for *un coup de dés*, as Robert Greer Cohn suggests, human reason does establish Identity through tautology ("A throw of the dice will never abolish a throw of the dice"), and, thus, Mallarmé's poem achieves the stasis implicit in the Absolute Idea.

13. James F. Mersmann, "Robert Duncan: Irregular Fire—Eros Against Ahriman," in *Out of the Vietnam Vortex* (Lawrence: University Press of Kansas, 1974), 169.

14. Mallarmé's "Don du poëme" is one of a constellation of poems that Guy Michaud sees as "a sort of presentiment of the poet's future esthetic" (*Mallarmé* [New York: New York University Press, 1965], 43). Very simply, if this can be said of a poem by Mallarmé, "Don du poëme" describes the birth at dawn of what, after a hard night's labor, at first seems a failed poem, "une horrible naissance." Dejected, the poet brings his wife this "enfant d'une nuit d'Idumée" (*Hérodiade*, according to C. Mauron) so that she may give the hungry infant, starving in the rarified atmosphere of the ideal ("l'air du vierge azure"), her milk ("blancheur sibylline"). What is so striking about the poem, however, as Michaud (40–42) and others have noted, is the extremely fluid and polyvalent nature of Mallarmé's images and the rapidity with which he proceeds from the real world—dawn and the finished poem—to a world of sensations evoked by those objects:

> Je t'apporte l'enfant d'une nuit d'Idumée!
> Noire, à l'aile saignante et pâle, déplumée,
> Par le verre brûlé d'aromates et d'or,
> Par les carreaux glacés, hélas! mornes encor,
> L'aurore se jeta sur la lampe angélique.
> Palmes! et quand elle a montré cette relique
> A ce père essayant un sourire ennemi,
> La solitude bleue et stérile a frémi.
> O la berceuse, avec ta fille et l'innocence
> De vos pieds froids, accueille une horrible naissance:
> Et ta voix rappelant viole et clavecin,
> Avec le doigt fané presseras-tu le sein
> Par qui coule en blancheur sibylline la femme
> Pour les lèvres que l'air du vierge azur affame?

Mallarmé sets forth an extremely complex interplay between the constellation of images in the opening of the poem. The poet gives birth, but it is a monstruous birth through parthenogenesis rather than through a cross-fertilization or dialectical synthesis of polarities, and the poet therefore initially considers disinheriting the poem and banishing it like Esau in Edom (Idumée). Wallace Fowlie, for example, sees this birth as "a blood-soaked birth of a bird" who will not be able to attain the ideal because its wing is torn and bleeding (*Mallarmé* [Chicago: University of Chicago Press, 1953], 142): "Noire, à l'aile saignante et pâle, déplumée." His black ink spurting out in driblets until it is finally exhausted, the poet, "de-penned," has failed, fallen, has unleashed a monstrosity. But Michaud, in a reading supported by the Nurse's Incantation in *Hérodiade* (*Oeuvres*, 41), sees the bird as dawn itself piercing the solitude of the poet's study and revealing to the still self-critical poet ("ce père essayant un sourire ennemi") the fruit of his "nuit d'Idumée." The result is a Palm (i.e., a laurel), but the poet's latest offspring still needs to be nursed by the reader who, as Fowlie maintains, must feed the poem, still breathing "l'air du vierge azur," with his or her own experiences and feelings (the life-giving "blancheur sibylline [de] la femme"). (The figure of "La Berceuse" is similarly ambiguous. Michaud insists on the entirely plausible biographical reading wherein Mallarmé takes his poem to Mme. Mallarmé, nursing their newborn daughter Geneviève. Fowlie emphasizes the more literary aspect of the "berceuse" as a singer of lullabies who will intone the poet's words and thus enable them to survive in the real world.) The reader closes the circuit and fills the void, "la solitude bleue et stérile," transforming an empty parthenogenesis into a fruitful conjunction of poet and reader, of male and female. Thus, "Don du poëme" permits two quite different readings: the first, that the poem is a failure because it is not a vehicle with which to attain the absolute; the second, that the poem, a product of a chance encounter with the real, requires the reader's real experiences, his or her "life-blood," to fulfill its destiny.

15. Duncan, "Letters on Poetry & Poetics," 107.

16. For an excellent discussion of Duncan's "law," see Mersmann, "Robert Duncan: Irregular Fire," *Out of the Vietnam Vortex*, 159–203.

17. See J. C. Milner, *L'Amour de la langue* (Paris: Editions du Seuil, 1978), 131: "Le recouvrement de la figure de la femme et de la langue pouvait s'imposer à Dante par les troubadours: chez ceux-ci, l'amour courtois a partie liée à l'hermétisme: pour suppléer à l'absence de rapport, feindre d'y faire, par choix, obstacle—tant du côté de l'inaccessible Dame que par une référence obscurcie."

INDEX

[Because French (post)symbolism is the focus of this book, the names of various (post)symbolists appear on nearly every page; I have therefore attempted to index only significant mentions—author.]